Co-
Leaders

Co-Leaders

THE Power OF Great Partnerships

David A. Heenan & Warren Bennis

John Wiley & Sons, Inc.

New York ▪ Chichester ▪ Weinheim ▪ Brisbane ▪ Singapore ▪ Toronto

To Nery and Grace,
co-leaders extraordinaire

This book is printed on acid-free paper. ∞

Copyright © 1999 by David A. Heenan and Warren Bennis. All rights reserved.

Published simultaneously in Canada.

This publication is designed to provide accurate and authoritative information in regard to the subject matter covered. It is sold with the understanding that the publisher is not engaged in rendering professional services. If professional advice or other expert assistance is required, the services of a competent professional person should be sought.

Library of Congress Cataloging-in-Publication Data:

Heenan, David A.
    Co-leaders : the power of great partnerships /
David A. Heenan & Warren Bennis.
        p.   cm.
    Includes index.
    ISBN 0-471-31635-0 (cloth : alk. paper)
    1. Leadership.   2. Chief executive officers.   I. Bennis, Warren G.
II. Title.
HD57.7.H397   1999
658.4'092—dc21   98-35142
                                                                   CIP

Printed in the United States of America.

10 9 8 7 6 5 4 3 2

Contents

The world can do without its masters
better than it can do without its servants.

SAMUEL GRIDLEY HOWE
Physician, reformer, and founder of
the Perkins School for the Blind

Preface

We live in a starstruck society. We love our heroes, be they astronauts, athletes, or chief executives. We honor their courage, covet their talent, and cherish their boldness. Whether it's on Main Street or Wall Street, celebrity status flows up the organization.

And yet we all know that cooperation and collaboration grow more important every day. In organizational life, those at the top need exceptional deputies as much as they need fresh air. The watchword today is co-leadership, where power and credit are freely dispersed throughout the enterprise. Society often depreciates the contributions of key subordinates, but successful leaders need them desperately.

"Where are the nation's leaders?" Robert Byrd recently asked his fellow senators. These leaders are not in short supply. They are superstars like Mark McGwire and Sammy Sosa, who defined a new standard of sportsmanship by openly professing their hope that the Great Home Run Chase of 1998 would end in a tie. They are the six astronauts and space pioneer, Senator John Glenn, who co-piloted the space shuttle *Discovery*. They are Berkshire Hathaway Vice Chairman Charles Munger, Charles Schwab co-CEO David Pottruck, Stanford Provost Condoleezza Rice, and many other gifted co-leaders who toil away in relative obscurity. To them, collaboration is not simply desirable, it is crucial.

Each of us came to appreciate the power and potential of great co-leaders at different stages of our lives. For Dave, it was typified by Jim Kelly, a fellow marine and worldclass executive at the College of William and Mary, who repeatedly turned down opportunities for advancement elsewhere to serve five presidents of an institution he truly loved. Warren's appreciation of the collective magic of co-leadership came at the University of Cincinnati, where he served as president. Working together with Board Chairman Ray Dotson, Warren's effectiveness soared. The partnership of a first-rate non-executive chairman and activist CEO propelled the university to new heights. When Ray retired, Warren lost an invaluable friend and ally.

Over the years, we have discovered that the genius of our age is truly collaborative. For all but the simplest tasks, we need teams of leaders working toward a common purpose. Co-leaders demonstrate this visceral strand of teamwork. They show why it's the only way things get done in today's complex, ever-changing organizations. Indeed, the shrewd leaders of the future are those who recognize the significance of creating alliances with others whose fates are correlated with their own.

Co-Leaders, therefore, lays to rest the destructive mania of the winner-take-all society. For five years, we examined dozens of great partnerships, from history and contemporary life. In the course of our research, we discovered how great lieutenants create great organizations as surely as do talented CEOs. As you will see, our heroes are as different from one another as chalk and cheese. However, they share an egoless commitment to cooperation and collaboration.

"We can do as partners what we cannot do as singles," Daniel Webster once said. Putting their talents in tandem, co-leaders are redefining leadership as a genuine partnership. Our stories show how and why.

David A. Heenan   Warren Bennis
Honolulu, Hawaii   Santa Monica, California

January 1999

1

The Case for
Co-Leaders

1

The Case for Co-Leaders

If a man aspires to the highest place, it is no dishonor to him to halt at the second.
— CICERO

An overseas visitor to our shores recently remarked: "If beings from another planet were attempting to learn about working in the United States by reading business magazines, they would have to assume that everyone in America is either a CEO or about to become one."

The point is well taken. Ours is a culture obsessed with celebrity, and so we have made superstars of Bill Gates and other fascinating leaders, just as we have made legends of favored rock stars and screen actors. Nevertheless, even as we read yet another article that implies that Microsoft *is* Bill Gates, we know better. We know that every successful organization has, at its heart, a cadre of *co-leaders*—key players who do the work, even if they receive little of the glory.

Take Microsoft's Steve Ballmer. According to insiders much of the software giant's unprecedented success is due to Ballmer, its relatively unknown second in command. Ballmer is Microsoft's president and top tactician, the person responsible for everything from getting the first Windows operating system shipped to keeping the company supplied with top-notch personnel. Although the average person hears his name and wonders "Steve who?" Ballmer has created Microsoft as surely as has his more famous boss.

"Microsoft could lose Bill Gates," former staffer Adrian King told *Forbes*, "but it could not survive without Steve's sheer will to succeed. That's what makes the company unique."

This book reflects our conviction that you must look beyond the Bill Gateses of the world to understand what will make organizations succeed in the new millennium. In this first comprehensive study of co-leaders and their often quiet power, we challenge the time-honored notion that all great institutions are the lengthened shadows of a Great Man or Woman. It is a fallacy that dies hard. But if you believe, as we do, that the genius of our age is truly collaborative, you must abandon the notion that the credit for any significant achievement is solely attributable to the person at the top. We have long worshiped the imperial leader at the cost of ignoring the countless other con-tributors to any worthwhile enterprise. In our hearts we know that the world is more complex than ever and that we need teams of tal-ent—leaders and co-leaders working together—to get important things done. The old corporate monotheism is finally giving way to a more realistic view that acknowledges leaders not as organizational gods but as the first among many contributors. In this new view of the organization, co-leaders finally come into their own and begin to receive the credit they so richly deserve.

Gates and Ballmer exemplify a relatively new type of alliance between a leader and his or her chief ally. In this scenario, so typical of Silicon Valley, the No. 1 and No. 2 associates seem more like buddies, or at least peers, than boss and subordinate. This new egalitarianism reflects a dramatic change in organizational life today. In Henry Ford's corporate America, the person at the top held all the power. He, and it was almost always a he, owned the company and all its assets. The workers were hired hands.

But on the cusp of the year 2000, economics is based on a very different reality. Microsoft and other high-tech companies are in the business of ideas. Good ideas belong, initially at least, to whoever has them, not to the company or the boss. Superior ideas can come from anyone in the organization, and they empower the people who have them, whether their business card says CEO or intern. If Microsoft is not a true meritocracy, it is nonetheless a company in which talent is valued and courted. Talent always has the power to walk (especially if, as in the case of Ballmer, the talent already has roughly $12 billion worth of Microsoft stock in its pocket). In such an environment, no chief executive would risk losing a key player by demanding unques-tioning obedience or any of the other outdated hallmarks of the rigidly hierarchical corporation of yesterday. This new egalitarianism isn't just a matter of style. It's a question of survival. In the new climate, every leader knows that the organization's best minds will take major assets with them should they walk out the door.

Co-Leadership Defined

Co-leadership is not a fuzzy-minded buzzword designed to make non-CEOs feel better about themselves and their workplaces. Rather it is a tough-minded strategy that will unleash the hidden talent in any enterprise. Above all co-leadership is inclusive, not exclusive. It celebrates those who do the real work, not just a few charismatic leaders, often isolated, who are regally compensated for articulating the organization's vision.

Although several leading companies from Citigroup to Daimler-Chrysler have restyled themselves around coequal CEOs, co-leadership should permeate *every* organization at *every* level. There are vivid demonstrations of successful power sharing from the Halls of Montezuma to the Hills of Silicon Valley. For example, the United States Marine Corps, with its fiercely proud tradition of excellence in combat, its hallowed rituals, and its unbending code of honor, personifies co-leadership. Despite its rigid command-and-control structure, the Corps' enduring culture screams togetherness: Semper fi. Esprit de corps. The few, the proud.

Such inclusive notions of leadership are not new. The Marines have been practicing their special brand of esprit for more than 220 years. But what is new are the changed realities of the twenty-first century. In a world of increasing interdependence and ceaseless technological change, even the greatest of Great Men or Women simply can't get the job done alone. As a result, we need to rethink our most basic concepts of leadership.

The prevailing winds blow in the direction of close-knit partnerships throughout the organization. In this new organizational galaxy, power doesn't reside in a single person or corner office. Rather power and responsibility are dispersed, giving the enterprise a whole constellation of costars—co-leaders with shared values and aspirations, all of whom work together toward common goals. As we look back at what we discovered in writing this book, one realization towers above all others: *Anyone* can be a co-leader—all he or she needs is talent and an organization that values and rewards co-leadership.

In researching this book, we spent five years scrutinizing dozens of gifted co-leaders, analyzing how they contributed to the greatness of their organizations. We studied how they related to the people above and below them and how they viewed the costs and rewards of being a costar. Because we believe personal stories are a lively, effective way to get important points across, we chose to make the case for co-leadership by telling the stories of a dozen outstanding adjuncts, from General George C. Marshall to Merrill Lynch's visionary Win Smith. Other co-leaders profiled range from Anne Sullivan Macy, Helen Keller's brilliant and devoted teacher, to legendary auto executive Bob Lutz.

Co-Leaders, then, is about truly exceptional deputies—extremely talented and dedicated men and women, often more capable than their more highly acclaimed superiors. No one illustrates this better than George Catlett Marshall. As important to his country as George Washington, Marshall brought unprecedented stature to a supporting role. With World War II looming, he rebuilt the United States Army despite extraordinary initial resistance. The architect of the Marshall Plan, he was President Truman's steady right hand as secretary of state and later secretary of defense. The first soldier to win the Nobel Peace Prize in peacetime, he was also a hero to the captains of his era. Truman, Eisenhower, and Churchill all said he was the greatest man they had ever known.

Routinely called on to do the work and forgo the credit, great partners sometimes have character where more celebrated leaders have only flash. Marshall is, again, the model. In retirement he turned down million-dollar offers to write his memoirs because he felt his reminiscences might trouble some of the people in his remarkable past. Such principled restraint is hard to imagine today when no tell-all memoir seems to go unwritten.

Again and again, *Co-Leaders* illustrates how the once yawning gap between the person at the top and the rest of the organization is closing because of rapid changes in the workplace and, indeed, the world. Although as a culture we continue to be mesmerized by celebrity and preoccupied with being No. 1, the roles of top executives are converging, the line between them increasingly blurred.

Called on to make more and more complex decisions more and more quickly, even the most daVincian CEOs acknowledge that they can't do everything themselves. Farsighted corporations and other organizations require their leaders to do more than put effective systems in place. Future-oriented enterprises have to be able to spot the Next Big Thing and respond to it before the competition. Such organizations are like organisms, constantly adapting to shifts in the global environment. As a result, the CEO's job doesn't get easier the longer he or she is in place; it typically gets even more demanding.

In 1997 famously capable Intel chairman Andy Grove, beset by lawsuits, a bout with prostate cancer, a flaw in Intel's Pentium Pro chips, and a dip in second-quarter earnings, admitted that he was on the verge of being overwhelmed. "I don't think I've ever worked as hard," he told *Fortune*. "I've been feeling very sorry for myself the past six months. Things are running at borderline out of control inside the company and out. . . . I go home spent."

In such an environment, first-rate co-leaders are a necessity, not a luxury. In May 1998 Grove chose as his successor Craig Barrett, Intel's superbly fit chief operating officer (COO) and the person responsible for perfecting the chip maker's manufacturing processes. Grove was the first to praise Barrett for having done the operations job at Intel far better than he. And why shouldn't Grove seek a successor of Barrett's caliber? When you know you are going to be facing challenges at every turn, you want the best there is at your side.

Once a sinecure, the corner office has become a revolving door, as boards and shareholders become ever more demanding of CEOs. Increasingly, heading an important organization in America is like being one of the kings in ancient Crete who had extraordinary power and access to every perk and pleasure—but only for a time. After his year of absolute power, the king was put to death. For contemporary CEOs the pay and the perks are unbeatable while they are in office, but they can't count on being in office for long. As the tenure of the average chief executive becomes shorter and shorter, the need for depth of leadership becomes even more crucial.

The untimely death in 1997 of Coca-Cola Enterprises, Inc. CEO Roberto Goizueta reminded the world that no complex organization can afford to rely too heavily on a single leader, however gifted and charismatic. Coke never stumbled in the days following Goizueta's death, largely because he had already groomed an able successor, M. Douglas Ivester, whom Goizueta had long referred to as "my partner." The company's major divisions were already reporting to Ivester, now CEO, when the Cuban-born chief became ill. The late chairman had also nurtured a dozen more key players under Ivester, who in turn had talented protégés of his own. In famed investor Warren Buffett's view, Goizueta's "greatest legacy is the way he so carefully selected and then nurtured the future leadership of the company."

Ivester has already gone far toward instituting a co-leadership culture at Coke. *Fortune* magazine's Betsy Morris recently described the atmosphere under Ivester: "Hierarchy is out—it slows everything down; he communicates freely with people at all levels. The conventional desk job is also out. Ivester prefers that employees think of themselves as knowledge workers—their office is the information they carry around with them, supported by technology that allows them to work anywhere. . . . A CEO on a pedestal is definitely out; a CEO as platoon leader is in." Ivester knows that co-leadership is a strategy for unleashing talent throughout the organization. Much more than rhetoric about teamwork, co-leadership is a commitment to partnering at every level, to serve the constantly changing needs of the organization. Yet even someone as committed to co-leadership as Ivester may be reluctant to share *all* his or her power. Ivester works closely with a team of 14 vice presidents but has not yet been willing to name a successor.

Contrast, too, China's smooth leadership transition with the sorry state of Russia, Cuba, and Malaysia. Deng Xiaoping's death quickly surfaced two talented co-leaders: President Jiang Zemin and Premier Zhu Rongji. Yet Russia, with ailing Boris Yeltsin acting more like a tsar than the country's first democratically elected president, desperately needs a succession plan. So, too, do autocratic Cuba and Malaysia.

Increasingly, corporations, countries, and other entities are realizing that top leaders and their co-leaders are not different orders of beings but essential complements: All are needed if the enterprise is to flourish. As college basketball's North Carolina Tar Heels were reminded in 1997, success, continuity, and survival depend on having a Bill Guthridge on board as well as a Dean Smith. Like athletic teams, all organizations need the bench strength, or deep leadership, provided by great co-leaders.

Paths to Co-Leadership

In the course of studying outstanding lieutenants, we were constantly reminded that co-leadership is a *role,* not an identity and certainly not a destiny. There is no single personality type that consigns people to careers in a supporting role rather than a starring one (indeed most CEOs and other leaders have done both). True, some strong-willed individuals must run their own shows. It's hard—almost impossible actually—to imagine Donald Trump, George Steinbrenner, or Leona Helmsley finding happiness in the trenches. But they are the exceptions.

Because all leadership is situational, we are leery about categorizing co-leaders. The social world isn't nearly as orderly as the physical world. People—unlike solids, fluids, and gases—are anything but uniform and predictable. As you will see, the co-leaders described in these pages have distinguished themselves in very different fields of endeavor: Amy Tucker coaches women's basketball at Stanford, while Merrill Lynch's Win Smith helped democratize the ownership of stocks and bonds, perhaps the most important change in the U.S. economy in 50 years. And each of these great partners had or has a distinctive, often colorful personality. But in the course of our research, we found that, however they differed, each had taken one of three distinctive career paths to successful co-leadership. Each was either a fast-tracker, a back-tracker, or an on-tracker.

- *Fast-trackers* are deputies on the way up. For presidential hopeful Al Gore and others, co-leadership is a rite of passage. Indeed being No. 2 is a time-honored way to become top dog. According to a recent survey, 86 percent of the heads of Fortune 500 companies were previous seconds in command.

  Upwardly mobile lieutenants understand that the route to the corner office is paved with achievement, loyalty, and luck. Savvy deputies also appreciate firsthand the need for superior bench strength. Fast-trackers tend to be good at what psychologist Erik Erikson terms "being generative"—that is, building their own cadre of talented lieutenants. Such co-leaders often understand, in the most visceral of ways, the value of sharing power.

■ *Back-trackers* are former chiefs who have downshifted. One of
history's most notable examples is Chou En-lai, who voluntar-
ily relinquished command of the Red Army to a gifted junior
officer, Mao Tse-tung. More recently, as few would have predicted, colorful cable pioneer Ted Turner seems to have found
happiness as a vice chairman at Time Warner.

Some back-trackers disdain elements of the No. 1 role:
deal making, strategizing, schmoozing with different interest
groups, and the like. Some find the pressure and lack of privacy
at the top to be major negatives. Others want to avoid the
nerve-rattling revolving-door syndrome of today's executive
suite. Generally speaking, these talented men and women find
greater peace being the quiet power behind the throne.

■ *On-trackers* are outstanding adjuncts who either didn't want
the top slot or weren't promoted into it. These people find
ways to prosper as supporting players. Passed over for CEO of
Chrysler, Bob Lutz called his stint as second in command
"absolutely the best period in my whole career." On-trackers
have the ego strength to be a costar. If they are offered top
billing, they will probably take it, as Harry Truman did a half
century ago and as Bill Guthridge did at North Carolina in
1997. But they are also comfortable remaining part of a
vibrant team of leaders.

Whatever their route to co-leadership, successful costars are consummate team players and, thus, valuable models for everyone interested in effective collaboration. Usually servant-leaders, they tend to
be self-reliant, yet committed to organizational goals. Outstanding
co-leaders "see themselves—except in terms of line responsibility—as
the equals of the leaders they follow," says Professor Robert E. Kelley
of Carnegie Mellon University. "They are more apt to disagree with
leadership and are less likely to be intimidated by hierarchy and organizational structure."

We have excluded any discussion of unsuccessful partners, or off-
trackers. These are people whose careers have derailed. Whereas fast-
trackers are on the way up, these poor souls are on the way out.

What motivates great co-leaders? Why, in particular, are they
willing to subordinate their egos, a sacrifice that seems all the more

remarkable in an age that celebrates the star? We found three main reasons, which led us to classify co-leaders as follows:

1. *Crusaders,* like General George C. Marshall, who serve a noble cause
2. *Confederates,* such as Bob Lutz and Stanford assistant coach Amy Tucker, who serve an exceptional organization or enterprise
3. *Consorts,* like Helen Keller's teacher, Anne Sullivan Macy, and Win Smith of Merrill Lynch, who serve an extraordinary person.

Of course, there is some overlap among categories. George Marshall as *crusader* was driven by the cause of freedom and world peace. Yet he was also a staunch *confederate* of the U.S. military establishment (the army, in particular) as well as a loyal *consort* to his mentor, "Black Jack" Pershing, and later to presidents Roosevelt and Truman. At different stages in Marshall's life, these loyalties enabled him to find satisfaction in a supporting role.

Critical Factors for Success

To be a successful co-leader, you need, above all, a champion who will allow you to succeed. Not every top gun is able to do that. Contrast Bob Lutz's success at Chrysler, thanks to the genuine partnership he had with CEO Robert Eaton, with Lutz's unhappiness at the auto giant when then CEO Lee Iacocca often undermined him. Great co-leaders are often born when leaders decide to do the one thing that most often distinguishes a great organization from a mediocre one— hire people who are as good or better than they are. As reserved as Lutz is flamboyant, Bob Eaton was perfectly comfortable with a partner who piloted his own jet fighter and who was a darling of the press. For Lutz's part, he long ago came to terms with being passed over for Chrysler's top job and found real happiness as Eaton's partner in everything but name. Indeed Lutz believes Eaton's willingness to share power was key to Chrysler's success. If Lutz had been made CEO in 1992, he said: "I would have had to have done it alone."

The ability to subordinate ego to attain a common goal is something both leaders and co-leaders need. Stephen Kahng built Power Computing Corp. into what *Business Week* described as the "fastest-growing computer startup of the 1990s." One of the industry's most respected technical experts, Kahng is also so nerdy and soft-spoken that his own staffers needle him about it. Knowing that he needed someone with different skills and a personality very different from his own to market the company's Apple clones and capture a greater share of the PC market, Kahng went after Joel Kocher, author of the winning marketing strategy, including direct sales, at Dell Computer Corp. Now Power Computing's president and COO, the exuberant Kocher is the antithesis of Kahng—in everything but their shared vision of market domination. Kocher is head cheerleader as well as marketing strategist, fond of such stunts as having Power Computing's staff wear camouflage fatigues every Friday on Fight Back for the Customer Day. A colleague of Kocher's at Dell told *Business Week* that he "demands, inspires, attracts, and coaches greatness"—the sort of description most people associate with CEO, not second in command. But Kahng had the wisdom and confidence to hire his complement, where a lesser leader might have been put off by Kocher's stronger charisma.

True leaders also know that the only deputies worth hiring are the ones good enough to replace them. And for their part outstanding co-leaders know that they don't have to be at the top of the organizational chart to find satisfaction—that exercising one's gifts and serving a worthy cause are far more reliable sources of satisfaction than the title on one's office door. Such people have acquired the rare ability to distinguish between celebrity and success. As that unlikely philosopher, the late Erma Bombeck, once wrote, "Don't confuse fame with success. Madonna is one, Helen Keller is the other."

Courage is one of the attributes of all great co-leaders, and one we rarely associate with that role. Deputies have to be able to speak truth to power, even when it hurts. (Real leaders demand honesty from their adjuncts, knowing that good information, even when it's unpleasant, is the basis of good decision making.) It was young George Marshall's courage in publicly correcting General Pershing that caught Pershing's eye and launched Marshall's extraordinary career. And candor like his own was one of the attributes Marshall always sought in his staffers. Yes-men may feed the boss's ego, but they serve no other useful function. Indeed they guarantee that the boss's knowledge will be limited to upbeat information and whatever he or she already knows. Good co-leaders protect their bosses when possible, but good bosses are willing to endure occasional discomfiture in order to find out what they *need* to know.

Creativity is almost as important an attribute of co-leaders as courage. Deputies have to go beyond the manual to find what best serves the organization. When George Tenet was named director of the Central Intelligence Agency in 1997, his former boss, John Deutch, told an instructive story about Tenet's ability to think on his feet and act decisively.

"George is a tremendously loyal and devoted public servant," Deutch told the *Wall Street Journal.* "The time I really realized how devoted a deputy he was was in an extremely important meeting with important foreign dignitaries. He cleared the room to tell me I needed to zip up my fly."

Every chief has the right to the loyalty of his or her deputies. Working at a leader's side, a trusted co-leader is often privy to information that could seriously compromise the boss's position if it were shared. As candid as great partners are in private, they are equally discreet in public. They can keep the boss's secrets—as long as they can continue to reconcile them with their own consciences. To some extent, all No. 1s depend on an image of excellence to maintain their positions. Good co-leaders may know about personal flaws or weaknesses, but they don't feel compelled to reveal or underscore them. Especially in crises, leaders have to know that their first lieutenants will maintain the illusion of superiority, which makes leadership possible. An example of this is Vice President Al Gore's unswerving public loyalty to a bruised Clinton, despite the pressure on Gore to distance himself from the controverial president as Gore himself seeks the nation's highest office.

Co-leaders need unusually healthy egos. That's a paradox really, because it would seem that they would need less ego strength than their leaders. But, especially in a society as obsessed with winning as ours, it takes extraordinary confidence to be No. 2 or No. 3. No matter how great a contribution a great co-leader makes, the majority of the credit is going to accrue to the top individual. That's the nature of the organizational beast. To some degree it may simply reflect the extent to which leaders function as symbols of their enterprises. But the fact is that even the best deputy will exist in the shadow of the boss. Bill Guthridge deserved considerable credit for Dean Smith's record-breaking 879 victories, but it was Smith whose name went into the record books, not the name of the man who spent 30 years as his assistant coach. As the self-effacing Guthridge told the press, "I knew my ego could take being lifetime assistant to the best coach around."

What does the organization get from a great partnership? A great many things. Two heads really are better than one when it comes to decision making. The psychological literature indicates that groups make better choices than do individuals. Last year Ford Motor's installation of the talented tandem of William Clay Ford, Jr., as nonexecutive chairman and Jacques Nasser as president and CEO was a ringing endorsement of co-leadership. "One of the nice things about this arrangement is that it does use the strength of two capable people," Ford told the *New York Times*. "Having watched how large this company has become, and how tough it is to manage, I think separating these jobs makes a lot of sense."

A first-rate deputy like Nasser can serve as an alternative model for the rest of the organization, one that other co-leaders may relate to more easily than to the person at the top. A great second can serve as institutional insurance in that he or she can quickly get up to speed to replace the person at the top. This is, tragically, one of the roles American vice presidents have had to play when presidents have died in office, and it is the role by which most people measure the vice president. Truman, whom as vice president FDR had kept in the dark about many important issues, including the development of the atomic bomb, proved surprisingly able in the nation's top job. The very thought of Dan Quayle succeeding George Bush so frightened many voters that it became a factor in Bush's failure to win a second term in office.

But heir apparent is just one of the many roles co-leaders play. Great partners may have strengths and skills that the boss lacks. The costar can compensate or complement. William Clark had superior cartographic abilities to Meriwether Lewis, for instance, that proved invaluable to the Corps of Discovery. Co-leaders can share the burden of leadership and lighten the workload. They routinely act as facilitators for their superiors. They almost always serve as advisers as well, at best providing the kind of candid, informed counsel that every leader needs. They are often conduits of critical information from elsewhere in the organization to the person in charge, and vice versa. They can also serve as sounding boards, counselors, confessors, and pressure valves. In bad times they may serve as lightning rods, even scapegoats. In the best of all possible organizations, they are genuine partners, though not necessarily equal ones, sharing responsibilities with the chief according to their individual skills and interests. Before Dean Smith's retirement in 1997, Bill Guthridge was responsible for the individual coaching at North Carolina, while Smith determined overall strategy—with Guthridge's quiet assistance. In the highly collaborative Clinton White House, Gore assumed major policy-shaping responsibility for several areas of national and international concern, including national security, environment, and technology.

Just Rewards

Although service is the paradigmatic responsibility of co-leaders, there comes a time in everyone's career when he or she asks, "What's in it for me?" Although co-leaders usually lack the name recognition and enormous salaries of CEOs and others at the very top, there are rewards in being No. 2 or No. 3.

For starters serving under someone else can be a marvelous education. As a young deputy to Pershing, Marshall attended a superb military college of one, where he was able to study a first-rate soldier in the flesh, day in and day out. Vice President Gore has been in a unique position to study President Clinton during his two terms in office. What better curriculum for a presidential hopeful than the chance to see how the incumbent handles the duties and pressures of the nation's highest office? Clinton himself stumbled badly in his first months in office as he learned on the job. Six years later came the infamous Monica Lewinsky affair. How much better for Gore to be able to learn from someone else's mistakes—and successes—before assuming that demanding office?

Some of the greatest rewards of co-leadership grow out of the relationship with the person at the top. Some co-leaders have warm, sustaining relationships with the people they serve, as Win Smith had with Merrill Lynch cofounder Charlie Merrill. Merrill was a demanding taskmaster, but a superb mentor, and, over the decades, he and Smith became closer than many fathers and sons. Some of the letters they exchanged after illness forced Merrill into semiretirement are as tender as love letters. Accomplishing something together can forge a lasting bond. As profoundly troubled as Meriwether Lewis was, he and William Clark became close friends in the course of their epic journey and remained so afterward: Clark and his wife even moved into Lewis's house for a time.

The relationships that develop in executive offices are enormously varied. Some CEOs and COOs have healthy rivalries that energize both of them. Others have the professional equivalent of bad marriages that distract and drain them. Camaraderie grounded in shared accomplishment is one of the pleasures of any happy workplace, and it can be especially gratifying for the people who are most involved in setting the agenda and steering the enterprise.

Another frequent source of satisfaction for co-leaders is the opportunity to revel in interesting work and the pleasures of craft. CEOs often barter power and responsibility for truly engaging work. It can be hectic at the top, especially on days when one meeting follows another and even meals involve professional obligations. Many contented alter egos have talent or expertise that they are able to exercise undistracted by the top person's daunting calendar and sometimes tedious responsibilities. Amy Tucker seems to have found joy in her craft as associate head coach of the women's basketball team at Stanford, despite having tasted triumph as interim head coach. Bob Lutz was happy at Chrysler as the hands-on creator of such eye-catching vehicles as the Dodge Viper, Plymouth Prowler, and Jeep Grand Cherokee. Successful co-leaders, especially those who have decided to remain No. 2, have often concluded that what they actually do is more important than making headlines.

As we shall see, some co-leaders find enormous satisfaction in serving a cause they believe in. Certainly Marshall is a superb example of someone who devoted his entire career to serving his country and indeed the world at large. For others, their work has many of the qualities of a religious vocation, and self-sacrifice is a price they are willing to pay. Born into island royalty, Bernice Pauahi Bishop believed that education could save her beloved fellow Hawaiians and devoted much of her life to creating the Kamehameha Schools. Eschewing the Hawaiian crown, she found another way to improve the condition of her people. As one observer said: "Refusing to rule her people, she did what was better, she served them."

Sometimes redefining power reflects a decision that there are more important things in life than other trappings of success. Princess Pauahi refused the crown because she believed accepting it would destroy her happy marriage to Charles Reed Bishop, who favored Hawaii's annexation by the United States. Amy Tucker is regularly offered head coaching jobs, especially now that women's basketball is booming, but she doesn't want to leave Stanford, a vibrant intellectual community in scenic Northern California.

As the happy buzz at visionary companies such as Steve Jobs's Pixar Animation Studios makes clear, the most exciting work being done today is collaborative, accomplished by teams of people working toward a common goal. Often there is still a Numero Uno, at least on the organizational chart. But in the growing number of global enterprises that trade in innovation, the real power is in the hands of the men and women who have the best ideas and the most valuable skills, whatever their job titles. In the workplaces of the new millennium, one of the leader's most important roles is to retain the necessary talent and unleash it. The rise of co-leadership reflects the fact that, despite the exalted terms in which we talk about No. 1s, they can actually accomplish things only when effectively teamed with other people.

Leadership Redefined

If we still treat some CEOs like celebrities, we are increasingly beginning to see them more as stewards than kings. No one has been more articulate on this change in our traditional view of leadership than management sage Peter Drucker, who said in praise of such non-imperial leaders as Harry Truman and GE's Jack Welch: "They both understood executives are not their own masters. They are servants of the organization—whether elected or appointed, whether the organization is a government, a government agency, a business, a hospital, a diocese. It's their duty to subordinate their likes, wishes, preferences to the welfare of the institution."

To some degree this more egalitarian understanding of leadership reflects a backlash against CEOs who earn far more than they deliver.

The surge in executive compensation in recent years has dismayed and infuriated the vast majority of people who work hard for modest pay. Thirty years ago the average chief executive in the United States earned 44 times as much as the average factory worker. According to the AFL-CIO, the ratio is now more than 300 to 1. Consequently, corporate boards as well as workers are beginning to question whether anyone deserves to make more than the budgets of some nations. Indeed Bob Eaton's $16 million annual compensation as CEO of Chrysler horrified German shareholder activists contemplating the 1998 merger of the Detroit automaker and Daimler-Benz AG. Eaton's German counterpart, Jürgen Schrempp, receives just $2 million a year.

Even *Business Week,* hardly a journal to foment revolution, huffed about the hubris of the chieftains of American business. "They are team leaders, not celebrities or one-man bands," the magazine editorialized. Yes, some extraordinary CEOs may deserve extraordinary compensation. "But usually, a chief executive works with a team of people who manage thousands of employees, each contributing to the success or failure of the company. A team leader requires respect to function. Making 200 times the average paycheck, simply because the market has a good year, doesn't generate respect."

That the American workplace needs to be rethought is increasingly obvious. The mounting anger over executive pay is only one piece of evidence. It is not a happy sign when the business best-seller list is topped by volumes devoted to Dilbert, the cartoon Everyworker, and the Orwellian hell in which he labors. This is organizational humor at its darkest, and one of its loudest messages is that it is time for sweeping change.

Although increasing numbers of firms are naming co-CEOs and showing other signs of embracing co-leadership, sharing power has its pitfalls. It will be interesting to see if Bob Eaton can work as comfortably with co-CEO Schrempp as Eaton once teamed with Lutz. The corner suite that houses incompatible executive peers can be an unhappy, unproductive place indeed. Boards can help keep the peace, but executive egos often make real partnerships impossible. You need only look at the vice presidency of the United States to see how hard it is for some No. 1s to share power. Even leaders who were abused as veeps had trouble treating their own vice presidents decently after becoming president. Truman, for example, was no better to Vice President Alben Barkley than FDR had been to him. Power is only shared by those who first choose to share it. In light of this first law of co-leadership, more and more organizations—and their governing boards—are realizing that willingness to share power is one of the criteria by which leaders must be judged.

As someone who knows both the executive experience and the subordinate one, the co-leader is a good model for a new, more egalitarian hybrid better adapted to the needs of the new millennium—people who can both command and follow, as the situation requires.

In American society the urge to be a star and the urge to achieve common goals as part of a community have always tugged us in different directions. As celebrity becomes less and less associated with genuine achievement, we need to think more clearly about what is best for our organizations and for ourselves. Great co-leaders remind us that we don't need to be captain to play on the team, that doing something we want to do and doing it well can be its own reward. That said, learning the secrets and skills of great No. 2s remains the surest path to becoming No. 1.

2
The Two Bobs
Sharing the Driver's Seat

Sharing the Driver's Seat: Bob Eaton (left), Chrysler chairman, with his trusted co-leader, Bob Lutz. (Photo courtesy of Chrysler Corporation.)

2

The Two Bobs

The most difficult instrument to play in the orchestra is second fiddle.
—LEONARD BERNSTEIN

Since its brush with bankruptcy at the beginning of the decade, Chrysler Corp. has risen from the ashes. Despite its erratic past, the smallest of the Big Three has become Motown's brashest, most successful automaker. For the past five years, the industry's low-cost producer has also been Detroit's profitability champion, generating the highest return on capital (18.2 percent)—remarkable for a capital-intensive business and well above its domestic rivals, General Motors Corp. (13.8 percent) and Ford Motor Co. (9.1 percent). Fueling buyers' insatiable enthusiasm for pickups, minivans, and trucks, the company raced to a market share of 15.5 percent of the U.S. automobile and light-truck market in 1998. Its hot-selling models—the Dodge Ram pickup, the Dodge Caravan, the Jeep Grand Cherokee, and the Durango sport utility vehicle—underpinned the $61 billion giant's revival.

Chrysler's success is due in large part to a new kind of organizational culture—the culture of co-leadership. It's a formula for success that, arguably, made Chrysler the world's hottest car company, a turnaround that did not go unnoticed by foreign investors. In a shake-up of unprecedented proportions, Daimler-Benz AG, Germany's luxury automaker and largest industrial firm, acquired a controlling interest in the 73-year-old company in November 1998. The combined entity, named DaimlerChrysler AG, ranks as the third largest maker of cars and light trucks in terms of revenues. However, this megadeal— 23 at the time, the largest industrial merger in history—would not have occurred without an earlier reversal of Chrysler's fortunes.

The architects of the automaker's amazing renaissance were two Bobs: chairman and CEO Robert J. Eaton and former president and COO Robert A. Lutz. For their remarkable efforts, *Fortune* ranked the company the "most admired" U.S. carmaker in 1997. Following suit, *Forbes* named Chrysler its Company of the Year and put co-leaders Eaton and Lutz on its cover. Not to be outdone, *Business Week* cited the two Bobs on its 1997 list of the world's best executives—the only twosome among such luminaries as Microsoft's Bill Gates, Andy Grove of Intel, GE's Jack Welch, and IBM's Louis Gerstner.

In many respects the two Bobs seem an unlikely pair. But despite their vastly different backgrounds, they have proved uncannily complementary. In 1993 low-octane Bob Eaton got the job high-octane Bob Lutz lusted after—the chairmanship of Chrysler. But when Lutz's longed-for promotion didn't come, the obviously bruised ex-Marine swallowed his pride. "Being a team player, which I am, you don't sulk and quit when someone else is selected captain of the team," he said at the time. Instead he found a kind of serenity as Chrysler's No. 1 co-leader. "The combination of Bob [Eaton] being chairman and me being president [was] the best period of my whole career," Lutz said. The inspiring tale of the two Bobs demonstrates Chrysler top management's ability to share the reins. It underscores one of the axioms of co-leadership: that true leadership can flourish outside the top job, to the benefit of both the individual and the organization.

Wild Geese

In an industry long associated with nerdy engineers, tightfisted controllers, and faceless bureaucrats, the automobile business has had its share of pioneering iconoclasts—men like Henry Ford, maverick GM founder Billy Durant, Walt Chrysler, Lee Iacocca, even (for better or for worse) John DeLorean. Robert Lutz was another of these creative highfliers.

Born in cosmopolitan Zurich, Switzerland, in 1932, Lutz grew up in affluence. The son of a wealthy banker, he spent a privileged childhood shuttling back and forth between Westchester County, New York, and a succession of Swiss boarding schools. After he was tossed out of one school, his father gave him a second chance on the condition that Lutz enlist in the United States Marine Corps immediately on graduation from high school. In 1954 young Lutz kept his end of the bargain and became an aviation cadet. Later as a commissioned officer he flew A-4 Skyhawks for five years. In 1959 he left active duty as a captain and, at age 27, enrolled in the University of California at Berkeley, where he graduated with honors and B.S. and M.B.A. degrees.

Shortly thereafter Lutz began his 36-year career in the automobile business as a product planner with General Motors Corp. His fluency in French and German soon earned him a European posting, where he rose to the rank of executive vice president (EVP) for sales and marketing of GM's Opel unit in Germany. However, eight years of suffering through the hidebound bureaucracy and arrogance of the world's largest carmaker prompted him to join Bayerische Motoren Werke AG at a salary eight times higher than that at GM. In three years he had climbed to EVP of sales and won the respect of his superiors. Eberhard von Kunheim, the former chairman of BMW, recalls Lutz's intuitive feel for a great product: "He could go into the styling studio and sense when you needed to change a line by a half millimeter here and a millimeter there. He was always right."

Ford, too, sensed something special in the cocky former jet jockey and in 1974 recruited him to run its German business. Five years later he vaulted to head of Ford Europe. Then in 1982, he returned to Dearborn to pilot the company's international operations. After another successful stint in Europe, it was back to corporate headquarters to run the truck division. "The nice thing about working somewhere else," Lutz recalls, "is that you begin to understand very quickly that, hey, we don't do everything right in the United States. People who were in Europe knew 20 or 30 years ago that American automobiles were going to become more like European automobiles. . . . They knew European cars were more fuel efficient and fun to drive."

Despite his rapid ascent, nonconformist Lutz was repeatedly warned that he had to tone down what Ford officials felt was his too-abrasive style. Chairman Philip Caldwell told him to stop talking to the press. Lutz's macho flamboyance was not for the faint of heart: He sometimes used his pocketknife to stir cream into his coffee, licking the blade afterward. For reasons that had more to do with style than substance, Lutz was passed over when the Ford presidency opened up in a major management shuffle.

In June 1986 Lutz, age 54, joined a bevy of Ford refugees who bolted to Chrysler. Feeling he was "running in place" at Ford, Lutz said "there was a lot about Chrysler that I found very appealing. Chrysler was seen, in those days, as sort of the last refuge of automotive malcontents, and I guess I pretty much fit that description. In fact, throughout my life, I've never really poured into the standard mold too well."

In Chrysler's blunt, plain-speaking CEO, Lee Iacocca, Lutz thought he had found the ideal soul mate. The cigar-chomping chairman had experienced firsthand the sting of seeing the top slot go to someone else. In 1978 Ford President Iacocca was the most likely successor to Chairman Henry Ford II, who had served 34 years at the helm. But Mr. Ford ultimately chose Philip Caldwell as the new CEO. Iacocca was furious, claiming surprise at the announcement, although company insiders say they believe he knew or should have known better. Ford's explanation to the dismayed Iacocca was brutally simple: "I just don't like you."

As head of Chrysler's truck operations, international activities, and component business, Lutz was an able and loyal lieutenant to Iacocca. But Lutz soon sensed that his boisterous boss might be more interested in blowing his own trumpet than in curing the company's ills. By the time Lutz was named president in 1991, his relations with the CEO were souring. Lutz openly opposed Iacocca's plans to link up with Italy's Fiat S.p.A. When the merger talks broke down, Lutz said publicly and none too diplomatically: "You really can't find a husband for a woman who is sick on her deathbed in the hospital."

From then on, Lutz admits, he "was given an abundance of not-too-subtle signals" that he would never get the No. 1 job at Chrysler. There is little doubt that his penchant for butting heads with Iacocca cost Lutz the top job. "It didn't take a rocket scientist to see I wasn't going to be Lee's successor," he recalls. "I had never been given any indication or any encouragement, not by the board and not by Lee himself."

On March 16, 1992, the 67-year-old Iacocca named as his replacement Bob Eaton, the head of General Motors' successful European subsidiary. The savvy Eaton had little horsepower in the charisma department, but he quickly revealed outstanding co-leadership skills. Upon Eaton's elevation to the chairmanship in January 1993, he sought to eliminate the political infighting of the Iacocca years, when warring camps—typically marketing, sales, and finance versus engineering, design, and technical support—undermined the company's progress. "It was horrible," one company insider said of the pre-Eaton culture at Chrysler.

Above all Eaton wanted to stem the exodus of key managers that had marked the Iacocca regime. Eaton knew that, especially in tough times, employees want their leaders to be a force of stability. Thus his top priority was to make Chrysler a more dependable, predictable organization, run by a cohesive team of co-leaders. His new order was the so-called Chrysler difference: a corporate culture that rejected bickering and self-aggrandizement and established and rewarded team-oriented goals.

To achieve this Eaton initiated daylong conferences and weekend getaways with his team of co-leaders. The preferred venue was the Thomas Edison Inn in Port Huron, about 60 miles north of Detroit. What's been termed "the Port Huron experience" was designed to get everyone involved and to foster collaboration. The atmosphere was collegial, not corporate. At one of these early meetings, one attendee recalls: "We sat in a room around a U-shaped table with easels and colored markers. Bob stood at one of the easels like a teacher or a coach helping us form our vision of the future. Can you imagine Iacocca doing this? No way!"

For many participants the initial reaction to the Port Huron retreats was complete surprise. "Instead of caution, he urged speed . . . ," Lutz said of his new boss. "Instead of drawing in our horns he urged us to be even bolder. . . . In the old days, only one person would talk. Dissenting voices were not easily tolerated and could be considered non-career-enhancing." However, under CEO Eaton commanding gave way to coaching, and the Chrysler difference began to take hold. "Before Bob, we had never tried to fundamentally change how we worked together," remembers former vice chairman Thomas G. Denomme. "He was the teacher. He was the catalyst."

While revamping the corporate culture, Eaton also understood the crucial importance of persuading the wounded Bob Lutz to stay.

As an outsider, Eaton needed his veteran No. 2's intimate knowledge of the company and, more important, his product expertise and vision. If Chrysler were to be truly different and bounce back from near bankruptcy, the incoming chairman would have to rely heavily on Lutz, the man Eaton had aced out of the top job. No easy task. "The betting in Detroit was that he and I would never get along," writes Lutz in his best-selling autobiography, *GUTS,* "that his presence would somehow upset the apple cart at the company, either by my doing my best to torpedo him or else his doing his best to change things just for the sake of change (and ego gratification). But people who thought that don't know me—and they certainly don't know Bob Eaton."

Letting Lutz Be Lutz

In mapping his approach to Lutz, Eaton first had to take his considerable measure. The larger-than-life Lutz lives in the fast lane. Patrician, ramrod straight, the former fighter pilot loves speed in all its forms. From his Swiss chalet–styled home on an 80-acre estate in Ann Arbor, Michigan, he often piloted his McDonnell Douglas MD500 helicopter to work. He also maintains a stable of other fast toys, including 6 motorcycles (one a 1952 Rumi Super Sport), 12 cars (among them a 1934 LaSalle convertible), and 6 trucks. Lutz would even drive the pace car—a Viper GT—in the Indy 500. In 1992 Lutz introduced the Jeep Grand Cherokee by driving then Detroit Mayor Coleman Young up the stairs of Cobo Hall Convention Center and right through a plate-glass window. Five years later, sporting a fake tattoo, Lutz played short-order cook while launching the wildly successful four-door Ram truck at the Chicago Auto Show.

For weekend entertainment Lutz still flies his own 600-mph Czech-built Aero L-39 Albatross jet fighter. In the past decade, he has had two near misses—once he crashed his helicopter at the Ann Arbor airport, another time he failed to deploy the landing gear on his jet. It is little wonder that he is known around Motown as Chrysler's top gun.

Together with third wife Denise, a filmmaker, advertising art director, and—yes—pilot, Lutz leads a high-profile life in Detroit and beyond. He is a sought-after speaker, and the press loves him. Chomping his ever present Cuban cigar, the martini-drinking vegetarian is outspoken and wittily acerbic. In retrospect the Eaton-Lutz chemistry is obvious. But in 1993 many skeptics wondered whether the quiet, unassuming Eaton could corral this brash, risk-taking maverick.

Yet from the start the two Bobs bonded. Perhaps the common ground was their mutual love of fast cars. For whatever reason Eaton made a crucial decision early on, to let Lutz be Lutz. "[A CEO] can't do it all. It's not fair to give somebody the job of president and chief operating officer and not give him autonomy." To his credit the new CEO acted in the very best tradition of co-leadership by freeing Lutz to exercise his remarkable talent without forcing him to modify his personal style. Had Eaton tried to change the guy once called "a common man's aristocrat," Lutz probably would have walked—to Chrysler's detriment. Instead Eaton realized that Lutz was a unique company asset, albeit an unusually colorful one. Eaton had the ego strength that all great leaders have to promote a co-leader at least as talented as him- or herself. Almost from the beginning, Eaton had no problem with Lutz's stronger charisma, nor did the CEO indulge in any authoritarian, noncollegial demonstrations of who was boss. Eaton seemed surprised when the press wondered if he planned to curb Lutz's aerial activities after his accidents.

As Micheline Maynard of *USA Today* put it: "CEO Eaton long ago gave up the idea of trying to rein in Lutz, whose antics would give other bosses sleepless nights. 'Bob Lutz without motorcycles and planes and fast cars wouldn't be Bob Lutz,' Eaton says. 'It would never occur to me even once to think about grounding him.' "

The partnership philosophy that Eaton created at Chrysler was an abrupt departure from the imperial atmosphere of the Iacocca regime. While pushing for greater efficiency and quality, Eaton decided to keep his hands off the product development process—refreshing news for the company's many passionate car guys of both genders. The new, consensus-minded CEO quickly approved the company's five-year product plan, largely developed by Lutz, and gave him free rein to execute it. Empowered as no Chrysler deputy had ever been, Lutz assumed complete control over day-to-day carmaking operations.

A true product visionary, Lutz nurtured and fought for the bold cars that underpin Chrysler's recent revival. He and the co-leaders he in turn developed (co-leadership tends to be contagious) reveled in the freedom that allowed them to create one eye-popping model after another. Among them: the Dodge Viper, Plymouth Prowler, and Chrysler's so-called LH cars—large, front-wheel drive, four-door family sedans that share key parts and are built at the same plant but have distinctive looks and are sold under different brand names.

"I just love the process of creating, helping create or guiding the creative team that creates this enormously interesting human artifact we call the modern car and light truck," Lutz said. From research and design to development, the company's brilliant No. 2 transformed the entire planning and production processes now envied by the rest of the auto industry.

At the heart of the firm's state-of-the-art production systems are its much vaunted, cross-functional platform teams. In the late 1980s, Lutz, with considerable help from engineering head François J. Castaing, pioneered a bold concept for bypassing the company's compartmentalized engineering tradition and using a focused team to develop a new car more quickly and for less money. Under their scheme a team of engineers, designers, suppliers, fabricators, and even marketers is created to develop each new vehicle, or platform, in industry parlance. They work together simultaneously. In the old system, each functional group—design, engineering, and so on—completed its own tasks and then turned the project over to the next group. By tearing down the walls between groups, the platform team approach made product development cheaper and faster by facilitating what Lutz calls, " 'real-time, right-now' problem solving." It had the added benefit of sparking the staff's creativity. Today Chrysler needs 31 months to ship a new model, down from approximately 40 months at the start of the decade. Its ultimate goal is to create vehicles in less than two years.

The introduction of platform teams "was a total 180-degree turn," recalls Robert S. "Steve" Miller, Jr., a former Chrysler vice chairman and chairman and CEO of Waste Management, Inc. "[Lutz's] product vision was different from anything we had seen before." The new approach "immediately clicked," says Lutz, who had experimented with a similar scheme at BMW. Nevertheless, the transition took its toll on Lutz. "It was probably during this period that I lost all hope of someday becoming CEO of Chrysler—even though, I'm convinced, we were laying the groundwork for saving the company," he recalls. "And, yes, I have no regrets whatsoever; in fact, I'd do it all over again in a heartbeat!" Sticking to his principles, Lutz and the company persevered. In short order the revamped process was giving the industry's smallest producer a $1,000 to $1,500 per unit cost advantage over its rivals.

True to his co-leadership style, the chairman kept his hands off the changes to Chrysler's product development systems. Eaton, who was involved with platform teams elsewhere, is quick to praise the Lutz–Castaing systems. "The ones at Chrysler work better than any I've ever been associated with," says Eaton. By listening to subordinates and not second-guessing them, Eaton soon created a new esprit at Chrysler. Eaton didn't just talk about empowerment, he actually shared power. "We don't want things coming to the top," he says. "We just don't get involved in all those decisions like other executives do."

With teamwork the new corporate mantra, the entire product design process became the subject of open, often heated debate. Chrysler's highly regarded head of styling, Tom Gale, recalls that these frank give-and-take sessions were rare elsewhere in the industry and "made us somewhat different." Gale thinks that Chrysler's emphasis on competing ideas, rather than chains of command, routinely produces superior products. Designs at other carmakers, he says, are often "more dictatorial." Gale argues the more consensual approach also caused morale at Chrysler to soar.

Rejecting Detroit's bureaucratic traditions, the co-leadership style of the two Bobs also made the carmaker more nimble and responsive to the marketplace. The partners jettisoned their pet peeves: lengthy pre-meetings, structured agendas, and paralytic planning sessions. "We've gotten rid of the ritualistic B.S. that does nothing but increase response time, add cost, and result in compromise solutions that are the lowest common denominator," Lutz told *Fortune*. Of the company's more informal, more collegial approach to decision making, Lutz added: "This isn't a love-in, but I've never seen guys work together like this."

Lutz credits Eaton with easing much of the internecine tension associated with Iacocca's tenure. "Bob Eaton is the least princely CEO

I have ever seen in my life," Lutz said. "He is a demanding boss, but he is not imperial. . . . Finally, I [had] a superior here I could respect." Mutual respect is invaluable in changing any organization's culture.

With Eaton as role model, Lutz seems to have overcome his superman complex and adopted a more trusting, decentralist philosophy. Lutz admits he's discovered it's better to trust everyone all the time and get burned once or twice than it is to distrust employees all the time, undermining them in the process. "Most highly qualified people can be trusted to work their tails off for the company, and make the right judgments," Lutz says. "They don't need constant supervision and control to do the right thing. That trust begets trust. And trust begets better performance."

And perform Chrysler did. For six years the two Bobs—Eaton, the diplomat, and Lutz, the hands-on operator—took a backseat to no one. On the operations side, Chrysler held a commanding lead in the industry. With the brassy Lutz overseeing its production methodology, the company imposed exacting technical standards without compromising the creativity or quality that have become Chrysler trademarks. The automaker consistently churned out a new roster of popular cars and trucks cheaply and quickly. Hot models like the Dodge Ram quadcab reflected Lutz's insight that pushing the customer's lustful gotta-have-it button is the key to selling cars, not price or fuel economy.

If only because co-leaders share the spotlight, Eaton repeatedly gave Lutz credit for his impressive contributions at Chrysler, describing Lutz as "integral to our success." "Bob Lutz will go down in history as the greatest president Chrysler has ever had," Eaton said. Lutz in turn gave Eaton the lion's share of credit for Chrysler's bounce back from near death to record profits. "An effective leader is able to inspire people with a clear vision," Lutz said, "an image of what the results will be and motivate them by describing what the rewards will be." Eaton, Lutz argued, not only has "the vision thing," he is uniquely focused on the future. In an interview with *USA Today,* Lutz lauded both Eaton's openness and his comfort in sharing power for the firm's turnaround. "What Bob has," Lutz said, "is self-esteem but no ego, as opposed to somebody who has ego but no self-esteem. . . . He's able to submerge his ego for the good of the enterprise—something a lot of executives just aren't able to do."

Closing Ranks Behind the Boss

In what would be the battle of Eaton's corporate life, the self-effacing CEO confronted his nemesis, Las Vegas billionaire and famed corporate raider Kirk Kerkorian, in 1995. In a long-running dispute, Chrysler's biggest shareholder, Kerkorian's Tracinda Corp., with just under 15 percent of the automaker's stock, wanted Eaton out. It constantly criticized him as bland, indecisive, and too ready to share power. What Chrysler needed, the anti-Eaton group argued, was a more forceful leader, willing to take charge and tighten reins. Its choice: the aggressive, whip-smart Jerome B. York. Then Kerkorian's top aide, York had served for 14 years at Chrysler, most recently as its chief financial officer.

Enlisting ex-chairman Lee Iacocca to his team, Kerkorian mounted a vicious assault on Chrysler and its embattled chairman. In an interesting tactic, Kerkorian insisted on a key role for Lutz, then 63, beyond the firm's mandatory retirement age of 65. Not to be outflanked, Eaton quickly countered, winning board approval to extend Lutz's tenure for the indefinite future. "Bob Lutz makes a hell of a contribution to this company," Eaton told *Business Week,* "and I intend to see he keeps doing that." Besides checkmating Kerkorian, Eaton appeased the many institutional investors who also held his chief co-leader in high regard.

Frustrated, Kerkorian then tried to appeal directly to Lutz. In trashing Eaton Kerkorian insisted that a Jerome York–led Chrysler would more fully exploit the talented lieutenant's abilities. Touting Lutz as "arguably the best product-development executive in the business on a worldwide basis," York pitched to no avail. "I would ten times rather work for a Chrysler run by Bob Eaton than a Chrysler run by Jerry York," Lutz said.

In retrospect the flaws in the takeover strategy are clear. Kerkorian failed to appreciate the earlier tensions between Lutz and York, both rivals in the race to replace Iacocca. Also, by allying with Iacocca, Kerkorian scored no points with Lutz.

After months of public bickering, Tracinda called it quits. Kerkorian agreed not to raise his stake in Chrysler, while the auto company agreed to give his forces a seat on the board. In quashing the takeover, Eaton demonstrated his resolve. "This guy is not a wimp," big, broad-shouldered Lutz said of his low-key superior. "Bob Eaton knows exactly what he wants." University of Michigan Professor David Cole, a leading expert on the global auto industry, agrees: "He's not a pushover."

Taking the gloves off against Kerkorian and company came naturally to the Colorado-born Eaton. The CEO is no child of privilege. His father was a brakeman for the Santa Fe Railroad, and his mother was a beautician, working out of their home. Whether young Eaton was delivering papers or harvesting wheat, he never had a spare moment. "Bob worked for absolutely everything he got," one boyhood friend recalls.

The fearless but unassuming Eaton, 10 years younger than co-leader Lutz, earned a B.S. in mechanical engineering from the University of Kansas in 1963 while working summers in an Oregon pea cannery. After college it was off to General Motors' Chevrolet Motor Division as a trainee. Eaton moved through a variety of engineering assignments, including running GM's sprawling technical center, which develops new cars and trucks. There he worked briefly for John DeLorean on the X-car, GM's first front-wheel drive auto. To broaden Eaton the auto giant sent him to Zurich to run its European operations in 1988. Under his leadership, GM Europe grossed $1.7 billion in 1991, when the company's North American operations were losing a staggering $7.9 billion. A year later Eaton traded in General Motors for Chrysler.

Although not as outgoing as Iacocca and never the publicity seeker he was, Eaton is no pushover. He made the No. 3 carmaker No. 1 in profits by cleaning up the balance sheet and revamping its culture. Eaton, in fact, may be the first CEO in decades who kept Chrysler from stalling out in a slowdown. He also molded a smart, disciplined management team with deep bench strength.

As the stabilizing force behind Chrysler's recovery, Eaton is finally receiving much-overdue recognition for his achievements. In a 1997 *Forbes*-commissioned Gallup poll of 400 corporate CEOs, he ranked fifth behind Jack Welch, Andy Grove, the late Roberto Goizueta, and Bill Gates.

Chemistry Lessons

What sets Eaton apart from many of his peers is his commitment to power sharing rather than power wielding. In order to forge a partnership with Lutz, Eaton redefined empowerment as genuine co-leadership, insisting that the two have crossover duties. "Sometimes I do aspects of the chairman's job, sometimes Bob does aspects of my job," Lutz told *USA Today,* while conceding that "Eaton's got a more conceptual, chairmanlike view of things." Able to laugh at himself, Eaton insists on give-and-take, even fun and games. In order to spark a meeting, Lutz says, "Sometimes I make fun of Bob. Sometimes he makes fun of me. No place is it written that we have to go at this in a grim way."

The depth of leadership Eaton has nurtured at Chrysler helped him trump Tracinda and make other difficult decisions. With his blessing the carmaker's co-leaders are encouraged to take risks. We believe, Lutz says: "The worst risk you can take is no risk." Eschewing "malicious obedience," Chrysler definitely takes risks. "They understand that this isn't a commodity business," says Christopher Ceder-gren, an automobile analyst in Thousand Oaks, California.

Chrysler executives are allowed to say "Oops!"—as they did in 1996 when the company decided to kill its long-awaited, rear-wheel drive luxury car. After considerable analysis and debate, Eaton blessed management's decision to walk away from the pricey design, code-named LX, which was targeted to go head-on against BMW, Mercedes, Jaguar, Lexus, and Infiniti. A more headstrong CEO might have flogged a dead horse in order to save face. Not Eaton. "It says a lot about the way Chrysler operates," Lutz says. "It really gets down to: What do we want to be? Do we want to be like everybody else? . . . The more you try to broaden appeal by attempting to please every whim of every consumer, the less you pinpoint the area in which your product, and only your product, can be of service." The highly competitive luxury car segment was already overcrowded, Lutz explains. "In the end we'd rather be first in a new place than seventh in the place everyone's rushing to."

Knowing when to say no is a critical trait of any world-class executive. And Eaton has it in spades. Besides nixing the luxury car project, he approved Chrysler's exit from Vietnam and backed away from huge additional investments in China, opting to concentrate instead on the North American market, where more than three-fourths of all Chryslers are sold. "One thing about Bob Eaton, he doesn't get carried away," says Lutz. "Other people give away more and more just to get the deal. Bob draws the line. That's it. . . . Strong leaders win respect by sticking to their guns. While a good leader can and does command a spectrum of styles, he or she should *never* succumb to consensus-driven management. That, to me, is a place leaders don't want to go!"

Although CEO Eaton listens carefully to his associates, there is no question who is in charge. Strong co-leaders want strong leaders, and Eaton has never been shy about vetoing his colleagues, including the highflying Lutz. When Lutz wanted to announce the retro-style Plymouth Prowler months before its official introduction, Eaton nixed the idea—not wanting to tip Chrysler's hand to its rivals. After hashing out their differences in private, Lutz agreed. "If we're at loggerheads, it's always strictly business," Lutz said. "It never gets personal." In true co-leadership ego is never as important as the shared mission and common goal.

For all its commitment to co-leadership, Chrysler is no democracy. "Leaders drive change!," Lutz bellows, viewing life "as a battle— or at least a heated conversation." He believes that a company can have too much togetherness, too much teamwork. "If you have 'groupthink', you may all love one another," he told *Automotive Industries,* "but it's usually not long before the amorous lemmings all run off the cliff together!"

In his last duties as a Chrysler vice chairman, Lutz continued to demand unlemming-like behavior. He fought hard to nurture strong, independent thinkers—people who rely on instinct and experience. In an interview with *Forbes,* he said: "[The industry] put so much faith in analysis and quantification and other areas of left-brain thinking we've often missed the forest for all the well-examined trees. . . . Over the past few years, I've been on sort of a personal crusade at Chrysler to legitimize . . . right-brain thinking."

At Chrysler, Lutz contends, right-brained thinking has played a pivotal role in the carmaker's recent success. For example, in designing the sassy 400-horsepower, two-seat, retro-roadster Dodge Viper, the company relied mostly on instinct, not analysis. "We didn't do any [market] research on that car at all: We just built it! Because that's what our intuition as 'car people' told us to do." Lutz believes the company's "dare-to-be-different product philosophy" has made Chrysler truly different, and better.

At Chrysler co-leader Lutz also took special pride in ridding the company of "numbers Nazis," control freaks who choke the operating people. "A worship of control for its own sake . . . denotes a company badly out of balance," he says. Recalling his days at "control-obsessed" Ford, Lutz argues that "with financial controls, looser is frequently better." Nevertheless, changing an environment of excessive control (in his words, "trying to move an extreme left-brained organization more in the direction of a left-right balance") is never easy. "Fear of the unknown," he says, "fear of loss of control [with all the horrors that term implies] will make change extremely hard." According to insiders Lutz was a major force in making Chrysler a more balanced, less buttoned-down enterprise.

For a host of reasons, industry analysts think Lutz's orneriness and daring-do will be hard to replace. "He's one of the last executives from the old school—one of those intense, car-oriented executives who makes decisions by the seat of his pants," said Kim Korth, president of IRN Inc., an automotive research firm in Grand Rapids, Michigan.

Until his retirement in July 1998, Lutz remained the carmaker's creative conscience. His last stint as vice chairman was as mentor or coach (in his words "Chief Coaching Officer") to the company's next generation of managers. From Chrysler's gleaming corporate headquarters in the Detroit suburb of Auburn Hills, he taught and inspired them. However, Eaton made sure that Lutz continued to focus on "making sure we retain our product edge," which was good news for Wall Street and for Chrysler shareholders.

Building a Dream Team

As Bob Lutz's career wound down, Eaton had a cadre of talented executives ready to take over. In December 1997 he tapped as his new copilot Thomas T. Stallkamp, a 51-year-old executive vice president and 17-year Chrysler veteran. On July 1, 1998, the new president promptly assumed day-to-day operations and became Eaton's most likely successor as CEO. Unlike Lutz, Stallkamp isn't a whiz at product creation, but he is credited with cutting more than $5 billion in costs as head of procurement and supply between 1989 and 1998. The outspoken No. 2 turned the unglamorous parts-buying opera-

tion into a major strategic initiative. A self-professed "regular guy,"
Stallkamp gets many of his efficiency ideas studying non-auto companies such as Intel Corp., Hewlett-Packard Co., and Motorola, Inc.
For marketing clues, he looks to retail giant Wal-Mart Stores, Inc., and
mail-order house Lands' End. Why? "There is more invention going
on outside of Detroit than there is in Detroit," he says, "and that's
what we want to tap into."

Stallkamp seems like the ideal replacement for the rough-and-
tumble former president. Lutz gave Chrysler its personality and
helped shape its image as Motown's brashest automaker. However, in
a mature market with long-term growth rates of only one percent a
year, new talents are required. Today's car buyers are uniquely savvy
since the Internet demystified pricing. They not only won't tolerate
price increases, they insist on generous incentives. So Chrysler's best
chances at improving earnings will come from trimming expenses.
Notoriously tough when it comes to costs, Stallkamp believes
"tremendous inefficiencies" have been built into the business of
building and selling cars and trucks. He estimates waste accounts for
as much as one-third of all spending at Chrysler. Therefore he
promises to redouble the company's efforts to slash expenses. His goal
for 1998: $1.5 billion.

Blind ambition? Perhaps, but Stallkamp knows the difference
between success and failure—the Chrysler difference—is people.
"You challenge your people to not be traditional and to find out-of-
the-box thinking" to solve problems, he says. No plodding penny-
pincher, Tom Stallkamp is a "brilliant integrator," according to Lutz.
"He makes people work together and get the job done. Some people
have good relationships, but can't get results. Some leave a wasteland
of destroyed people behind him." Stallkamp is results-oriented without being toxic. He is, Lutz says, "a guy who has the hard edge to get
the job done."

Few people expect President Stallkamp to have difficulty managing a bevy of outstanding lieutenants. Although there is always some
resentment among people who didn't make the cut, Chrysler's carefully nurtured co-leadership culture should minimize friction. Every
Monday, Stallkamp gathers his six EVPs together for their input. He
meets each one individually later in the week. "We operate as a unit,"
he says, noting that the automaker's team-oriented management

approach gives all key executives a voice in decision making. "The old style that there is a general and all his troops report directly to him is out of vogue—at least at Chrysler."

The Spoils of Second Place

Although Bob Lutz didn't achieve his lifetime dream of holding the No. 1 job at a Big Three auto company, he long ago made peace with himself. "I'd be telling less than the truth if I said I was happy to have been passed over for the top job at Chrysler. But I knew I had to make a decision: whether to sulk or quit or maybe even try to undermine my new boss; or as the Marines say to 'suck it up' and continue on, fighting for what I saw to be the company's right course." Then in an admission uncharacteristic of many senior executives, he adds: "I never really expected to rise as high as I did." Being passed over "was easy to come to terms with. . . . [But] things turned out for the best. . . . Too many people in this business look at winning to mean getting yourself promoted to the highest level possible. We [need to] focus on the idea of the *entire* team winning against the competitors."

In many respects Lutz is especially proud of reversing the self-absorbed, inward-looking "Me! Me! Me!" culture that once governed Chrysler (and, he regrets, much of corporate America). The company "now has what many people consider to be the fastest moving, most efficient, and most successful product-development organization in the auto industry," he says. "And one big reason for all that, I'm convinced, is that as a company we've strived to achieve the same unique mixture of personal empowerment and group discipline so well exemplified by the U.S. Marine Corps."

Displaying his perpetual esprit, Lutz says he found fulfillment in a co-leadership role, simultaneously leading and following. Life is all about balance, he reminds us. On December 1, 1998, Lutz's high-profile career took a new twist when he was renamed chief executive of the struggling Exide Corp. Look for the 66-year-old executive to quickly reverse the fortunes of the nation's biggest battery maker.

■

Working together, the two Bobs put Chrysler in overdrive. Bob Eaton understood then as now that the best thing any leader can do for an organization is to allow its co-leaders to discover their own greatness. "Today, it's the strongest team that wins," he said. "I want to be known for having led the best team of any company in the world."

Ironically, as Eaton charts his own future in the newly merged DaimlerChrysler, his experience in co-leadership should serve him well. Although officially a co-CEO of the $130-billion colossus, Eaton seems destined to emerge as the No. 2 man. After a three-year transition period, he plans to step aside, with co-CEO Jürgen Schrempp from Daimler taking command. With Bob Lutz as a model, Eaton should have few problems adjusting to a supporting role.

One lesson of the two Bobs is that you don't have to be in a high-tech business to exhibit superior leadership—not just at the very top but deep down in the organization. Even in mature industries, skillfully led teams of talented individuals can succeed spectacularly. Conversely, corporations still in the grips of myths about the Great Man or Woman will forever lag behind.

3

Cyberstars

Ballmer Is to Gates What Barrett Is to Grove

Gates Passes the Ball to Ballmer: Billionaire Bill (left) enjoys a "high bandwith" relationship with fellow billionaire, co-leader Steve. (Gamma Liaison)

Cyberstars: Intel chairman Andy Grove is right behind heir apparent Craig Barrett. (AP Wide World Photo)

41

3 | Cyberstars

*There are two kinds of people: Those who
do the work and those who take the credit.
Try to be in the first group; there is less
competition there.*
—INDIRA GANDHI

"Any sufficiently advanced technology," wrote futurist Arthur C. Clarke in the early 1960s, "is indistinguishable from magic." Until recently technology and magic were synonymous for many folks, who thought semiconductors were part-time orchestra leaders and microchips tiny snack foods. Leave it to Microsoft's Bill Gates and Intel's Andy Grove to take the gobbledygook out of the New Economy. More than anyone else, these two high-tech impresarios are responsible for integrating digital age technology into the American culture.

Today almost half of U.S. homes have personal computers. Indeed the home is the site of these cyberstars' greatest success. In an alliance known as Wintel, Microsoft's Windows operating systems and Intel microprocessors joined to make the personal computer the dominant feature of the New Economy. Microsoft's stronghold on PC operating systems is legend. Doubling in size every two years, the Redmond, Washington, colossus represents roughly 60 percent of the value of the entire software industry and, to most observers, the most highly valued company in the world. Its earnings and sales have risen at a rate of more than 30 percent a year for the past five years.

Intel's hegemony in personal computing is even more pronounced. The Silicon Valley powerhouse supplies close to 90 percent

43

of the world's PCs with its microprocessors. Worth almost $125 billion (more than IBM), with $6.95 billion in net income (the third most profitable business in the country), Intel has seen its sales head skyward, growing 20 percent to 50 percent for each of the past five years. Since Grove took over as CEO in 1987, the chip maker's average annual return to investors has been an astounding 44 percent.

For the King Kongs of the New Economy, celebrity is part of their jobs. William Henry Gates III, who has more than a billion dollars for each of the 40-some years of his life, became a cult hero by creating Microsoft. Two decades older Andrew S. Grove, *Time* magazine's 1997 Man of the Year, came to America a Holocaust survivor and penniless refugee and went on to make Intel the world's largest chip maker. As the economic center of gravity shifts westward, Gates and Grove represent the ultimate success of modern American capitalism. As powerful as they are, neither man runs his company alone; both promote environments where co-leadership thrives.

In the digital age, co-leaders count. Intellectual property—people—matter most. As the postindustrial revolution embraces speed and change, it requires ample stores of fresh-faced knowledge workers who can alter the environment in new and exciting ways. Microsoft and Intel are high-paying meritocracies where geniuses flourish. Both companies blend brainpower with cultures that emphasize lifetime learning, risk taking, accountability, and closeness to the customer. In addition to the charismatic men at the top, both companies have deep reservoirs of first-rate talent that help account for their strong earnings and seemingly impregnable market positions. Witness, for instance, the significant contributions of co-leaders Steve Ballmer and Craig Barrett.

Bill's Brain Trust

Harvard Yard has rarely boasted a better intellectual match than Bill Gates and Steve Ballmer. In 1973 the unlikely twosome met at the movies when both lived in Harvard's Currier House. Gates, the eccentric introvert from a wealthy Seattle family, never found his niche in Cambridge. Brilliant, but bored and boorish, he cut required classes to audit graduate courses in economics and math. Playing poker became a favorite pastime. Then a big, blustery but socially adept Steve Ballmer took Gates under his wing. The muscular, energetic six-footer nurtured Gates, getting him to join the Fox Club, a men's eating and drinking society, and make the occasional foray into New York City. But in the spring of 1975, Gates's old high school pal Paul Allen persuaded him to become Harvard's most famous dropout and to join Allen in starting the world's first microcomputer software company. Eventually they dubbed it Microsoft.

Ballmer stayed on at Harvard to graduate magna cum laude in applied mathematics. (Earlier he had bested Gates in the Putnam national mathematics competition for undergraduates.) After Harvard, Ballmer went to Procter & Gamble Co. for a short-lived career in consumer marketing. There he served as an assistant product manager, overseeing, among other things, a dessert flop called Coldsnap (a package of which he still keeps in his office as a reminder of why concepts fail). But Ballmer had his successes as well. As James Wallace and Jim Erickson write in *Hard Drive,* their best-seller on Gates and Microsoft: "At Procter & Gamble, Ballmer had become known for redesigning the company's Duncan Hines cake mix box so that it sat on store shelves horizontally rather than vertically to grab more space. Ballmer would later say that's what he wanted to do at Microsoft— help Gates squeeze out the competition."

After two years at P&G, Stanford Business School beckoned. There Ballmer won prestigious first-year student awards from the Boston Consulting Group and its rival, Bain & Co. But midway through Ballmer's first year at Stanford, Gates persuaded him to join the fast-growing Microsoft. Demand for Microsoft's services exceeded what the company could supply. The fledgling firm was swamped with, in Gates's words, "all kinds of interesting projects that had the potential to turn into something big." Ballmer was just the kind of smart, tough non–techie Gates needed to drive the business side of the company. After some haggling, Ballmer dropped out of business school and signed up for $40,000 a year, plus 8.75 percent (now diluted to 5.1 percent) of Microsoft stock.

In 1980 Ballmer was the first nonprogrammer hired by the company, and Gates gave him wide berth in his initial assignments. Almost immediately Ballmer became the company's recruiting coordinator, a job he knew to be key in any information business and a job he loved. Ballmer sought new hires at such elite campuses as Harvard,

MIT, and Carnegie Mellon, wooing candidates with the promise of
stock options, not huge salaries. He looked for people with enormous
intelligence, energy, and drive. In a 1983 interview with *InfoWorld,*
Ballmer explained Microsoft's recruiting philosophy. "There's a standing policy here," he said. "Whenever you meet a kick-ass guy, get
him. Do we have a head-count budget? No way. There are some guys
you meet only once in a lifetime. So why screw around?"

In addition Ballmer oversaw the purchase of Seattle Computer
Products' operating system, QDOS (for "quick and dirty operating
system"), for the bargain-basement price of $50,000. Renamed MS-
DOS, this system has been the core of Microsoft's software success.

Ballmer's next task was to win over the techies. No small feat,
because, as Gates remembered: "We didn't really believe nonprogram-
mers should manage programmers." Nevertheless, in 1983 Ballmer
was given his first opportunity to manage software developers. The
original Windows concept was stalled, and Ballmer's job was to get
the techies moving the product off the line. Physically imposing,
Ballmer blends vast amounts of energy and raw intellect with a willingness to listen. "The developers accepted him early on because he
was smart," Gates recalled. "He would sit and listen to them, understand the things that they really liked to do." Besides listening,
Ballmer demanded 100 percent effort. As he told *Forbes,* "I learned
that you have to get the right guys, and you've got to look them in
the eyes and listen, and find the guys you can trust. Then ride them."

With Ballmer cracking the whip, the Windows team went into
overdrive, moved sleeping bags into their cubicles, and got the job
done. In Microspeak these frenzied periods of activity before a ship
date are called Death Marches. According to a lexicon of insider jargon, Death Marches are fueled by flatfood, described as food "mostly
from vending machines, that you can slip under people's doors so
they can keep working."

If Ballmer has a shortcoming, it is relentlessly riding himself and
others. Sometimes The Embalmer, as the bellicose No. 2 is called by
some insiders, presses too hard, as he did at a company meeting in
1991 when he actually blew out his vocal cords (they had to be sur-
gically repaired). Yet it is Ballmer's zealotry, as much as Gates's leadership, that has enabled Microsoft to achieve its remarkable market
power.

For all his bluster, Ballmer is a co-leader very much in the style of Helen Keller's teacher, Anne Sullivan Macy, who did whatever was necessary to serve her beloved pupil. According to a Microsoft official, Ballmer often talked about the time he spent as head equipment manager for the Harvard football team. The executive speculates: "I think he saw himself as . . . someone who loved making sure the bucket of water was there so the team could win. Bill was going to be the quarterback, and Steve was going to be the guy who would do any damn thing it took to make this work." When asked to describe their 25-year partnership, Ballmer confessed: "It's like a marriage." Just how far will Ballmer go to serve Gates and Microsoft? It was allegedly Ballmer who, at Gates's request, asked Melinda French to sign a prenuptial agreement before her marriage to Gates in 1994.

Bashing Big Blue

As Bill Gates endeavors to find new markets, Steve Ballmer figures out ways to dominate them. "If Gates is the grand strategist," wrote *Forbes*'s Jeffrey Young, "Ballmer is the master tactician."

On numerous occasions Ballmer's brass-knuckle tactics have served Microsoft well. IBM, among others, learned a sobering lesson about software competition and innovation and what it means to confront steamroller Steve and his cohorts at Microsoft. In 1980 IBM, the unchallenged leader in computer hardware, decided to enter the personal computer market. To jump start the project, Big Blue scrapped its tradition of creating all its own hardware and software. After intense negotiations, Microsoft emerged as the exclusive software licensee of MS-DOS. Better yet, Microsoft, along with Intel, which provided the microprocessors that are the powertrains of most PCs, were allowed to license their technology to companies other than IBM. This produced the PC-clone industry that dominates the market today.

Within a few years, IBM dominated the personal computer market. Microsoft's operating systems became the industry standard, not only on IBM but also on IBM-compatible machines. However, by 1983 Gates was convinced that the character-based MS-DOS technology was outmoded. Future interfaces would be graphical, with icons that allowed users to communicate more easily with their PCs.

That same year Microsoft announced its plans to bring graphical computing to the IBM PC with a product called Windows. The new product would allow consumers to use a mouse to engage graphical images on the screen and would feature on-screen windows, each of which could run a different program.

After much cajoling, Ballmer convinced IBM to collaborate on a replacement for MS-DOS, called OS/2. The terms of the alliance allowed Microsoft to sell the same operating system that IBM was using to other manufacturers. Each party could also further extend the operating system beyond what they had developed together. But when Ballmer wanted to make Windows the standard operating software for OS/2, IBM balked.

IBM repeatedly rebuffed Microsoft's pleas to oversee the operating systems project. Although Microsoft continued to develop OS/2 applications, its confidence in the sluggish system faded, and so Microsoft pressed on its own with Windows. "We hedged our bets; we had to," Ballmer told *Forbes,* clearly delighted at the prospect of bashing IBM. Over time the worse OS/2 looked, the better Windows seemed.

In 1990 Microsoft launched its much superior Windows 3.0, thereby dooming IBM's clumsy OS/2 system. The move not only hurt Big Blue's standing in the PC business, it also threw into confusion the leaders in the applications software industry—Lotus and WordPerfect—who had been creating new spreadsheet and word processing products for OS/2. With Windows 3.0 Microsoft became a key player in the applications software business, grabbing the lion's share with its Excel spreadsheet and Word word processing programs. Roughly two-thirds of Microsoft's present sales come from applications, and the company is by far the biggest, most profitable vendor in the industry.

As IBM learned the hard way, Microsoft's slogan "Windows Everywhere" became reality—thanks, in large part, to Steve Ballmer's incessant promotion. More than 90 million units of Windows were sold in 1998, and Windows is now installed in roughly 400 million PCs. In the high-performance corporate market, Windows 95 and Windows NT Workstation 4.0 are installed in more than 200 million machines. Yet co-leader Ballmer, like Gates, is never satisfied. "We need to . . . continue to broaden out the places in which those Windows applications can be delivered—more platforms serving more market opportunities, more niches," Ballmer said in his keynote address to the 1997 PC Expo.

When it comes to the competition, Ballmer gives no quarter. As his interactions with IBM suggest, Ballmer is ruthless in defending Microsoft's turf. In recent years he has led the charge against Internet rival Netscape Communications Corp. Worried that Netscape, using the Java language, could turn its dominant Internet browser into a virtual operating system, Microsoft built its own browser, Explorer, into Windows 95. Prior to the America Online–Netscape merger, Microsoft had eroded Netscape's market share to 41.5 percent. Microsoft had grabbed a dominant 43.8 percent share of the browser segment in less than four years, in part by giving its Internet Explorer away free and by pressing PC makers to ship it as a condition of licensing Windows (practices that resulted in the 1998 antitrust actions against the company by 20 state Attorneys General and the U.S. Justice Department). Meanwhile Java remains a technological work in progress.

It's small wonder Scott McNealy, chairman and CEO of Sun Microsystems, which developed Java, called Microsoft "the centrally planned economy." In equally strong language, he referred to Microsoft's top two co-leaders as "Ballmer and Butt-head." Such tough lingo only seems to encourage the Microsoft duo to press on with the attack.

Cloning Co-Leaders

For almost two decades, Steve Ballmer has been Microsoft's biggest champion. He is clearly Gates's alter ego ("No one should doubt that he's number two in the company," Gates said). On July 21, 1998, Ballmer was promoted to the presidency, solidifying his role as Gates's heir apparent. Nevertheless, co-leadership permeates the entire organization. "This is an amazing group," said Gates of his co-leaders. "These are all supersmart guys who've grown up with the business. None of these people are trying to push, or care that much about their title, or even care how they are perceived externally." Besides President Ballmer, several other key players include: Chief Operating Officer Bob Herbold, age 55, an ex–P&Ger, who oversees finance and operations while helping systematize Microsoft's strategic planning; frizzy-haired Nathan Myhrvold, who, with a Ph.D. in physics from Princeton, serves as the company's chief technology officer; Pete Higgins, who directs all new initiatives in interactive media; Paul Maritz, ex-Intel exec, who runs most of the product groups; chief counsel Bill Neukom; and Ballmer's right-hand man, Jeff Raikes, who came to Microsoft from Apple Computer in 1981 and now serves as group vice president for sales and marketing. This impressive cast of co-leaders is as important to Microsoft's continued prosperity as the company's outstanding R&D operation, known as Bill Labs.

Gates's brain trust extends far beyond Ballmer. Early in his career, the introverted Gates recognized the need for a close inner circle of topflight co-leaders. "I always knew I would have close business associates like Ballmer and several of the other top people at Microsoft and that we would stick together and grow together no matter what happened," Gates said. "I just decided early on that was part of who I was."

Business rivals like Steve Jobs, cofounder of Apple Computer and now its interim CEO as well as the No. 1 at Pixar Animation Studios, grudgingly admire Gates's ability to create a deep co-leadership team: "Bill has done a great job of cloning himself," Jobs said. "Now there are all these aggressive 'Little Bills' running the various product groups and divisions, and they keep coming at you and coming at you. . . ."

But to characterize the Microsoft team as a band of Little Bills does a disservice to Gates and his chief lieutenants. Microsoft has always hired on intelligence or, in company lingo, "intellectual bandwidth." "Bill is not threatened by smart people, only stupid ones," explains technology chief Myhrvold. Moreover, Gates and Ballmer value and reward contentiousness. Conventional wisdom has no place in their world. "Bill brings to the company the idea that conflict can be a good thing," said Ballmer. "He knows it's important to avoid gentle civility from getting to the heart of an issue quickly. He likes it when anyone, even a junior employee, challenges him, and you know he respects you when he starts shouting back."

In his long tenure at Microsoft, Ballmer has stood toe to toe with the boss on numerous occasions. Within a few weeks of his arrival in Redmond, Ballmer insisted that the fledgling company, which then employed about 30 people, hire an additional 17 folks—and fast. Gates was flabbergasted: He thought taking on so many new people would bankrupt the company. The argument raged for hours, with Ballmer, who was Gates's housemate at the time, moving out in a huff. Fortunately Gates's father calmed both men down. The next day Ballmer got permission to hire his new employees. "To this day," Gates said, "we've been hiring smart people as fast as we can find them."

Besides encouraging dissent, a hallmark of effective co-leadership, Gates practices the kind of egalitarianism that fosters a partnership culture. Working out of a rather modest office, Gates is a relaxed, informal leader who personally answers all e-mail from employees. Khakis and flannel shirts are the uniform of the day in the campus-like office complex. The atmosphere is relentlessly nonhierarchical. The most junior and senior staffers engage in spirited give-and-take in windowless conference rooms filled with standard-issue furniture. Company picnics, complete with rodeos and rock bands, give employees at all levels a chance to bond with each other, and annual off-campus retreats allow all employees to ponder the software maker's future.

"We win because we hire the smartest people," Gates has often said. But attracting the best and the brightest is only the first step at Microsoft. Gates and his co-leaders strive to keep their workers productive and happy. That's where self-actualization—in plain English, rewarding work—kicks in. Microsoft wins by combining cutting-edge technology, challenging assignments, a spirit of egalitarianism, and esprit de corps. Its staffers exude pride in themselves and the company.

Money also talks. From day one Gates has recognized that stock options are the currency of the New Economy. "Shared ownership through stock options has been more significant and successful than anyone would have predicted," he said of his employees. "Literally billions of dollars of value have accrued to them." Stories of Microsoft millionaires abound. Roughly 80 percent of company employees get stock options, and most professionals hired before 1992 have become millionaires. Not counting Gates and Ballmer (worth $58 billion and $12 billion, respectively, at last count), the three most highly compensated Microsofters have an average net worth of at least $20 million.

Despite the material rewards, Gates is a constant worrier. "He still feels he must run scared," Ballmer said. No doubt maintaining one of the world's great businesses—with 25,700 employees and $14 billion in sales—requires constant vigilance. "Success is a lousy teacher," Gates has warned. "It seduces smart people into thinking they can't lose. And it's an unreliable guide to the future."

The path along the information highway is indeed treacherous. But Gates takes comfort in his band of loyal co-leaders. Bonded by a common vision and a piece of the action, co-leaders such as Steve Ballmer maximize Microsoft's chances of maintaining its nearly unshakable franchise.

Andy's Ally

"It is an admission of bankruptcy . . . to have to go outside to recruit top management," Peter Drucker once wrote. He believes that seamless succession planning is a hallmark of any great enterprise. Simply put, any organization that is propped up by a single Great Man or Woman is bound to fail.

Since Intel's founding in 1968, it has excelled at orderly leadership transitions. Each of the chip maker's three legendary founders—Robert Noyce, Gordon Moore, and Andrew S. Grove—served for about a decade as chief executive. On May 20, 1998, the baton passed smoothly once again as Grove, age 61, handed the CEO role over to his well-groomed successor, Craig R. Barrett, age 58, Intel's president and chief operating officer. The charismatic Grove is not planning to disappear. He will continue to work full-time as chairman, spending more time on strategic issues, especially new growth opportunities. "I need to understand the issues that limit the growth of the industry," Grove told USA Today. "That takes time, and that's not consistent with the role of being chief executive officer."

Barrett replaced the hyperaggressive Grove as president in 1997, a move that prompted speculation that Barrett was Grove's heir apparent. Grove had overcome a well-publicized bout with prostate cancer, but he said he did not step down for health reasons. "I am feeling great," Grove said. "I am not putting aside work, but I wanted to put aside the rigidity of Intel management responsibilities . . . to have more flexibility in what I want to pay attention to."

As able as Barrett is, measuring up to Grove won't be easy. During his 11-year reign, Intel grew from $1.9 billion to $25.1 billion in annual revenues. The chip maker thrived in the face of numerous challenges, including the importation of Japanese chips, the emergence of clone chip makers, and competition from rival microprocessor designs, especially the Power PC, a joint venture of IBM, Apple, and Motorola. Under Grove's stewardship, Intel's market value exploded twentyfold, to $125 billion. "Without Andy Grove, Intel might have been a less intense, more friendly company, but it would also be a smaller, less profitable company," said cofounder Moore, Grove's mentor.

What is more, the slender, combative Grove made Silicon Valley all but synonymous with the entrepreneurial spirit that drives the New Economy. The author of three best-selling books, a popular Stanford Business School lecturer, and a regular speaker at major computer industry events, he has come to symbolize a generation of entrepreneurs who founded the Valley's most important companies. Over the past few years, Grove led Intel to invest in more than 100 high-tech start-ups, making it one of the biggest venture capitalists in the world. Yet for all his achievements, Grove said his tenure is over: "It's time, and I'm ready."

Barrett could not have emerged from Grove's shadow at a more critical time. His elevation comes with the company at a crossroads. While its lock on the chip market seems secure, the explosive growth of the Internet and the surge in popularity of low-cost PCs mean that Intel needs to find new markets for its microprocessors in a range of new devices. In recent years the company has seen its blistering profit margins begin to fade—from $235 a chip for most of the '90s to roughly $150 a chip today. With high-end PC sales and margins under pressure, Intel must also grapple with collapsing foreign markets, missed opportunities in consumer appliances (especially the 3Com PalmPilot and WebTV), and antitrust charges by the Federal Trade Commission. The pressure for earnings is across the board.

Clearly these are gut-wrenching times at Intel. "We are concerned that their growth in earnings is going to be stalled for a while," said Dan Scovel, an analyst at Fahnestock & Co., after reviewing Intel's earnings warning in 1998. More critical was Matt Stichnoth, editor of the *Wall Street Companion,* who said: "Their best days are behind them," and postulated that Grove was getting out while the getting was good. A less gloomy but nonetheless concerned Drew

Peck, managing director of the investment firm SG Cowen Securities, predicted: "Intel is facing one of its greatest challenges in the last 10 years." But, Peck added: "Barrett should be the right person for the job."

The first man outside of Intel's founding troika to be CEO, Barrett is up to the task, according to Grove. "He is ready to flex his muscle," Grove said. "He's paid his dues and has lots of ideas, so it's only fair that he have enough time in the job to accomplish what he thinks needs to be done."

The Path To the Top

Craig Barrett grew up south of San Francisco, one of three kids in a lower-middle-class family. A scholarship brought him to Stanford, right up the road from Intel's headquarters in Santa Clara. Stanford Professor William Nix remembers Barrett as a "fiercely competitive" track star who "wanted to be at a place where he could change the world." After receiving his Ph.D. in materials science, Barrett joined the Stanford faculty for what appeared to be a distinguished career in academia. Barrett was a tenured professor there when he got a call from a friend at Intel, asking if he had a student he could recommend to the fledgling company.

"I said no, but could you use a bored professor?" Barrett remembers. Barrett took a one-year leave of absence from Stanford for what he believed would be a temporary post at Intel. As an academic, Barrett felt somewhat intimidated by the Silicon Valley crowd and returned to the comfortable confines of The Farm, as Stanford is known, the next year. But he soon had regrets. "I was back [at Stanford] for about a day when I realized I had made a mistake," he confessed. So The Professor, as he is sometimes called, rejoined Intel full-time in 1974 as a technology development manager. Barrett jumped to vice president in 1984, senior vice president in 1987, executive vice president in 1990, COO in 1993, president in 1997, and CEO a year later.

The six-foot two-inch Barrett's big break came in 1985, the year Intel decided to exit the memory chip business and focus on microprocessors. Named head of manufacturing, Barrett set out to double output. By 1988 he had exceeded that goal, and by 1996 productivity had soared sevenfold.

One of The Professor's breakthrough concepts was the McDonald's-like "Copy Exactly" program, which ensures that all Intel plants use precisely the same equipment and procedures (right down to the color of the paint) to reduce variation and enhance quality. The scheme worked so well that Intel was able to convince customers like Dell Computer Corp. that they didn't need alternative sources of supply for chips—a major breakthrough because computer makers typically shun relying on a single supplier. "Copy Exactly" allowed Intel to produce standardized chips in volume, eliminating the usual long waits between chip introduction and production. This in turn led to Intel's remarkable market dominance and enviable profits.

Boosting both quality and output are passions of Barrett's. A no-nonsense manager with a 7 A.M. to midnight schedule, he personally checks equipment inside each factory for particle contamination. The tall, thin CEO insists that every Intel plant be immaculately clean. Barrett misses nothing, and he never stops pushing. It was Barrett who came to Intel's rescue in 1994 when it was coping with the infamous Pentium flaw, which caused the company's microprocessor to miscalculate certain mathematical equations. Under his watchful eye, Intel now leads the chip-making industry in productivity and quality control. Even Grove, king of the nitpickers, conceded: "I had the operations role before Craig and I thought I was pretty good at it. But I hang my head in shame at how well he's done."

When Barrett was running day-to-day operations, he was given most of the credit for coordinating the company's huge plant expansion, as well as introducing new chip-processing technologies. Intel spends lavishly to stay ahead of its rivals—typically $5 billion a year on new chip plants, or "fabs." "It's a risk to go out and spend billions of dollars on these manufacturing plants," Barrett told *Business Week*. "But if we didn't, we couldn't possibly reap the benefits." With 12 plants (in Grove's words, "our fields of dreams") in such diverse locations as California, Ireland, Israel, Malaysia, and China, Intel does what no competitor can match: build state-of-the-art microprocessors by the millions. It is this manufacturing clout that gives the chip maker its most feared weapon: size.

"That is where the great fortunes have always come from, with economies of scale," said Alfred Chandler, professor emeritus of business history at Harvard University. "No one can compete because the barriers to entry are there. That is what Ford did, what Rockefeller did and what Carnegie did." And that is what Intel has been doing for the past decade under Barrett's direction. To many industry watchers, he is the executive most responsible for transforming Intel into a high-tech manufacturing powerhouse.

"Andy was the visionary, but Craig made it happen," said James Allred, CEO of Eskay Corporation and an Intel veteran. David B. Yoffie, a Harvard professor of business administration and an Intel director, agreed: "The ability to turn Intel from a technology company with adequate-to-poor manufacturing to a leading manufacturer is largely due to Craig Barrett's leadership."

Staying On Top

To Barrett, whose ability to get the job done is combined with a sarcastic wit, the Intel formula is straightforward: "The way we work is very simple. We build factories, and we design products and we create process technology. And our factories crank out product." Like Grove, Barrett is unlikely to become complacent. "I'm every bit as paranoid as Andy is," he often says. "We recognize that the technology treadmill doesn't stop. You fall off and you get run over."

As CEO, Barrett is also every bit as pugnacious as Grove was when it comes to defending Intel's turf. In the rough-and-tumble world of chip making, Intel plays hardball every day. Frequently it has taken a high-handed, litigious approach to its customers, particularly for copyright or patent infringement. In 1997 Intel took on Digital Equipment Corp., which had sued Intel for infringing on patents for Digital's Alpha microprocessor. Intel responded with a countersuit, threatening to withhold supplies of Intel chips from Digital. Eventually DEC agreed to a $700 million settlement and contracted with Intel to manufacture the Alpha chip. (Compaq Computer Corp., DEC's new owner and Intel's best customer, must now decide whether to continue the arrangement.)

In these tussles the tough-as-nails Grove was often portrayed as the bad cop to good cop Barrett. However, Barrett's donnish looks can be deceiving. The unassuming, but hard-driving Barrett has been known to carry a baseball bat into meetings in order to get everyone's undivided attention. "He's one tough cookie," NB Montgomery Securities semiconductor analyst Jonathan J. Joseph said, particularly when it comes to safeguarding the company's technology. "I won't defend Intel's intellectual property any less than Andy Grove," Barrett insisted.

Although there is steel underneath the velvet, Barrett has a more mild-mannered demeanor than his feisty, often inflexible chairman. Indeed Barrett's diplomacy makes him a better candidate than Grove to restore the industry's trust in Intel. Barrett helped negotiate the previously mentioned DEC settlement and some others. More recently he assumed the primary role in Intel's regular meetings with its key partner, Microsoft. Perhaps because Barrett's wife, Barbara, is a lawyer and politician (who ran unsuccessfully for Arizona's governorship in 1994), he is less outspoken than Grove, who once characterized Washington politicos as "those people who control our fate and flunked freshman calculus."

As unforgiving as Grove and Barrett are to their enemies, they are equally passionate about preserving the company's partnership philosophy. In Silicon Valley much has changed in the 30 years since Grove, Moore and Noyce formed Intel. Rebelling against corporate bureaucracy, the three were determined to create a successful business without the customary trappings of managerial elitism. Those same egalitarian virtues apply today. Office space for the most senior executives (Grove and Barrett included) consists of cramped Dilbertian cubicles, surrounded by shoulder-height dividers. No preferred parking or chauffeurs here. Canteen food is hastily consumed during meetings in colorless conference rooms. Corporate attire—typically open-necked shirts and short-sleeved pullovers—is the antithesis of the traditional suit and tie. As for material rewards, the company's generous stock-option plan has turned more than 1,000 employees into millionaires.

Of Intel's co-leadership culture, Grove contends: "A business like ours has to employ a management process unlike that used in more conventional industries. . . . We at Intel frequently ask junior members of the organization to participate jointly in a decision-making meeting with senior managers. This only works if everybody at the meeting voices opinions and beliefs as *equals,* forgetting or ignoring status differentials. And it is much easier to achieve this if the organization doesn't separate its senior and junior people with limousines, plush offices, and private dining rooms."

In its relentless quest to come up with new ideas, Intel values directness. Its internal debates, Grove wrote, "are vigorous, devoted to exploring issues, indifferent to rank and include individuals of varied backgrounds." "If you are in middle management, don't be a wimp," he urged every staffer. "Don't sit on the sidelines."

Despite their warm relationship, the soft-spoken Barrett has had more than his share of debates with Grove. When Grove gave him his first performance appraisal many years ago, Barrett said, "I threw it back at him and said he could do better than that!" Somewhat taken aback, a rare condition for Grove, he redrafted the appraisal.

"I learned that, working with Andy Grove, you take advantage of his brilliance, his drive, his creativity, and you don't hesitate to tell him when he's wrong," Barrett said. Over the years these spirited give-and-takes have forged a close bond between the two men. Grove has told friends that he and Barrett are so much in sync that they often finish each other's sentences. "He's become my partner in everything," Grove told the *Wall Street Journal*.

Looking Ahead

Like Microsoft, Intel's success attracts the best people—and the best people sustain success. "It sounds commonsensical, and it is," Barrett said. "If you want to get great people, start by being great at what you do. People perceive us as leading-edge, successful, and visible in the marketplace, and they want to be part of that." But in the New Economy, attracting great people is only half the job; the other half is unleashing them to do great things. Here, too, Barrett excels. "I don't run Intel," he continues to insist. "I delegate and Intel runs itself. I try to rally people around a goal and get them all aimed at achieving it." As for the company's tradition of sharing power, Barrett said: "Intel has always been guided by a collective personality, first with Bob and Gordon, then with Gordon and Andy, and now with Andy, Gordon, and me."

Though no one talks about Barrett's successor, he is already building an impressive management legacy, with the counsel of Grove and Moore. Behind the new CEO is a cadre of bright, driven co-leaders eager for advancement. Possible front-runners include executive vice presidents Frank Gill, Gerhard Parker, and Paul Otellini. The favored son appears to be Otellini, who heads the microprocessor business. "All of these guys make for a very strong bench," said Rob Chaplinsky, a partner at Mohr Davidow Ventures, a Palo Alto–based venture capital firm.

Whoever eventually succeeds Barrett, shareholders needn't worry about a leadership vacuum. Chairman emeritus Gordon Moore, who still pops into Intel's headquarters, recently noted its depth of leadership and quipped: "I'm not sure I could get a job here today."

4

Winthrop H. Smith

A Breed Apart

A Breed Apart: CEO Charlie Merrill (left) and co-leader Win Smith (here on the terrace of Merrill's Manhattan apartment) met regularly to chart the course of Merrill Lynch. (Merrill Lynch)

4

Winthrop H. Smith

*It's the men behind who make
the man ahead.*

—MERLE CROWELL, Twenty-First Century Editor,
  Writer, and Publicist

Merrill Lynch, Pierce, Fenner & Smith: The caboose on this tongue-twisting train was Winthrop H. Smith, the longtime co-leader of the famous brokerage house. For two decades Smith was the low-keyed adjutant to hard-driving Charles E. Merrill. And when Merrill was incapacitated during most of the '40s and '50s, Win Smith ran the business—helping make Merrill Lynch one of America's leading financial institutions. In doing so he helped transform the country's stock markets from a rigged game for wealthy speculators to a source of capital and income for John and Jane Doe. Turning the middle class into financial players was good for the firm, good for industry, and good for the economy.

Promoting People's Capitalism

At the turn of the century, America's rough-and-tumble financial markets were in disarray. Wall Street was every bit as wild as the American West. Only gamblers and manipulators dared venture into the market. Charles Edward Merrill, more than any other financier, would transform this speculators' sport for the affluent few into an investment choice for millions.

The son of a small-town Florida doctor, Merrill studied at Amherst and Michigan. In the summer of 1907, he went to New   63

York to seek his fortune in the textile industry. There he met another
22-year-old, Edmund C. Lynch, a Johns Hopkins graduate who was
hawking soda fountain equipment. Two years later Merrill scrapped
the rag trade for his first Wall Street job as a bond trader with George
H. Burr & Co. Early on he had unconventional ideas about the investment business. An unalloyed capitalist, Merrill rejected the notion
that the world of investing was the exclusive province of the well-
to-do. He believed strongly that the opportunities of the markets
should be accessible to everyone. Preaching "people's capitalism,"
Merrill set about his life's work of bringing Wall Street to Main
Street.

In 1914 the street-smart contrarian founded Charles E. Merrill &
Co. The following year he changed its name to Merrill, Lynch & Co.,
after he convinced Ed Lynch to join him. In those days the company
was not so much a retail broker as a distributor of new securities for
growing companies. Merrill foresaw an exciting opportunity in the
newly emerging chain store industry. He had watched the industry
since his days in textiles, and he was certain that the convenience,
choice, and value offered by these innovative merchandisers would
appeal to the public—provided the chains could get expansion capital.

"Chain stores were no mystery to the investing public we
reached," he later wrote. "I saw an opportunity to render a real public
service and at the same time to make a great deal of money." In the
mid 1920s the firm acquired a controlling interest in Safeway Stores,
Inc., and Merrill and Lynch soon became multimillionaires.

Enter Win Smith

With its newfound success, Merrill, Lynch & Co. prospered and grew
rapidly. In 1916 Merrill spotted a new hire sorting prospect cards of
likely clients. "Is your name Smith?" the cofounder asked. "My name
is Charlie Merrill." Little did Merrill know that Smith would prove
to be one of the acquisitive financier's most important acquisitions.

Born of quintessential Yankee stock, Win Smith grew up in South
Hadley Falls, Massachusetts. He attended Phillips Andover Academy
and graduated from Amherst College, his father's alma mater, in 1916.
After a brief stint in investment banking in Boston, Smith headed to
New York, where he took a job as a runner for a brokerage at $7 a

week. In September 1916 he joined Merrill, Lynch as a file clerk at $10 a week. The firm would turn out to be his life's work.

World War I interrupted the partnership's growth spurt. Merrill saw duty as a flight instructor, while partner Lynch served in a cavalry unit. Young Smith, for his part, was commissioned a second lieutenant in the army. However, much to their chagrin, the trio never saw combat because hostilities ended in 1918.

The Great War established New York as the world's new financial hub. During the Roaring Twenties, large numbers of Americans discovered Wall Street for the first time. Whether on the golf course or the commuter train, men liked to brag about being in the market. It was more a matter of vanity than of greed for these casual investors. Toward the end of the decade, several million unsophisticated investors would get burned.

In 1928 Charlie Merrill turned economic Nostradamus and warned of a possible stock-market apocalypse. "The financial skies are not clear," he said. Worried about the irrational exuberance of the market, Merrill advised his clients and his partners to get ready for an economic downturn. When the great crash of October 1929 came, Merrill, Lynch had already chopped its overhead and invested in low-risk areas. Despite the firm's foresight, the big bust caused "terrific physical, mental and emotional strains," Smith recalled. Many overzealous investors "ended up owing the firm money they were never able to repay."

Merrill, Lynch & Co. weathered the Great Depression with its reputation intact and its partners on solid financial footing. Nevertheless, Merrill sensed that the aftermath of the crash would be a protracted period of subpar performance. He decided to lighten the firm's load. In February 1930 he sold its retail brokerage business, transferring its branches, several partners, and most of its employees to E. A. Pierce & Co. Merrill, Lynch operated with a skeleton staff, concentrating on refundings. In semiretirement, Merrill focused on Safeway Stores, building it into the country's third largest grocery chain.

Smith, like most of his Merrill, Lynch colleagues, plunged into the task of making E. A. Pierce the nation's No. 1 "wire house"—that is, an investment firm that depends on its private telegraph wires for broad-based business. Early on Smith was posted to Boston to turn around its troubled office. In September 1931 he took over the important Chicago office. Two years later Smith revolutionized financial record keeping, introducing early IBM technology to the company's back-office operations.

But even Smith's passion and innovation could not save Pierce. Like most brokerage houses, the firm was always undercapitalized and struggled throughout the depression. Its worst setback: the untimely death of Ed Lynch in 1938. Merrill grieved to one close colleague: "Eddie's death has been a terrific blow to me. For 31 years, Ed and I were the best of friends and for 29 of these years the closest of business associates. I truly don't know how I am going to get along without him."

Eventually Winthrop Smith would fill that void. After the spin-off in 1930, Smith saw little of Merrill except for annual pilgrimages to the Merrill estates in Palm Beach, Florida, and Southampton, New York, and an occasional Amherst-Williams football game. Later Smith and Merrill spoke more frequently about the declining fortunes of E. A. Pierce, in which Merrill retained a minority interest. Knowing the firm's days were numbered, Smith—with Pierce's permission— initiated merger discussions with Merrill in October 1939. Smith told Merrill that with some fresh capital and aggressive reduction of overhead the troubled retail house could easily produce a million dollars in profits.

Merrill "became very much interested," Smith wrote later. "We went backwards and forwards over the figures." As the number-crunching continued, Merrill was analyzing various public opinion polls. The results were dramatically similar: Average Americans continued to misunderstand and distrust Wall Street. Stockbrokers were widely regarded as dishonest insiders. Where others saw only bad news, the ever entrepreneurial Merrill saw an opportunity. He was convinced that an honest, customer-oriented retail brokerage could convert the disbelievers to his brand of people's capitalism.

With Smith's patient prodding, Merrill decided to reenter the retail business. On April 1, 1940, Merrill Lynch, E. A. Pierce & Cassatt opened its doors, dropping the comma between Merrill and Lynch for the first time and adding Cassatt, a Philadelphia firm in which Merrill, Lynch and Pierce already had an interest. As directing partner and the firm's biggest investor, Merrill headed the combined entity.

Smith became managing partner, second in command, and chief co-leader.

At a historic meeting of the 68 partners and office managers at New York's Waldorf Astoria Hotel, Merrill fulfilled one of a leader's key responsibilities. He shared his vision of the modern Merrill Lynch—giving clients a square deal and putting their interests first. "Merrill made a tremendous impression on the visiting managers," Smith wrote later. "They had come to New York thoroughly bewildered by the merger and thoroughly downhearted because of the poor business that they had been experiencing for years. He inspired them, put new hope into them and sent them home full of confidence and ready to lick the world."

Reshuffling Power

Having pumped up morale, Merrill "rolled up his sleeves and began to work as he never worked before," Smith remembered. Merrill had made a fortune as an investment banker specializing in chain store financing. Now he began a national campaign to create a "department store of finance," whose "shelves" were stocked with equities. Through its newly acquired branch network, Merrill Lynch would demystify Wall Street for ordinary Americans.

Merrill Lynch's campaign helped renew the national interest in stocks and bonds by bolstering the public's confidence that it would get a fair deal. Before the end of 1940, more than 12,000 new accounts had been opened—impressive, considering that its total customer base numbered only 50,000. Slowly but surely Merrill's strategy of supermarket selling was taking hold.

Merrill's populist philosophy was articulated in the firm's Statement of Policy, known in house as The Ten Commandments. The first and foremost commandment: "The interests of our customers *must* come first." The other commandments also reflected the firm's commitment to provide red-carpet treatment to all customers, large and small. Today Merrill Lynch's customer-first manifesto is expressed in five principles: client focus, respect for the individual, teamwork, responsible citizenship, and integrity. After more than half a century, the consumer-oriented approach that Merrill pioneered and Smith implemented still underpins the company.

With Merrill focusing on marketing, Smith searched for new growth opportunities. In 1941 Smith engineered another merger that would win the now booming brokerage the nickname, the Thundering Herd. Seeking greater economies of scale, Win initiated merger discussions with Fenner & Beane, a New Orleans–based commodities and investment house. Negotiated by Workaholic Win in just seven days, the compact was a perfect fit. Fenner & Beane was the country's leading commodities trader and second in securities—the mirror image of Merrill Lynch. The marriage of the two largest firms in the brokerage industry expanded the combined house to 93 cities and membership on 28 exchanges.

During World War II, the new Merrill Lynch, Pierce, Fenner & Beane benefited greatly from the economic recovery and the sharp rise in personal income fueled by increased military spending. In 1943 the partnership reported record earnings of $1.1 million. Merrill and Smith divided duties according to their separate strengths. With Smith, the detail man, overseeing day-to-day operations, the outgoing Merrill "made extensive trips visiting many of our offices, holding sales meetings with account executives and putting new life into the organization." But in April 1944, after an arduous business trip to the West Coast, the 58-year-old Merrill suffered a heart attack. Later that summer he had a second, more severe attack. From then on Merrill's loyal lieutenant would lead the firm.

Merrill's incapacitation could not have come at a worse time. The bull market of the postwar period created tremendous opportunities for every American mass marketer. Merrill Lynch, with its preeminent distribution network, stood to benefit more than any other brokerage. The rebuilding of war-torn Western Europe, Asia, and the Pacific also promised significant growth. But Merrill knew that his precarious health made it impossible for him to lead the firm in this dynamic period.

In the 1940s coronary bypasses, angioplasty, beta blockers, strict diets, and the like were not part of a cardiologist's arsenal. Patients with chronic heart disease were simply placed on light duty. Rest and relaxation was the prescribed therapy. Strenuous exercise, even sex, was out. Stress was to be avoided at all costs. As a result, Merrill would spend his remaining 12 years in deluxe semiretirement in Southampton, Florida, and Barbados.

The downshifting that his health required did not come easily to Merrill. At his most vigorous, he conjured up images of Teddy Roosevelt, the champion and epitome of "the strenuous life." Despite Merrill's frequent bouts of angina, he couldn't detach himself from the Thundering Herd. With Smith's support, Merrill forged a new role that enabled him to contribute from afar.

Although Merrill remained the directing partner, the low-keyed Smith now ran the company. Economic historian Edwin J. Perkins writes of Smith: "He was the de facto CEO. At first, Merrill and Smith shared strategic decision making, but, over time, Smith assumed added responsibilities." As managing partner, he ran the firm's daily operations, aided by two other key executives, Michael W. McCarthy and Robert A. Magowan.

McCarthy had not come up as a Wall Street man. Instead the North Dakotan got his training in the chain store industry. He came to the firm in 1940, when Merrill reassigned him from Safeway Stores to take over backstage activities—Wall Street jargon for operations, communications, and other administrative services. Bob Magowan was Merrill's son-in-law. He had also received his early training in retailing, including a three-year stint at Safeway. In 1938 Magowan joined Merrill Lynch as head of its attention-getting advertising and sales promotion departments.

Under Smith's direction the new leadership team vowed to stick with Merrill's supermarket strategies. Despite Merrill's illness, he remained the dominant personality in the firm, in part because he was far more charismatic than Smith. As Merrill Lynch's cofounder and its largest investor, Merrill insisted on staying involved in company affairs. Though his ailment kept him away from the office, he kept a sharp eye on the business via an endless exchange of memos, telephone calls, and frequent informational visits from Smith. Whether Merrill was at his summer estate in Southampton or winter homes in Florida and the Caribbean, he was at the heart of Merrill Lynch right up to his death in 1956.

Merrill's system of remote-control management depended on outstanding co-leaders. In Smith and his lieutenants, McCarthy and Magowan, Merrill had the ideal team to put his pioneering ideas into action. In no time the firm shook tradition-bound Wall Street to its very spats. Among its innovations: making financial information

widely available. The firm erected a permanent Investment Information Center in Grand Central Station, distributed jazzy educational
brochures, ran catchy ads with titles like "What Everybody Ought to
Know About This Stock and Bond Business," sponsored the first
investment seminars for women in San Francisco, and published the
first annual report on Wall Street. These new ideas, supported by a
$1.5 million annual budget, made Merrill Lynch the best-known
investment house of the day.

In 1945 the company revolutionized Wall Street once again,
establishing the industry's first training school for stockbrokers (now
known as financial consultants). Noting that the average broker was
52 years old, Smith recruited young people and trained them in Merrill Lynch's ways. To this day its two-year training program remains
one of the most rigorous in the industry. Merrill Lynch also insisted
that its "account executives" (Merrill's term) be bright, earnest, and,
above all, public-spirited. Engagement in charitable or civic affairs
was a must. In Merrill's view such participation was not only good in
itself, it also helped win over the average American.

In another industry first, Merrill Lynch eliminated sales responsibilities from its branch managers. They could not compete with the
account executives on their staffs, eliminating a traditional source of
bickering. The firm's innovative profit sharing, bonus plans, and top
salaries also kept staff turnover at an industry low—still true today.
Insiders, including current CEO David H. Komansky, also knew they
would have priority at promotion time.

In a business famous for prima donnas, outsized egos, and job-
hopping, Merrill became a cocoon of team players. "We do consider
ourselves to be an organization where the whole is more important
than the individual," Komansky said of values nurtured over half a
century. "For many years, we have stridently avoided encouraging the
star system." At Merrill Lynch, the firm is the star.

The 1950s started with a rush—for the market and for the company. Under the benign administration of President Eisenhower, business was good and inflation was low. Prosperity was in the air, and
confidence in stocks was creeping back. In 1954 the Dow Jones
Industrial Average finally eclipsed its previous record from the fall of
1929. Merrill Lynch continued to educate prospective investors, and
its relentless promotions worked. At the start of the decade, 6 million

individuals owned equities; by the end of the decade, more than 12.5 million did. (Today, directly or through mutual funds or retirement plans, between 75 and 85 million Americans own stock.)

Economic experts point to another event that lured many new investors into the market. In 1956 Ford Motor Co. common stock was offered to the public for the first time. The sheer size and sterling reputation of the company helped reassure the public about the maturing market. The record-setting $660 million offering gave Merrill Lynch its first billion-dollar underwriting year, setting a record that would stand until 1965. Although other big IPOs would follow, "Ford was the landmark that firmly placed Merrill Lynch among the underwriting leaders," according to the company history, *A Legacy of Leadership*.

Commodities trading also exploded during the 1950s. Merrill Lynch produced a popular educational film on hedging, "Marketplace, U.S.A.," and took it, along with easy-to-understand informational brochures, on a 40-city promotional tour. In the mid 1950s, the firm also energized its international business by establishing correspondent relationships with several commodity houses in Europe. These ventures became the nucleus for other overseas offices: Geneva in 1951, Paris and Rome six years later. Merrill Lynch's flag flew higher than ever as more and more foreigners flocked to U.S. stocks and bonds.

Behind the scenes Smith made sure that the organization's back office, or operating systems, kept pace with its growth at home and abroad. Besides its burgeoning overseas trades, Merrill Lynch was handling more than one million transactions a year from 300,000 customers, served through 120 branches in 90 cities across the country. Smith "introduced much of the electronic equipment that has greatly increased the speed and accuracy of executing orders for customers," wrote *Business Week*. Working closely with IBM, Smith and his colleagues led the company—indeed the industry—into the computer age.

Remote-Control Management

After his two heart attacks, Merrill reconciled himself to a reduced role in the firm. A third coronary in September 1945 left no doubt that the rigors of command would have to be borne by younger, heartier individuals. Though not an invalid, Charlie knew he couldn't overtax his frail constitution. From time to time, he plunged back into the fray of business. But Merrill admitted to Smith that these interventions took their toll.

"Every time I attempt to stick my nose into something that has to do with the firm, I end up by getting worried and upset," Merrill confessed. "This is really just silly of me, and so far as humanly possible, I am just going to let you and your gang run the business and let the 'chips fall where they may.' "

The old warhorse remained more than a mere figurehead, though. "His evolving role became reasonably similar to the position of an activist chair of the board of directors in a large corporate enterprise—a chair who had only recently relinquished his CEO duties to protégés, but who still tried to stay apprised of recent developments and to influence decision making," writes Edwin Perkins. "Charlie was an absentee directing partner who nonetheless remained involved in the firm's affairs. Since Charlie had the largest capital investment in the firm, his opinions, when offered, could not be ignored or easily dismissed."

Indeed the cantankerous Merrill often voiced his opinions on company matters. Sometimes he had relatively minor concerns—the design of a sales brochure, the bonus for a particular manager, the recommendation that executives be allowed to have radios in their offices. But often Merrill gave Smith enormous discretion, even over Merrill's personal affairs. Thus Smith supervised Merrill's charitable contributions and even acted as go-between in a divorce settlement with Merrill's former wife. As a result of Smith's flexible co-leadership, the incapacitated chief was able to focus on more weighty strategic and philosophical issues.

"I . . . think that we are paying too much attention to the thermometer, and too little attention on the patient," Merrill wrote Smith, in disgust at industry proposals to hike sales fees. "Higher commissions only mean that we will be putting an umbrella over the heads of our poorer managed and weaker competitors, and I feel that we must take a very strong position against it."

As the firm grew, Merrill also worried that it was losing its entrepreneurial flair. "The bureaucratic spirit must be squashed," Merrill told his younger partner. "It can be fatal to any outfit. [We need] to promote *new ideas, efficiencies,* and *self-reliance*." A strong proponent of international expansion, Merrill prodded Smith: "I hope you won't mind me nagging you about our proposed offices in Canada and overseas!"—and then proceeded to nag him repeatedly.

Nothing perturbed the remote-control CEO more than "the tendency of a few to veer away from our basic principles." In memos to Smith, Merrill insisted: "I think it is a great deal better for everybody to read the Ten Commandments than it is to have a Bible on the shelf and never look at it. . . . This is a good time to restate our policies and objectives in simple, straight-forward English."

In many respects Merrill's physical distance from Wall Street enhanced his contributions to the company. "In some ways [his absence] was an advantage," Smith explained, "because he had a better perspective of what was happening to the business as a whole, and to our firm in particular, than he might have had had he been actually participating in the day to day events."

Yet the frustrations this former dynamo felt because of his poor health are evident in virtually every communication. In one "Dear Winnie" letter, Merrill lamented: "I am full of sedatives and painkillers. . . . I wish that I were more philosophical of accepting with grace the facts of life. It would be silly for me to tell you otherwise, because you are too close to me not to have understood the waves of resentment and despondency that too often threaten to swamp me."

Mindful of good health as only those who have lost it are, Merrill begged Smith to minimize the dangerous stresses of the workplace. "Please pardon the renewed suggestion that you examine and re-examine your own personal executive staff," he cautioned Smith in 1954. "I shudder to think of how much extra pressure would be forced on you and the other top executives at 70 Pine Street [if the firm's rapid rate of expansion continues]." In another letter Merrill wrote: "I doubt very much whether you have taken the time to evaluate the extra burdens that have been put on you by the growth of the business and the general pressure which comes from a big increase in activity. . . . Please for your sake . . . and my sake, use your best brains to safeguard the health and happiness of Winthrop Hiram Smith."

Though often intolerant of other colleagues, Merrill's affection for Smith bordered on love, which he expressed openly and honestly.

"I want you to know how grateful I am to you for the job which you have done since the new firm started out on the long hard campaign which, except for your character, courage, capacity and infinitesimal fortitude might so easily have ended in disaster," Merrill wrote from his Barbados hideaway. "To sum it all up, Win, I for one am determined that you shall not escape receiving the lion's share of the gratitude and pride that is in my heart." In the same letter, he added: "When next you see your mother, be sure to tell her that I love her very much and that I know the fact that her boy Winnie who works for Merrill Lynch is responsible for what Merrill Lynch is and hopes to continue to be."

In 1953 Merrill received a brief reprieve from semi-invalidism. Dr. Samuel Levine of Peter Bent Bingham Hospital in Boston prescribed an experimental treatment that entailed regular doses of radioactive iodine. The protocol ended Charlie's angina attacks, enabling him to attend a two-day company conference at Manhattan's Hotel Statler. There, in what would be his last hurrah, Merrill paid tribute to his devoted co-leader.

"Just imagine what would have happened to this firm if we had an avaricious, smart-aleck, stuffed shirt, old poop [like me], running this business since 1944! We wouldn't be here," Merrill told his colleagues, most of whom he had not seen in 10 years. "If I started to tell you what I thought of Win Smith, I would be here for the next couple of weeks. . . . I have met many fine fellows, but I have never met a more lovable, more dependable, more thoughtful, just decent guy in my life. I thank God practically every night that it has been my good fortune to have Win take over and help sell me the idea of working for you bums."

When Merrill finished speaking, he sobbed openly. "The audience," Smith recalled, "was profoundly moved and tears appeared in the eyes of practically everybody there." The Statler conference was Merrill's last company function. Although Dr. Levine's miracle cure lessened his angina, he suffered from a recurring case of the shingles. The once legendary carouser spent his last years as, in his words, "one sick cookie." He died in Southampton on October 6, 1956, at age 70.

When asked to describe his longtime partner, Smith said: "Few human beings have possessed more frailties than he, yet, on the other hand, few humans have had the objective ability to recognize better than him their own frailties. . . . On balance, after some 37 years of intimate relationship, I know that CEM was innately a kindly gentleman, a financial genius, a courageous pugnacious man, an individual who just plain liked people and one who could be an easy touch to an old friend."

Even in death Merrill remained an easy touch. Philanthropy was a passion with him. His will specified that his capital interest remain in Merrill Lynch, while his share of the profits be left to a long list of charitable institutions, with Amherst College the major beneficiary. The Charles E. Merrill Trust closed its books in 1981, having distributed a grand total of $113.6 million.

Merrill's reputation eventually caught up with his achievements. A year before his death, Martin Mayer, author of *Wall Street: Men and Money*, wrote: "He is the first authentically great man produced by the financial market in 150 years. . . . Merrill brought in the public, not as lambs to be fleeced, but as partners in the benefits. The climate of the 1930s helped, the New Deal laws helped, and many individuals helped, but the prime mover was Charlie Merrill."

Though Merrill's was the name usually associated with Merrill Lynch's spectacular progress during the '40s and '50s, Wall Street pundits understood that Smith was the co-captain. In many respects this great partnership was much like Chrysler's two Bobs—Eaton and Lutz. At Merrill Lynch, the gregarious, flamboyant Southerner was tempered by the principled, soft-spoken Yankee. *Barron's* described Merrill as having "the physique of a Plymouth Rock rooster, the savvy and courage of a horse trader, and the soul of a poet." Impulsive and intuitive, he was very much of the Ready-Fire-Aim school of management.

Smith, however, was more analytical and deliberate. "He wasn't very fast-moving," recalled Edmund Lynch, Jr., son of Merrill Lynch's cofounder. "But he was very thorough and thought everything out. . . . He wouldn't shoot from the hip or give you an arbitrary decision." Robert Rooke, who worked with both Merrill and Smith for almost four decades, described Smith as "not bombastic," like Merrill and Lynch, but "a pacifier and consolidator."

With a round face and ready smile that made him look somewhat like actor Carroll O'Connor, Smith had qualities we sometimes fail to associate with effective leadership: a genial personality, unaffected naturalness, and unfailing optimism. One of Smith's premier skills as an executive was his ability to stand above the fray and disarm antagonists. Company executives report that Smith was *the* driving force behind the smooth functioning of the disparate elements that comprised Merrill Lynch. It was Smith who was able to reconcile the big egos and competing interests of the newly acquired brokerages. In doing so he was a "wonderful umpire," said Herbert H. Melcher, a partner at the firm. "He [would] listen to any opposing view and understand it." Whereas most big Wall Street houses were loose confederations of super egos with super paychecks, Smith turned Merrill Lynch into that rare outfit that was bigger than the sum of its parts. That kind of synergy is what co-leadership is all about.

Louis H. Engel, the firm's advertising director, once said: "Win Smith was the only man who, after Charlie Merrill had his heart attack, could have held this thing together. He was an incredible man. He was absolutely one of the most quiet, unassuming men you ever met in your life. . . . In those early days, the partners came from all these different firms. They still had their old ties, their old loyalties, and their particular buddies down the hall. But it was Win Smith who welded this thing together and made it one organization."

Like co-leader Bob Lutz at Chrysler, Smith had enormous influence over decision making. He was the only partner with direct access to the absentee CEO. "As the chief spokesman for Merrill, Smith's authority was supreme," notes historian Perkins. "In many ways Smith was cast in a role similar to that of a loyal prime minister who devotedly served an ailing and aging, but still strong-willed, monarch—an enlightened leader who had been forced by uncontrollable circumstances to reside permanently at a distance from the seat of power."

In wielding his authority, Smith never sought to upstage the throne. Eight years junior to Merrill, the loyal second in command was always respectfully deferential to his mentor and benefactor. Smith was especially grateful that Merrill had lent him the funds to cover his capital contribution to the partnership in 1928. Reflecting on their 37-year association, Smith said: "My early relationship with him was a combination of boss and father; later, it developed into an older brother relationship and then as a partner and a close friend."

Carrying the Ball

After Merrill's death in 1956, Smith assumed the dual roles of directing and managing partner. A year later he named longtime associate Mike McCarthy managing partner. In 1958 the firm juggled names again. Alpheus Beane, Jr., son of the late cofounder of Fenner & Beane, withdrew from the partnership—taking his name along with him. In deference to Smith, the enterprise was renamed Merrill Lynch, Pierce, Fenner & Smith.

Meanwhile the pressures of growth were severely straining the capital needs of the company and the industry. Since its birth under a buttonwood tree in 1792, the New York Stock Exchange had insisted that member firms be partnerships. Each partner assumed personal liability for any debts or lawsuits his or her house incurred. This was the traditional way of doing business on Wall Street, a stronghold of tradition.

Merrill Lynch, of course, had always delighted in tradition breaking. As early as 1940, Merrill called partnerships "antiques." Brokerages, he argued, needed the ability to retain their earnings to fund future growth. Under partnership law each new partnership agreement required the approval of every partner. As Merrill Lynch grew, this proved cumbersome and impractical. As one partner put it: "We were running a streamlined operation from a surrey with a fringe on top."

In 1953 the New York Stock Exchange allowed its brokers to incorporate. The vote: 594 in favor, 538 opposed. That summer the small firm of Woodcock & Hess became the first corporate member. But the legal complications of incorporating 117 partners prevented Merrill Lynch's immediate change. In 1959 Smith was finally able to fulfill one of Merrill's lifetime dreams—making the Thundering Herd the first major Wall Street brokerage to incorporate.

Chairman Smith emerged as a formidable head of the 6,500-person powerhouse. After leading the company through the complex process of incorporation, he explored ways to improve the organization's efficiency. "We are not content with being big," Smith told his management team. "We also want to be the best."

At a meeting of Merrill Lynch executives during the 1940s, Smith suggested the firm trade Wall Street for the suburbs, where employees would be "only ten minutes from home. . . . One of the greatest weaknesses of some of our managers is habitually leaning on New York—using the Home Office as a crutch!" Smith argued. Long before others had, Smith recognized that the greatest potential for growth, both for the company and the industry, lay outside the major cities—in the suburbs and small towns. Geographical diversification required more local decision making and less guidance from the top—principles of co-leadership that Smith passionately believed in. Anticipating a strategy that would make Sam Walton a legend and a billionaire, Smith established branch offices of Merrill Lynch beyond the urban ring. The first mall outlet opened in Paramus, New Jersey, in 1958. Smith also continued to champion overseas expansion. The London office opened in 1960. A year later Merrill Lynch became the first U.S. brokerage to establish a presence in Tokyo.

Away from the office, Smith led a simple life. He had no yacht, no Florida palace, no stable of racehorses, no valet, no chauffeur. He abhorred ostentation. Like all true Yankees, he also had a visceral hatred of waste. Smith usually carpooled to work from his Manhattan apartment or drove from the family's 100-acre farm in Morris, Connecticut. "He was incredibly simple," said son Winthrop H. Smith, Jr., an executive vice president with Merrill Lynch. "I don't know whether economics dictated that because his investment was stock in the firm or whether [it] was just his Puritan background. I suspect it was the latter."

Toward the end of the 1950s, Smith learned that he had Parkinson's disease, a disabling disorder caused by progressive deterioration of nerve cells in the brain. As is typical, the condition didn't affect Smith's mental abilities, and for a few years medication controlled its symptoms. Nonetheless, he began to transfer more and more power to his No. 2, Mike McCarthy. By 1959 Smith could no longer devote full time to the firm. Ironically McCarthy assumed virtually the same role Smith had when Merrill became ill. With Smith forced to be less and less active, the next in command ran the firm.

Bullish on America

Winthrop Smith died at his Connecticut home on January 10, 1961. As Merrill Lynch's guiding light and moral compass for almost two decades, Smith won national recognition. He was named one of America's 50 top business leaders by *Forbes* magazine in its fortieth anniversary issue—just as Merrill had been a decade earlier.

An executive whose light touch was the perfect foil for his boss's bravado, Smith understood the meaning of complementary leadership—and used it brilliantly. Look at some of his more notable achievements. He engineered the company's major acquisitions and assimilated them into Merrill Lynch's innovative culture. He accelerated Merrill Lynch's overseas expansion. He led the push for incorporation and set the stage for the firm's public offering in 1971. He modernized its primitive office and administrative systems. He introduced fresh talent to the organization and trained them in its co-leadership culture. He identified and developed key executives, including several of his successors. Deep leadership and seamless succession were two of his highest priorities.

"Two very important things in every person's life are love and money," Merrill once said. "We can't help much with the love but we can help manage and perhaps increase the money." During Smith's tenure, Merrill Lynch produced market-topping returns for both its clients and the firm. The modest brokerage that earned $200,000 in 1940 reported $12 million in net earnings 20 years later. In fiscal year 1997, the global giant earned $1.9 billion on $31.7 billion in revenue. Taking stocks and bonds together, Merrill is currently the world's largest underwriter and boasts the largest sales force in the business, blanketing the United States with 14,800 brokers serving 4.5 million households. It was the first brokerage firm to have more than $1 trillion in customer assets.

"I think [Dad] had . . . as great an influence as Charlie Merrill did on the firm—maybe, in many ways, a greater influence," said Win Junior, who has been at the company for more than 20 years and now heads its international operations.

Decency and integrity were important ingredients of Smith's personality. He was principled but not pious, compassionate but not sentimental, moral but not moralistic. Regrettably his plain-spoken, above-board manner seems at odds with the current Gordon Gekko ("greed is good") culture of Wall Street.

"He was the gospel, a man of great stature," said Ed Lynch, Jr. "A tremendous amount of the credit [for the firm's success] goes to him."

One of Smith's successors, chairman emeritus William A. Schreyer, agrees: "Some people get respect, some affection. Win Smith got both."

■

When Charles Merrill and Winthrop Smith entered Wall Street, Americans were wary stock buyers. At most, only 15 percent of households were in the market. Today almost half of the adult population has money socked away in equities—either directly or through a 401(k) retirement program. The financial world has changed, in large part because of these farsighted co-leaders. Investor confidence is at an all-time high. More people have money in the stock market than ever before.

Working together, Merrill and Smith made ordinary people bullish on America. Thanks to them, people's capitalism is a reality. Besides democratizing investing, they helped provide U.S. industry with much-needed capital for expansion. In tandem they were truly, in Merrill Lynch's famous catch phrase, "a breed apart."

5

Chou En-lai
The Elastic Bolshevik

Long March Warriors: Mao Tse-tung (left) and Chou En-lai forged a formidable partnership. (AP Wide World Photo)

81

5 | Chou En-lai

Radical changes require adequate authority.
A man must have inner strength as well as
influential position. What he does must
correspond with a higher truth.
—CONFUCIUS

The first of October, 1949, Founder's Day of the People's Republic of China: Premier Chou En-lai stood a dutiful half step behind Chairman Mao Tse-tung on the giant balcony of the Gate of Heavenly Peace, the entrance to the ancient imperial palace in Beijing. Before them a sea of red flags were waved enthusiastically by scores of thousands representing the 650 million citizens of the world's newest nation. In his harsh Hunanese dialect, Chairman Mao proclaimed: "The People's Republic of China is now established! The Chinese people have stood up!"

The celebration marked the end of 2,500 years of struggle against European colonialism, Japanese imperialism, and Soviet adventurism, as well as years of infighting by the nation's many warlords. In the 500-year-old Beijing palace, Founder's Day also marked the end, for Chou and Mao, of years of filthy jails, hairline escapes, secret meetings, and soups spiced with shoe leather. A great partnership forged during the infamous Long March of 1935 had brought them to this historic moment of triumph.

The unlikely pair were a study in contrast. Disheveled, robust, and earthy, 54-year-old Mao Tse-tung had none of the polished elegance of most world leaders. It was Chou who looked that part, with his handsome demeanor and commanding presence. Chou had sculp-

tured features; shiny black hair, intense eyes; a dark, almost Mediterranean complexion; and his beltless uniform was smoothly pressed.
His slim figure and handsome face belied his 51 years and countless
hardships. As dashing as Chou was to China's masses, the pecking
order was crystal clear: The brutish Mao was China's unchallenged
leader; the debonair Chou his loyal co-leader.

For the next quarter century, Chou En-lai would continue to
play the role of Chairman Mao's political consort. As Mao's alter ego,
Chou assumed the demanding positions of premier and foreign minister. Over time the affable, pragmatic, and persuasive deputy would
see his reputation and popularity eclipse those of his gruff, quixotic
superior. Today many sinologists regard Chou En-lai as China's finest
leader—a man of extraordinary intellect, tireless energy, and selfless
devotion to his people. Although officially only a costar, Chou was, in
many ways, China's guiding light.

The Birth of the Revolution

At the outset, few could have predicted that the Chou-Mao partnership that endured for four decades would have lasted for a day. For
starters both men had dramatically different early lives and career
paths.

Mao Tse-tung was born on December 26, 1893, in the tiny vil-
lage of Shao-shan in Hunan Province. The son of a once poor peasant
who later became a well-to-do farmer and grain dealer, Mao rebelled
against parental authority, leaving home in his early teens to study in
the provincial capital, Changsha. There he first came in contact with
new ideas from the West and the famed Nationalist revolutionary Dr.
Sun Yat-sen, whose political message led to the overthrow of China's
last emperor in 1911. It was during this period that Mao formed his
much-cited belief: "Political power grows out of the barrel of a gun!"

Years of frustration and uncertainty followed. After soapmaking
school, a stint at the police academy, and other apprenticeships, Mao
went to work as a librarian's assistant at Beijing University, China's
leading intellectual center. After intense self-study, he began to abandon Western liberalism and favor Marxist-Leninism as the answer to
his country's problems, particularly the oppression of rural peasants by
warlords and rich landowners. In 1923 Mao became a full-time revo-

lutionary. Shortly thereafter he met Chou En-lai, although nothing more is known about their initial encounter.

Chou came to communism along a very different route. Born in 1898 to an aristocratic family in Huaian, Kiangsu Province, Chou En-lai (*En-lai* means "coming from grace") graduated from a well-known middle school in Tientsin, then in 1917 he went to Japan for further study. Ironically his first choice for study abroad was the United States, but he failed the entrance examination. In 1919 he (and Mao) participated in the famous May Fourth Movement in Beijing in which students protested against imported ideologies and foreign intervention in China's affairs. Chou was arrested, released from jail after four months, and eventually went to France on a work-study program.

Chou found Europe seething with revolutionary ideas and calls for social change. He was quickly pulled into the ferment. In Paris Chou shared croissants and communism with Deng Xiaoping and other comrades who had joined the Chinese revolutionary movement. It was in Europe that Chou made a lifetime commitment to communism and became European organizer for the Chinese Communist Party (CCP), which was founded in Shanghai in July 1921.

In late 1924 Chou returned to China from France to join Sun Yat-sen's revolutionary Kuomintang (KMT, or Nationalist Party), then allied with the Communists against the warlords. Chou was appointed deputy director of the political department of Whampoa Military Academy, whose commandant was a talented young officer named Chiang Kai-shek. Impressed with the articulate and dashing Chou, Chiang named him chief commissar of the KMT's military campaigns and sent him to organize a series of urban uprisings.

In early 1927 Chou En-lai became director of the military department of the CCP's Central Committee as well as a member of its Politburo. His star was rising in both the Nationalist and Communist camps. However, when Chiang Kai-shek took Shanghai later that year, he turned his guns on the now feared Communists within his ranks, including Chou, who barely escaped with his life.

The next several years saw Chou's ascendancy and Mao's relative stagnation. In 1928 Chou was invited to the Soviet Union—then the major sponsor of the CCP—for the Sixth National Congress, where he was elected an alternate member of the Comintern's Executive

Committee. Two years later he addressed the Congress of the Soviet Communist Party—an unprecedented honor for a foreigner. In January 1931 Chou returned to Shanghai to assume a major role in the newly restructured Chinese Communist Party, now dominated by Moscow-trained internationalists. During those years he served on the CCP's Central Committee and ran the military affairs department, sometimes doubling as organizational chief.

Chou was outdistancing most of his comrades, including Mao. He built the CCP elite—forging the brain trust of the Red Army by cultivating and converting to communism many of Chiang Kai-shek's most promising young officers and best-trained troops. Chou organized bands of ragtag rebels to take over major cities. A pragmatist and a detail man, he also overhauled the party's key management and administration systems.

One of many rivals who watched Chou's rise with both admiration and envy was Mao Tse-tung, then a minor figure several rungs down the organizational ladder. Shunned by the Soviet-trained clique of CCP leaders, Mao recalled that he had "no voice at all" in party affairs. Mao's talents as a specialist in the peasant movement were not taken seriously by the elitist leadership. Frustrated, Mao broke with the party hierarchy in Canton and returned to his home province of Hunan to pursue his lifelong ambition of organizing the peasantry.

In many respects Mao Tse-tung's return to Hunan marked the turn in his fortunes. Seeing how courageously China's rural poor dealt with terrible injustices, Mao developed great admiration for them. Respected in turn, Mao began to channel their mounting anger into a network of militant organizations. Soon, he predicted, China's several hundred million peasants would "rise like a tornado or tempest—a force so extraordinarily swift and violent that no power, however great, will be able to suppress it."

Mao rejected traditional Marxist-Leninist dogma that dismissed the rural poor as ignorant and incapable of revolution. To him peasants, not the urban proletariat, were China's sleeping tiger. He believed that when China's revolution came, it would be fought largely by the farmers who made up 80 percent of its population. Mao also scorned Soviet military practices, including full-scale attacks on urban targets of opportunity. Because the Chinese revolutionaries had fewer resources than the enemy, they had to rely on escapist hit-and-run tactics—depending on smaller, more mobile cadres of bare-footed peasants led by sympathetic members of the educated elite. Selective retreat, Mao argued, was another important war tool. His infamous scorched land strategy called for feigning weakness by withdrawal. After the enemy was drawn into rural areas, the revolu-tionaries cut enemy supply lines and picked off individual soldiers.

Initially the Chinese Communist hierarchy rejected Mao's revi-sionist ideas. Chou En-lai, in particular, criticized his enthusiasm for the peasantry. The rural poor, Chou argued, suffer from "selfishness, narrow-minded conservatism and a lack of discipline." To embrace them, he said, "runs totally counter to the revolutionary principles and organizational discipline of the Party."

Under Chou's leadership the Red Army continued to practice its long-standing, Soviet-inspired strategy of massed attacks on big cities. As Army commander, Chou had to consolidate scattered bands of untrained, ill-equipped fighters into a unified central force. Chou frequently chastised Mao for his undisciplined, highly personalized leadership style, insisting that Mao "overcome [his] many incorrect tendencies."

When the Star Becomes Costar

Eventually Chou En-lai became exasperated with Soviet-style con-ventional warfare. After several failed attempts to dislodge Chiang Kai-shek's elite KMT units from selected cities, Chou regrouped his battered and demoralized Red Army in the south-central province of Kiangsi. During the so-called Kiangsi period of the early '30s, Mao had little control over policy making, especially in military matters.

However, in October 1934 Chou sided with Mao for the first time—electing not to wage a headlong frontal attack against the Kuomintang's reinforced army of one million men. Instead the Red Army abandoned Kiangsi and set out for the northwest of China on a year-long, 6,000-mile retreat known as the Long March. Death from exposure and frequent attacks trimmed the Communist army from 70,000 to 30,000 as it passed through treacherous and hostile country.

In January 1935 the Chou-Mao partnership was solidified further in Tsunyi. Although clearly superior to Mao in the party hierarchy,

Chou began to recognize in Mao leadership qualities that he lacked. Perhaps most important were Mao's appeal with the peasants and his ability to speak their language. As recounted by historian John McCook Roots, Chou recognized that Mao "has a way of presenting a most complicated subject so that even the uneducated can seem to understand it. He never talks above the heads of his audience. He never talks down to them either. There is a real flow of intimacy between him and the people."

In assessing Mao Chou may have remembered the Confucian proverb: "While the advisers of a great leader should be as cold as ice, the leader himself should have fire, a spark of divine madness." Chou saw that Mao had the fire that he lacked as well as a profound appreciation of the grassroots Chinese, their hopes, and their dreams. Chou also came to appreciate Mao's wisdom in recognizing that China was essentially agrarian. Through Mao's eyes Chou saw that Moscow's proletarian hard line wouldn't work in China. At the Tsunyi conference, Chou astonished the party hierarchy by admitting to past strategic errors. In one of the most remarkable examples of back-tracking in co-leadership history, Chou recommended that Mao Tse-tung take over leadership of the Red Army, while Chou retire from the Military Council. In an emotional plea, Chou told his colleagues that Mao "has been right all the time—and we should listen to him."

If Chou En-lai had qualms about downshifting from the top slot to No. 2, he didn't show it. In one stroke he lifted a former subordinate from obscurity—a former underling whom Chou had criticized harshly over the years and whose championing of the peasantry did not constitute the sophisticated leadership of Chinese communism that Chou had once struggled for. Chou could easily have maintained his No. 1 position had he wished. But he recognized that Mao alone possessed the leadership traits and charisma needed for China's future—a style that combined head and heart, emotion and intellect. Chou sensed that Mao was the only one who could rally the masses and lead the revolution.

By taking a step backward, Chou En-lai was moving his beloved China forward. "The helmsman must guide the boat by using the waves," Chou once told Henry Kissinger in explaining his decision to transfer power to Mao. To historian Roots, Chou En-lai's "rare mixture of political prescience and personal self-effacement" made possible this pivotal changing of the guard. "A man of immense charm and poise . . . [Chou] was totally dedicated to the goals that governed his life, and he was willing to justify the use of anything that would advance those goals," Roots writes. An expert in balancing his personal goals with national goals, Chou became known as the elastic Bolshevik. As a result of his selflessness, Chou won the confidence and admiration of his comrades, who instinctively trusted the purity of his motives. His credo was simple: "To serve the people"—a phrase that appeared on a button he wore on his uniform for the rest of his life.

Unlike most of us, Chou always "knew when—and how—to climb down," one observer said. The elastic Bolshevik was a "round man"—"one who is smooth in his dealings, who is good at making friends, and who always adapts himself to the existing situation."

Shaping the Partnership

In an alliance that would last 42 years, Chou En-lai and Mao Tse-tung left the Tsunyi conference as formidable co-leaders. Mao, the peasant, fought against the oppression of landlords and warlords. Chou, the intellectual, fought against inequality and foreign encroachments. They represented the two dominant elements in Chinese society— the common people and the educated class of civil servants—and together they masterminded the defeat of the Japanese and later led a national revolution and achieved their vast country's independence.

The Tsunyi conference was the start of Mao Tse-tung's rise to unchallenged supremacy. It was a position he relished. "Beauty lies at the top of the mountain," Mao often remarked. When his elevation to supreme commander was announced, a massive ovation rose from the ranks of the Red Army. "Chairman Mao, Chairman Mao!" the 30,000-man militia roared.

Meanwhile Chou deferred to the leader he had created. With characteristic grace, "he had taken good care to be a little behind the others, behind everyone else," writes Han Suyin, in *Eldest Son,* a biography of Chou. "He let Mao ride ahead—and followed behind."

Tsunyi was Chinese communism's prelude to national triumph. To succeed co-leadership depends on shared values. During the Long March, Chou and Mao developed a joint manifesto that would shape their lives and those of millions of others. First and foremost, they embraced the principles of Marxist-Leninist determinism. They believed that history would inevitably lead to world communism, and it was their job to hurry it along. Next, both men pressed for a strong, united front against Japan, urging the end of the civil war with the Nationalist Party. "The Chinese do not fight Chinese," Chou said. "Inhuman is he who slays his own brother to feed the wolf."

In addition Mao and Chou sought to replace rigid Soviet ideology, with its emphasis on the urban proletariat, with a uniquely Chinese strand of communism that made heroes of its peasants. This indigenous interpretation later became known as the Sinofication of Marxism. Furthermore, both men advocated the reversion of land ownership to the peasantry, but in an orderly manner. Whenever possible, Chou and Mao tried not to alienate decent local landlords. Unlike most party members, they recognized the importance of property rights as a necessary condition for open trade and efficient commerce—both critical to China's modernization. They also strove to avoid direct confrontation with friendly, noncommunist intellectuals. Later this position was reflected in Mao's pronouncement to "let a hundred flowers bloom"—that is, to encourage the expression of many diverse ideas. Finally, both men believed Sun Yat-sen's dire description of prerevolutionary China: "We have become a heap of sand." Only rigid discipline, the co-leaders agreed, could unleash the extraordinary potential of the Chinese people.

Crafting a Co-Leadership Role

During the Long March, Mao had observed in Chou two talents he lacked: obsessive attention to detail and great political sophistication. As the CCP's new leader, Mao turned to Chou to cement relations with the Kuomintang. After the outbreak of the Sino-Japanese War in July 1937, Chou worked diligently to shape an all-China victory against Japan. He also led the negotiations for peace with his archenemy, Generalissimo Chiang Kai-shek, at the end of World War II.

In December 1945 American General George C. Marshall was sent as a special envoy to China to mediate the Chinese Civil War between the Communists and the Nationalists. With Chou and Chiang, Marshall worked tirelessly for a cease-fire on both sides, but to no avail. Despite their tremendous ideological differences, Chiang Kai-shek once described Chou as "the most reasonable Communist he ever knew." So impressed was the Generalissimo with Chou's grasp of national issues that he told his highly influential wife, Madame Chiang: "Apart from myself, there is no one more capable of being the leader of this country."

When it became clear to Chou that rapprochement with the Nationalists was no longer possible, he quickly won over the majority of Chinese intellectuals and politicians, who had become increasingly disenchanted with the widespread corruption of the KMT and Chiang. Chou's success in organizing a united front against the Nationalist government was a central factor in Chiang Kai-shek's downfall and in Mao's victory in 1947.

As premier of the Beijing government from its beginning in October 1949, Chou became the chief administrator of the huge civil bureaucracy of the People's Republic of China. But his absorbing interest was always international relations, which he pursued with genius and endless vigor. He served as foreign minister from 1949 to 1958 and subsequently played the primary role in shaping China's global strategy. His appointment as China's senior ambassador— "Mao's scout in the tower," as historian Theodore White called him— reflected Mao's good sense. Chou was better informed about world affairs, he was better connected with foreign dignitaries, his language skills were sharper (he was fluent in English, Russian, French, and Japanese), and he was psychologically more attuned to the need to open China to the outside world than any of his contemporaries.

Throughout his life Chou fought against the forces of xenophobia, no small task in a country marked by alternating periods of isolation and foreign intervention. He daringly spoke in favor of interracial marriage to a people intoxicated with nationalism and ethnocentrism. "It is said that Chinese girls do not want to marry foreigners," Chou wrote, "How can we contribute more to humanity unless there is intermarriage? How can we practice internationalism? We must now cultivate a new spirit!"

Tough language in a new nation. In many ways Chou was a latter-day Confucius, the Chinese sage who died 2,500 years earlier. Like Confucius, Chou extolled the virtues of the "upright and superior person" and a sovereign who governs with morality—a link between heaven and mankind—a mandate that Mao occasionally failed miserably to fulfill.

The elastic Bolshevik's personal magnetism, intellectual vigor, and congenial reasonableness secured many allies for the new China. So many, in fact, that Henry Kissinger later described Chou as "the greatest statesman of our times." Yet Chou's negotiating principles were deceptively simple: Win friends to isolate the enemy and never push to extremes. Applying these principles, he systematically convinced a growing number of nonaligned nations of the merits of Chinese communism. Chou made his debut as a major statesman at a Geneva conference on Indonesia in 1954. Next, he caused a stir at an Afro-Asian conference in Indonesia. Trips to Poland and Hungary in 1957 marked the beginning of Chou's influence in Eastern Europe. His first visit to Africa in 1964 signaled Beijing's growing influence in the Third World.

Thucydides had it right 2,500 years ago when he said that rising powers challenge the international order. Thucydides was talking about Sparta's challenge to Athenian dominance. In the 1960s it was the People's Republic of China that threatened the status quo. China's people's war became a model for restless underdogs in Asia, Africa, and Latin America. Chou's reputation as a world-class statesman and negotiator grew even greater when U.S. envoy Henry Kissinger made a historic visit in July 1971.

After jointly engineering the Sino-Soviet split in the early '60s, Mao and Chou realized that only the United States could help China industrialize swiftly. Without U.S. support, it would be a long, hard climb out of misery to prosperity. So Chairman Mao instructed his chief lieutenant to press for an American détente. "It takes a long rope to catch a whale," Mao said, "and you, En-lai, shall weave that rope."

Weave Chou did. On June 2, 1971, Richard Nixon received what proved to be the most important communication to an American president since the end of World War II—Chou's invitation to visit the People's Republic of China. The following year Nixon, accompanied by Henry Kissinger, met the 73-year-old Chou in Beijing. During their lengthy negotiations, Nixon was enormously impressed by Chou's wit and vitality and his total lack of conceit or arrogance. "Many hours of formal talks and social conversations with Chou made me appreciate his brilliance and dynamism," Nixon recalled.

"Unlike many world leaders and statesmen who are completely absorbed in one particular cause or issue, Chou En-lai was able to talk in broad terms about men and history." Similarly Kissinger observed that Chou was "equally at home in philosophic sweeps, historical analysis, tactical probing, or light repartee. His command of facts and, in particular, his knowledge of American events was remarkable."

Nixon and Kissinger were also impressed that Chou ably performed hundreds of different tasks, from reading the page proofs of China's official daily newspaper to monitoring the cleanliness of Beijing's streets without ever losing sight of the big picture. "Though [Chou] tended personally to each tree, he always was able to see the forest," Nixon recalled.

What also became clear to Nixon and Kissinger was the high degree of trust between Mao and Chou, especially in foreign affairs. When asked about specific language in a joint Sino-American communiqué, the aging Mao told them: "Those questions are not questions to be discussed in my place. They should be discussed with the Premier. I only discuss philosophical questions."

By and large Mao shunned day-to-day affairs. He was the new China's self-professed visionary, its ideological beacon. Mao was "a colossus . . . a man inhabited by a vision, possessed by it," observed French writer André Malraux. Frequently the elusive chairman remained away from public view for prolonged periods of reflection and introspection. So it was left to his pragmatic partner to move this turbulent young nation into the twentieth century. Many of Mao's most important documents were drafted by Chou. The impulsive Mao would outline his grand visions, and Chou would bring precision and clarity to them.

"Mao was Chairman of the Board. Even in his declining years, he was still recognized as the leader," Nixon writes. "But Chou was the Chief Operating Officer."

On the one hand, Mao was a visionary and an ideologue whose love of the struggle had the quality of an addiction. Chou, on the other hand, saw revolution as a tool that could be used to achieve important societal goals. A negotiator by nature, he tempered ideology with pragmatism. "I am more Chinese than Communist," he told one visiting journalist. The elastic Bolshevik was a realist who refused to be doctrinaire. In what must have sounded almost treasonous at the time, Chou once told a journalist to remember: "Confucius was not a Marxist."

Indeed Chou En-lai was always proud of his Confucian background. And the defining attributes of Confucius's superior man, including grace as well as firmness, unquestionably helped Chou to achieve so much for China in its relations with the rest of the world. After a seven-hour interview with him in May 1960, Britain's Lord Montgomery concluded: "[Chou] is a very different person from Mao. . . . I would describe his brainpower as brilliant. . . . He is a very intelligent, likeable man, with charming manners. . . . I liked him so much that I invited him to come and stay with me in my home in England as my private guest."

Chou's triumph as a diplomat was largely due to his personal magnetism and his willingness to work 16- to 18-hour days. He always had time for a foreign visitor, with whom he might chat for hours. In his final 18 months, despite an ongoing battle with stomach cancer that included six operations, Chou continued to make China's case to the world by meeting with more than 60 foreign leaders and dignitaries.

Yet for all his tact and other Confucian virtues, Chou possessed incredible toughness. A colleague once remarked: "It is fascinating to watch how Chou En-lai operates at the negotiating table. When you study his statements afterwards, you realize that he hasn't made any substantial concession on any important issue." Sinologist Theodore White contended that Chou was as "ruthless as any [leader] the Communist movement has thrown up this century." Kissinger, too, recognized Chou's dark side. As Nixon writes, Kissinger saw Chou as "a cobra that sits quietly, ready to strike at the opportune moment."

Survival Skills

It was Chou's willingness to serve as Mao's alter ego that allowed China to develop politically and economically. Of all the men who had been senior to Mao in the party's early days, only Chou En-lai managed to survive as a member of the team. His partnership with Mao was unprecedented in its intensity and significance. It was, in the words of Chou biographer Roots, "the most vital factor in the birth and survival of the People's Republic."

Why did the relationship succeed? Perhaps most important, Mao never felt threatened by Chou. Although Chou became Mao's one essential co-leader, Chou stayed largely in the shadows, the faithful functionary who made the machinery run. He was *houtai*—in Mandarin, "the man behind the stage"—a figure of great influence whom the public does not appreciate fully. Interestingly, Chou was the only major Communist leader who refused to give a first-person account of his career.

Chou En-lai was as trustworthy as he was self-effacing. He never forged a personal clique in the CCP and never organized a faction against Mao. Nor did Chou ever seek presidential power, although he was asked to do so on several occasions. He believed China would gain nothing from an internecine struggle against Mao. A better alternative, Chou believed, was to try to contain China's volatile, but charismatic leader. Chou En-lai, wrote Roots, "was able to appeal to the middle ground of Mao's personality, which on the one hand distrusted sycophancy yet on the other hand was apprehensive about potential betrayal. Chou could skillfully assuage these insecurities." As a result, he always came through the occasional internal power struggle unscathed.

"Symbiosis is perhaps the best word to describe the [Chou-Mao] relationship," writes Edgar Snow, the American journalist and author of *Red Star Over China*. "Very different in working style and personality, Mao and Chou complement each other as a tandem based on thirty-seven [eventually forty-two] years of trust and interdependence." Incomplete separately, they formed an unstoppable team. "There was total harmony, ocean and shore come together," writes Han Suyin.

Over the years the men came to work so easily together that they sometimes startled casual observers. A French diplomat once met with Mao while Chou sat next to the Chairman and read a newspaper as if nothing else were happening in the room. "Imagine anyone reading a newspaper next to de Gaulle!" the Frenchman exclaimed.

Aesop once said a doubtful friend is worse than a certain enemy. Over the years Chou never wavered in his friendship for or loyalty to Mao. The faithful No. 2 protected his leader in every conceivable way. Traveling together through China's vast countryside, Chou often gave Mao his sun helmet to protect the Chairman from the burning rays. Chou personally arranged Mao's quarters, meals, and itinerary—and often tasted food and drink intended for the Chairman.

Inevitably Chou's willingness to defer invited derision from some party members. They called him the Housekeeper. But Chou was not subservient. His strength "lies in the fact that when he is teamed up with another leader, he was not his man and he is not Mao's man now," writes Chou biographer Kai-yu Hsu. Chou never resorted to flattery in his alliance with Mao, and he urged others to see their leader clearly. For all Mao's greatness, he should not be regarded as "a born leader, a demi-god, or a leader impossible to emulate," Chou told a youth group in Beijing.

That is not to say there were no frictions between China's two great men. The Mao-Chou years were often strained, even antagonistic. The Long March warriors disagreed, sometimes violently, on many subjects. Back talk came easily to Chou. In 1958, for instance, he forced Mao to back down on his Great Leap Forward campaign, the catastrophic policy of mandated egalitarian communes and small labor-intensive enterprises as vehicles for economic modernization. Chou also roundly criticized the gigantic upheaval known as the Great Proletarian Cultural Revolution, which probably set China's progress back at least a generation. Especially troublesome to Chou was the rising power of the Red Guards, young people whose loyalty to Mao bordered on the deranged. More than anyone else, Chou deserves credit for bringing order and reason to this deranged period of 1966 to 1969.

Author Han Suyin likens Chou and Mao to the "perpetual shield-and-spear." Always insecure, the cunning Mao didn't allow any potential successor to enjoy perfect ease. Despite Mao's longtime admiration for Chou, he referred to him on more than one occasion as "the little donkey." During the Cultural Revolution, Mao turned a deaf ear on repeated Red Guard attacks on Chou, whom they labeled "the rotten boss of the bourgeoisie." On August 26, 1967, a mob of Guards kept Chou under house arrest for two and a half days without food or sleep—leading to his first heart attack and the eventual decline of his health. Mao refused to intervene on Chou's behalf. Also, after the Cultural Revolution, Mao made Lin Piao the party's only vice chairman, in effect relegating Chou to No. 3.

In Chou's final days, Mao abandoned his ever loyal lieutenant. The Chairman reportedly chose not to visit as Chou lay dying in the hospital, and Mao did not attend Chou's funeral. When Mao was informed of Chou's death on January 8, 1976, he said nothing at all. But that night Mao's nurse and companion noticed that tears were running down his face.

In time the legacy of Chou En-lai may eclipse that of the often brutal Mao Tse-tung. From all accounts Chou's death drew more spontaneous grief from the Chinese than Mao's passing nine months later. A million people lined the streets to mourn "the beloved," as Chou is still known today. On the first anniversary of his death, thousands took his portrait—draped in black—to Tiananmen Square to swear their fidelity. "Chou is alive!" they shouted. "He is among us!"

China-watcher Dick Wilson described Chou as "the best loved, the most accomplished, the most successful, and the most unerring political leader in twentieth century China." For most Chinese Mao was more of a deity, an abstract mystical figure, than a man. Chou was a revered, but very human leader who could be depended on in times of trouble. "In him the Chinese found their ideal 'ruler,' " Han Suyin writes. "He was a revolutionary, but . . . in the Confucian mold . . . [a] man of total integrity, the father and mother of his people."

A modern career counselor might say that Chou's greatest failing was his lack of ego and his insistence on devoting himself entirely to the betterment of others. Yet Chou's behavior was consistent with an ideology—communism—that subordinates individual satisfaction to the greater good. Unlike Mao, Chou was willing to contribute in quiet ways as an adviser and implementer. As historian James Mac-Donald notes, in China these roles were traditionally demeaned as those of servants, making Chou's achievements that much more remarkable.

The consummate co-leader, Chou En-lai lived a life informed by the Confucian values of integrity, self-sacrifice, and dedication to the people's welfare. If public service detracted from personal enhancement, so be it. During the Long March, the elastic Bolshevik realized that Mao Tse-tung could lead a revolution, but he could not build a nation. For that Mao would need Chou's help.

Make no mistake, Mao Tse-tung was the principal architect of the new China—a man of tremendous strategic insight, tactical ability, and daring. His legacy: leadership of the largest peasant revolution in history and dominance of the Chinese scene for 30 years. But it was Chou who made sure that the People's Republic survived.

"Without Mao, the Chinese revolution would never have caught fire," Richard Nixon observes. "Without Chou En-lai, it would have burned out, and only the ashes would remain."

6 | George C. Marshall
Selfless Leadership

Man with a Plan: Perhaps America's greatest co-leader, Secretary of State George C. Marshall (right) with President Harry Truman in 1948. (AP Photo)

6

George C. Marshall

*I rate the capacity of man by: first, courage
and ability; and second, real experience
under fire.*
—WINSTON CHURCHILL

"The President is on the phone, dear," Katherine Marshall called to husband George, who was expertly pruning the upper boughs of a peach tree at their Leesburg, Virginia, home. With some difficulty the retired U.S. Army Chief of Staff descended through a thicket of wavering branches and, as fast as his 65-year-old legs could carry him, strode in to answer the call from his commander in chief. It was November 27, 1945.

In characteristic fashion Harry Truman got straight to the point. Civil war loomed in China, where Mao Tse-tung's Soviet-backed Communists threatened the Nationalist forces of American ally Chiang Kai-shek. With Eastern Europe quickly becoming a laboratory for Marxist-Leninism, the free world could not tolerate the defection of Asia's strongest and most powerful nation to socialism. To worsen matters Truman's popularity was ebbing, a slump that probably reflected the nation's postwar weariness as much as anything. Moreover, one of the Republicans' favorite themes was that the Democrats were growing soft on communism and were not providing Chiang with the support needed to smash Mao's revolutionaries. Only Marshall, the president argued, could negotiate with these two impassioned strong men and put the Chinese civil war to rest.

President Truman's choice of George Catlett Marshall as his special emissary to China seemed a safe bet. After all, the indomitable general's skills as administrator, commander, and strategist had gained him worldwide acclaim, the trust of Truman, Roosevelt, Churchill, and other world leaders, and unparalleled respect from Congress and the nation as a whole. Against almost insurmountable odds, the General of the Army (which also included the air forces) had organized and equipped the largest ground and air force in U.S. history. When Marshall became Army Chief of Staff on September 1, 1939 (the day Germany invaded Poland, starting World War II), U.S. troop strength stood at fewer than 200,000 men, making it the nineteenth largest army in the world, smaller than the armies of Greece, Portugal, and Switzerland. In the next five years, Marshall would expand that relatively weak army into a well-trained, well-equipped force of 8.3 million.

Under Marshall the United States armed itself and its allies as no other fighting force ever had. America produced almost 300,000 combat planes, more than 87,000 warships, millions of guns, and billions of rounds of ammunition. Simply put, Marshall was the most influential military leader of World War II. He was, in the words of Winston Churchill, "the true organizer of victory." When Marshall was named *Time*'s Man of the Year in 1943, the magazine declared that "George Marshall had armed the Republic." "In general's uniform," *Time* wrote, "he stood for the civilian substance of this democratic society. *Civis Americanus*, he had gained the world's undivided respect. In the name of the soldiers who had died, General George Catlett Marshall was entitled to accept his own nation's gratitude."

Nor did the general's accomplishments go unnoticed by ordinary citizens. It came as no surprise in 1945 that when Americans were asked who was most responsible for the successful implementation of the war effort, they chose Marshall over everyone else, including President Franklin Delano Roosevelt. The consummate co-leader, Marshall was living proof that leadership was a matter of skill and commitment, not simply a function of rank or office.

However, World War II had taken its toll on the aging soldier. For six years he had fought with every branch of government to mobilize peacetime America against the Axis powers: Germany, Italy, and

Japan. Initially he had to win over the isolationists, who controlled Congress and public sentiment. Later he battled rivals in other branches of the armed forces and even within the U.S. Army itself. Once America entered the war, Marshall became the president's chief military representative at international conferences at Casablanca, Quebec, Cairo, and Teheran, as well as Washington, D.C. Among his most important contributions to the Allied victory: He led the fight for the Allied drive on German forces across the English Channel, in opposition to the so-called Mediterranean strategy of the British.

A superb negotiator and brilliant public speaker, Marshall proved he could manipulate the most stubborn, difficult, and politically astute men of the time, including Roosevelt, Churchill, and Stalin. But Marshall was especially deft at handling such military prima donnas as George Patton and Douglas MacArthur. When the Allied victory was at hand, Marshall's responsibilities shifted to planning the successful conclusion of the war, including the peacetime realignment and rebuilding of the defeated nations.

So after four decades of military and public service, Marshall, at age 65, was ready to retire. He and his beloved second wife, Katherine, yearned for some quiet time together in the Virginia countryside. But when President Truman's call came (only one day after Marshall had made his retirement address at the Pentagon), the former leader of the greatest army in the free world said that he would go to China at once.

To be sure Marshall knew full well the risks of this, his first diplomatic assignment. He had firsthand knowledge of China. From 1924 to 1927, he had commanded a garrison in Tientsin, where he acquired a working knowledge of Mandarin. Thereafter he had made it a point to stay abreast of Chinese affairs of state. Recently he had taken to heart the advice of Generals Albert C. Wedemeyer and Joseph W. Stilwell, who argued that the pervasive corruption surrounding Chiang Kai-shek rendered futile any American attempt to prop up the Generalissimo over the long run. Marshall understood that the task would be all but impossible. As one commentator said of the mission: "Talleyrand, Metternich and Castlereagh could not have pulled it off."

Why then did this American icon, fully aware of the pitfalls, abandon a cozy retirement to get involved in the vicious Chinese imbroglio? "Duty, honor, country" were sacred principles to George Catlett Marshall. When the presidential call came to serve the nation, Marshall had no choice. He would simply do his best—as he had always done.

Historian Drew Middleton offers a useful analogy to explain Marshall's unconditional acceptance of Truman's assignment. "The Duke of Wellington, on being reproached for accepting a relatively minor position, explained, 'I am *nimmukwallah,* as we say in the East; that is, I have ate of the King's salt and therefore, I conceive it to be my duty to serve with unhesitating zeal and cheerfulness, when or whenever the King or his government may think proper to employ me.'" Like Wellington, Marshall would always do what his country asked.

We know the unfortunate outcome of the general's first foray into international diplomacy. After arriving in China in late 1945, Marshall found the Nationalist armies engaging, but not defeating, the Communist forces. Marshall soon realized that Mao's greatest weapon was Chiang Kai-shek's dismal record of corruption. In short order Marshall recommended that all future U.S. aid to the Nationalists be limited and strictly supervised by American officials. This, of course, enraged the Generalissimo. The Communists, for their part, viewed any U.S. support for the Kuomintang as an assault on China's sovereignty. They, too, fell out with Marshall.

Civil war was inevitable. No outsider, however skilled, could have reconciled the monumental differences between the Chinese leaders and their millions of followers. Despondent, Marshall returned home from his failed mission in January 1947.

However disappointed Marshall was by the outcome in China, he would never have defined it in purely personal terms. Marshall always acted with a higher purpose. Duty transcended ego. Like the Roman generals of ancient times, Marshall practiced *nobilitas.* To him its twin components were service and subordination. In 1902 when he took the oath of national service during his commissioning as an army second lieutenant, Marshall committed himself to placing his country first. If that required self-sacrifice, so be it.

For all that Marshall put a true leader's original spin on the principles such as subordination that he was committed to. The command-and-control features of the army, the nation's most hierarchical organization, demanded that every member strictly adhere to the chain of command. But to Marshall following meant more than snapping to, more than robotically giving or taking orders. Like Chou Enlai, Marshall understood the importance of speaking his mind, of dissenting—vehemently in some cases—when he believed those in power were mistaken. To the chagrin of many of his more conventional subordinates, he always demanded that his aides challenge his directives, if they could do so out of conviction. Those who failed to do so were dismissed. Expunging self-interest from his decisions, Marshall often sacrificed his personal ambitions and dreams (including running for the presidency), in the nation's best interests. "America first," not "Me first," was chiseled indelibly in Marshall's psyche.

The Early Years

George C. Marshall, Jr., was born in Uniontown, Pennsylvania, on the last day of 1880, only 15 years after the end of the Civil War. The third child of a relatively wealthy purveyor of coal and coke, young George was overshadowed by his older brother and sister. An awkward, unimposing child, he absorbed the conservative values of the small-town America he knew and loved. According to biographer Forrest C. Pogue, Marshall's was an era that spoke often of "responsibility, duty, character, and integrity," and Marshall took these "Victorian values" to heart.

Marshall decided early on that he wanted to be a professional soldier. West Point was closed to him because he lacked connections, and his grades were mixed. Instead he went to Virginia Military Institute (VMI). Just before he started in 1897, Marshall caught typhoid fever. He was still weak as he began his first, or rat, year.

The sandy-haired freshman endured the normal hardships of the Institute, including incessant hazing. VMI was a spartan place. The barracks had no running water or flush toilets. Windows were left open at night, and, in the harsh winters, snow sometimes accumulated on students' cots over night. Reveille was at 5:30 A.M.; taps sounded long after dark. Rats never had a moment to themselves. They cleaned toilets, did countless push-ups, and were ordered about by upperclassmen—all this in addition to a rigorous program of academic study. Liberty, or free time, was granted only on Saturday afternoons, and rats were confined to the local countryside. Any cadets who ventured into downtown Lexington were subject to immediate expulsion.

After a wobbly beginning, Marshall began to shine. He showed proficiency in military subjects and was judged excellent in drill, discipline, decision making, and leadership. He finished his first year at VMI as first corporal of cadets and, two years later, was unanimously named captain of the Institute, taking command of the assembled cadets at all major ceremonies. The tall, lean, handsome 20-year-old already displayed the characteristics that would mark him as a mature adult. His simplicity of living and air of crisp reserve were strengthened by the harshness of the VMI experience.

"He was certainly not a scholar or an intellectual, and he would not have been considered academically intelligent," writes leadership expert Howard Gardner. "His strengths lay more in the sphere of 'personal intelligences,' in well-considered judgements about people and events. An extremely hard worker, he was very disciplined and reflective, and he expected these features in others as well."

Marshall graduated from the Institute in June 1901. He was commissioned as a second lieutenant in 1902, the same year he married a Lexington woman, Elizabeth Carter Coles, six years his senior. Marshall then embarked on 18 months of service in the bloody Philippine Insurrection, which followed the Spanish-American War. From 1906 to 1908, he studied military strategy at the Cavalry School and Army Staff College in Fort Leavenworth, Kansas, where he graduated at the top of his class. When World War I broke out in 1914, Marshall was 34 and had already been an Army officer for 12 years and had served in 14 different billets at home and abroad.

In every instance Marshall performed admirably, winning the praise of his superiors. "This officer, for his years of service, age and rank, is one of the most completely equipped for military service it has been my lot to observe," said one evaluator. "He has excellent tactical sense, is keen of perception, prompt to decide and act, and quick to take advantage of opportunities for improvement. . . . Should the exigencies of active service place him in exalted command, I would be glad to serve under him."

Kudos notwithstanding, George Marshall remained a lowly first lieutenant. Understandably, he was frustrated by his syrup-slow progress in the peacetime Army. Unable to fully exercise his carefully honed abilities, Marshall complained to his old mentor, General E.W. Nichols, the superintendent of VMI: "The absolute stagnation in promotion in the infantry has caused me to make tentative plans for resigning as soon as business conditions improve. Even in the event of an increase as a result of [congressional] legislation next winter, the prospects of advancement in the Army are so restricted by accumulation of large numbers of men of nearly the same age all in a single grade, that I do not feel it right to waste all my best years in the vain struggle against insurmountable difficulties."

General Nichols urged the antsy lieutenant to "think twice and think long" before resigning his commission. "You are an eminent success in your present line of endeavor, highly esteemed by everyone who knows you, and with a standing in the service of the very highest bar none. Stick to it," the general advised. "I am very sure in time you will be among the highest ranking officers in the service."

As often happens, it was the advent of war that accelerated Marshall's military career. He entered World War I in 1917 and was soon promoted to lieutenant colonel (temporary) and then major. However, the combination of a minor injury and his "special fitness for staff work" kept him from the European front lines. As chief of operations to the First Army's Commanding General Robert Lee Bullard, Marshall proved himself a uniquely talented briefer. (Marshall was unrivaled at making a battle plan and then articulating it, in Bullard's view.) In the fall of 1918, Marshall mobilized the gigantic Meuse-Argonne offensive, consisting of 500,000 men and 2,700 guns—all in less than two weeks. As a result, Bullard called him "the wizard" of "the most magnificent staff operation of the war."

A year earlier Marshall's defense of his chief had almost ended his career. In October 1917 General John J. "Black Jack" Pershing, the commander in chief of the American Expeditionary Force in Europe, chastised Marshall's commander, Major General William L. Sibert, for the division's sloppy performance on field maneuvers. Without any hesitation the red-faced lieutenant colonel spoke up, arguing angrily that Pershing's remarks were blatantly unfair and that the general's staff "didn't understand what they were doing." Taken aback, Black Jack spoke somewhat defensively of troubles at his command post. The straight-shooting Marshall immediately responded, "Yes, General, but we have them every day, and they have to be solved at night." Later, in his official diary, Marshall expressed regret: "I made a great mistake . . . [and] learned the lesson then I never forgot afterwards." He resolved not to let his anger get the better of him again. In the future he would speak his mind, but in a more moderate tone.

Instead of being angry with the blunt young officer, General Pershing was impressed by Marshall's loyalty and his courage in speaking truth to power—invaluable qualities in any lieutenant. It was Pershing who resuscitated Marshall's career at the end of World War I. As Army Chief of Staff, Pershing tapped the talented, outspoken officer as his principal aide-de-camp. For five years Marshall served his master well, developing a strong bond with America's foremost war hero. Pershing in turn found Marshall both able and simpatico in temperament. Both were tough taskmasters and tireless workers who failed to suffer fools gladly. During this period Pershing was almost like a father to Marshall, counseling and supporting him for the rest of Pershing's life.

After serving in Washington with Pershing, Marshall was assigned to the 15th Infantry Regiment in Tientsin from 1924 to 1927. Although Marshall found his China years "delightful, interesting and several times, exciting" and "more instructive than anywhere else in the army," he was unhappy with his lack of command responsibilities. Marshall seemed destined for a lifetime of staff assignments. The problem was one that faces many talented subordinates today—heated competition for too few top slots. "Administrative desk jobs have always been my pet abominations," Marshall lamented, "but with so few regiments and so many lieutenant colonels, one has little choice."

As if disappointment over the trajectory and pace of his career were not enough, Marshall lost his beloved wife, Elizabeth, in 1927. But Marshall soldiered on. For the next five years, he served as an assistant commandant (i.e., head of instruction) at the Infantry Officers' School at Fort Benning, Georgia, where he strongly influenced army practice, particularly in the areas of training and modernization. He also started his famous "black book," which identified high-potential young officers, many of whom would become outstanding commanders in World War II. It was also at Benning, writes History Professor Lance Morrow of Boston University, "that Marshall developed the reputation—later a sometimes rueful Army legend—for ruthlessness in judging officers and sacking even the most experienced men in favor of junior officers who, in his judgement, were up to leading a modern army."

A New Beginning

On October 15, 1930, George Catlett Marshall remarried. Katherine Tupper Brown was a widow with three children—an instant family for Marshall. General Pershing was his best man. Despite the giddiness of the moment, Marshall was still a lieutenant colonel at the age of 50. In contrast, his longtime rival, Douglas MacArthur, was an acting four-star general and chief of staff of the U.S. Army.

Marshall's prospects began to improve. In 1933 he attained the rank of colonel and was named chief of staff of the Illinois National Guard Division, based in Chicago. Next, he commanded the Fifth Brigade in Vancouver, Washington. Notwithstanding his exceptional performance, he found himself blocked for promotion to brigadier general by his nemesis, MacArthur. To MacArthur, Marshall was a Pershing man and, hence, not to be trusted. Pershing's repeated appeals to get Marshall promoted, plus the ringing endorsement of President Roosevelt, fell on deaf ears. It was not until 1936 when MacArthur resigned as Army Chief of Staff to become commander in chief of the Philippine Defense Forces that Marshall's career began to take off. MacArthur's successor as chief of staff was General Malin Craig, a longstanding member of the Pershing clique and, thus, favorably disposed to any deserving disciple of Black Jack. On August 24, 1936, Craig awarded the 55-year-old Marshall his first star.

In 1938 General Craig summoned Marshall to Washington to serve as his chief deputy. The military establishment was desperately concerned about the weak state of the country's defenses. America, the top brass felt, had to rearm and to recruit and train manpower. The White House, however, recognized the public's strong isolationist tendencies. Mindful of American people's reluctance to participate directly in the war, President Roosevelt nonetheless advocated supplying Britain and France with the matériel needed to stave off the advancing Germans.

At a November 1938 conference, Roosevelt proposed to his cabinet members and military advisers that the United States build 10,000 airplanes. It was one of FDR's pet programs, and, by and large, those in attendance nodded their heads in agreement with the commander in chief. But when the president asked "George" whether he supported the plan, Marshall replied, with characteristic honesty: "I am sorry, Mr. President, but I don't agree with you at all." In Marshall's opinion the task of building and staffing so many warplanes was not only overly ambitious, it was totally unrealistic. And Marshall felt duty-bound to let Roosevelt know it.

A startled FDR left the room in a huff, and the meeting ended abruptly. Marshall's friends predicated his tour of duty in Washington would soon come to an end. "Well, it's been nice knowing you," Secretary of the Treasury Henry Morgenthau whispered to Marshall.

To Roosevelt's credit he never referred to the incident again. Instead FDR took a new interest in the career of this outspoken junior general. A few months later, when Army Chief of Staff Craig's retirement was imminent, the president put Marshall's name on the short list of potential replacements. Lobbying for the position was intense, and tremendous pressure was put on Roosevelt to appoint the more senior General Hugh Drum. In Marshall's corner were several influential backers, including Pershing and longtime FDR confidant Harry L. Hopkins. When a number of leading journalists wanted to mount a public relations campaign for Marshall, he responded: Thanks, but no thanks! "My strength with the Army has rested on the well-known fact that I attended strictly to business and enlisted no influence of any sort at anytime," he wrote one prospective champion. "That, in Army circles, has been my greatest strength in the matter of future appointment, especially as it is in strong contrast with other most energetic activities in organizing a campaign and in securing voluminous publicity. Therefore . . . the complete absence of any publicity about me would be my greatest asset, particularly with the President."

Marshall's instincts were right. His quiet self-confidence, lack of self-aggrandizement, and talent for presenting his case to both soldiers and civilians carried the day. On Sunday, April 23, 1939, Marshall was summoned to the White House. FDR had chosen Marshall over 33 more senior men as the new Chief of Staff of the Army.

When informed by the president of his appointment, Marshall reminded his commander in chief: "I have the habit of saying exactly what I think. And that, as you know, can often be unpleasing. Is that all right?" FDR said he would not only tolerate Marshall's bluntness, he expected Marshall to speak his mind.

Shortly thereafter Katherine Marshall sent the president a letter of thanks. "For years I have feared that [George's] brilliant mind and unusual opinions were hopelessly caught on more or less of a treadmill," she wrote. "That you should recognize his ability and place in him your confidence gives me all I have dreamed of and hoped for. I realize the great responsibility that is his."

Marshall's responsibilities never loomed larger than on September 1, 1939, when his swearing in as Army Chief of Staff coincided with Germany's invasion of Poland. Now a temporary four-star general, Marshall reported immediately to the White House to begin planning America's expanding role in World War II. Marshall knew the anemic current state of the army. The United States, if pushed, could muster a meager five fully equipped divisions. The Germans, however, claimed 136 divisions, many of which were battle-hardened. Less than 0.5 percent of the U.S. population (504,000 men) were on active duty or in the reserves. In contrast, nearly 10 percent of the population of Germany, or 6.8 million men, was combat trained.

Marshall's early days as Army Chief of Staff were spent making the American people aware of the dangers of Nazism and the need to mobilize quickly. Working behind the scenes, he was incredibly effective at making the case for building "the most efficient army in the world."

But Marshall was troubled by his commander in chief's apparent ambivalence about beefing up the country's military muscle. Frustrated by FDR's insensitivity to the country's lack of preparedness, Marshall asked Secretary of the Treasury Morgenthau to arrange a special meeting with the president. On May 13, 1940, Marshall, Morgenthau, and a few other senior officials went to see the president. After FDR testily rejected several proposals for modernizing the nation's defenses, an angry Marshall requested a three-minute meeting on the subject.

Not mincing his words, Marshall told the president just how poorly prepared existing U.S. forces were to counter the German threat and the danger that lack of readiness posed for the free world. Marshall described the sorry state of the U.S. military and quickly and deftly offered proposals for achieving the proper levels of readiness, complete with tentative budgets. The next day, FDR granted the general's request.

That evening Secretary Morgenthau told Marshall, "You did a swell job, and I think you are going to get about 75 percent of what you want." In his personal diary, Morgenthau went further, saying he was "tremendously impressed with General Marshall. He stood right up to the President."

Two days later President Roosevelt forwarded the bulk of Marshall's recommendations to Congress, with a covering statement: "The developments of the past few weeks have made it clear to all our citizens that the possibility of attack on vital American zones [has made] it essential that we have the physical, the ready ability to meet these attacks and to prevent them from reaching their objective." Shortly thereafter the lawmakers approved the request that Marshall had persuaded Roosevelt to make.

Now Roosevelt and Congress were finally on board, and America could begin the military buildup needed to win the coming war. Marshall later described this event as a defining moment for the nation and the event that cemented his own relationship with the mercurial Roosevelt. Marshall had done what great co-leaders do. He had taken the initiative and convinced his president to follow a superior course of action.

Strange Bedfellows

In many respects Marshall and his president were polar opposites. On the one hand, the gregarious FDR was a people person, even a schmoozer. Constantly grinning, he was on a first-name basis with everyone. Marshall, on the other hand, was naturally aloof—some said cold—by nature. ("I have no feelings except for those I reserve for Mrs. Marshall," he once admitted.) He tended to work grim-faced, and, from all reports, he never addressed anyone by his or her first name.

FDR was Mr. Nice Guy. He found it virtually impossible to fire anyone, except for gross misconduct. In contrast, Marshall imposed extremely high standards on his subordinates. Underperformers were quickly cashiered out of the service. Historian Doris Kearns Good-win recounts a telling story about Marshall. He once ordered a friend to a foreign post. The man said he was sorry but he couldn't report immediately because his wife was out of town and he needed to pack his furniture. When the man apologized, Marshall snapped: "I'm sorry, too, but you will be retired tomorrow."

Largely instinctual, Roosevelt's disorderly management style frustrated many of his top aides, including Marshall. The sometimes Machiavellian president liked to foster creative ambiguity—frequently assigning the same task to competing units within his administration. While this practice caused considerable uncertainty and confusion among departments, it did give Roosevelt the benefit of multiple opinions.

The president also abhorred organizational charts, rigid policy guidelines, lengthy memoranda, or any of the other trappings of a traditional organization. "Roosevelt's America," observes Goodwin, "was not an organization at all. There was no master plan, no neat division of responsibility, no precise allocation of burden. . . . A lesser man, a smaller ego, would have sought greater control, rigid lines of responsibility and authority."

Marshall, in contrast, relied on rigorous analysis, not intuition, in his decision making. A stickler for detail, he approached every issue with order and discipline. "He could listen for long periods when he was being briefed," recalled his deputy chief of staff, General Tom Handy, "and it was astounding how much he could remember, even the little things. He once came back from a session before a congressional committee on the Hill, when he had been asked some prickly and meticulous questions on minor but complicated matters. He reeled off the answers with ease and authority."

FDR's informality was a scourge to the precise and disciplined Marshall. The general was also suspicious of any politician who cared so much about public opinion. As Goodwin points out, Roosevelt "studied public opinion: he read a variety of newspapers; he analyzed polls; he travelled the country when he could and he dispatched his wife [Eleanor] when he could not; he brought in people of clashing temperaments to secure different points of view, he probed visitors at dinner; he tried out his ideas on reporters. . . . He was able to sense what people were thinking and feeling."

Marshall had reservations about FDR's fondness for taking the public pulse. In Marshall's stern view, decisions that reflected popular sentiment involved unnecessary risks, including the temptation to shade unpleasant truths. Marshall worshiped at the altar of integrity. He never lied, either in his own interest or the nation's. Rigorously nonpartisan, he embodied the disinterested public servant.

Marshall's credibility and immense moral authority made him what Howard Gardner describes as "the most sought-after witness in Congressional history." "His testimony became legendary as time after time, he addressed a skeptical committee and won it over to his cause," Gardner writes. "Marshall knew how to address proud congressmen as equals, never condescending to them and always taking their concerns seriously, yet sticking to his guns as well. . . . An observer who had heard many presidents address the Congress said, 'Not one of them could hold a candle to General Marshall when he wanted to make people do things.' "

Idealism and integrity were the constants of Marshall's thinking. In his 1941 commencement address at the College of William and Mary, the nation's No. 1 soldier said: "At a time when civilization, according to our crude appreciation, reached a summit in achievements, we find ourselves in a great catastrophe in which all our ideals are in dispute. The relationship between the individual and the community, between citizens and the government, between man and their God—all are questioned, all are attacked. The things of the spirit which have enabled this college to endure, which guided the great men of its early days, these seem to be trembling on the verge of the discard. The times demand courageous men with unselfish purpose and truly great ideals."

While FDR was given to grandstanding, Marshall was self-effacing. He declined seven-figure offers for his life's story. He believed soldiers should not write their memoirs, especially if it meant sometimes wounding old colleagues.

When it was unclear whether Roosevelt would seek an unprecedented fourth term, various groups wanted Marshall to head the democratic ticket. He refused all such overtures, contending that military personnel had no place in politics. "So long as the various servants of the Government in important positions concerned with national defense devote all their time and all their thoughts to the straight business of the job, all will go well with America," he wrote one booster. "But just as soon as an ulterior purpose or motive creeps in, the trouble starts."

Marshall never sought honors. Several representatives in the House wanted to have him elevated from general to Field Marshal, a practice common in many other countries. Marshall squelched the idea. "I asked them, 'How it would sound for me to be addressed as Marshal Marshall,' " he recalled dryly.

Not surprisingly the low-keyed Marshall found the boisterous FDR to be somewhat unnerving. Socially Marshall kept his distance from his commander in chief. Despite Harry Hopkins's urgings, Marshall never visited Roosevelt in his retreats in Hyde Park, New York, or Warm Springs, Georgia. "I was not on an intimate relationship with the President," Marshall later recalled.

Although Marshall zealously served FDR, the soldier had personal reservations about him at first. Anyone who rose to the White House had to be somewhat devious, Marshall initially reasoned. Presidents operated in a sea of flattery and guile; such was the nature of Washington politics. Eventually, however, the general not only came to trust FDR, he developed a deep-seated respect for him. Among other things Marshall respected the President's courage in making tough decisions, such as in encouraging the Doolittle bombing raid of Japan, in positioning the U.S. Fleet at Pearl Harbor, in deciding to invade North Africa, and in securing $2 billion for the development of the atomic bomb. Marshall also applauded his commander in chief for not interfering with the military during the entire war, even when it was tempting to second-guess the brass. "In times of great stress," Marshall said, "Roosevelt was a strong man."

For all their differences, Roosevelt and Marshall shared several key traits that made their partnership truly great. Perhaps most important was their commitment to a common cause, so strong a commitment that both were willing to suffer whatever discomfort they experienced working together. Both recognized that you don't have to be buddies to be effective co-leaders. Other common strengths: Both men were superb at identifying talent. In addition to his highly regarded cabinet, the president also assembled a first-rate military team, including, in addition to Marshall, Admiral William Leahy, the president's own military representative. Once FDR's team was in place, he let his experts operate as they saw fit.

Similarly Marshall either named or helped to name the leading generals of the army and army air forces in World War II. From Dwight D. Eisenhower to Omar N. Bradley, Marshall sent into combat men whose work was well known to him. Other outstanding commanders whose careers Marshall helped shape included Mark Clark, Walter Bedell Smith, J. Lawton Collins, Alexander Patch, Lucian Truscott, and Matthew B. Ridgway. In the Pacific Marshall's theater commander was General MacArthur. A lesser man might have dwelled on MacArthur's role, years before, in thwarting his career. Not Marshall, who urged Roosevelt to summon MacArthur back from retirement. For the China-Burma-India campaign, Marshall strongly recommended Joseph Stilwell, while Albert C. Wedemeyer won Marshall's enthusiastic endorsement to serve as chief of the China Theater and as deputy to Lord Louis Mountbatten.

Marshall gave every subordinate strong and unconditional support. "Although he believed that a commander should select good men and then give them his confidence, he was also prepared to proffer assistance when it might be of value," Pogue writes. "Often a commander facing a crisis in the field found a steadying message from the Pentagon promising complete support in whatever decision he had to make."

Both Roosevelt and Marshall had an all but limitless capacity to inspire trust, but in different ways. Eloquent, aristocratic FDR possessed an uncanny sensitivity to his followers, a rare ability to assess public sentiment, and a genius for rallying people behind him. "No one understood better than he," historian Eric Larrabee observes, "the inner dynamic of American strength: how to mobilize it, how to draw on it, how to gauge its limits. Once mobilized, it did not need to be driven; it needed only to be steered."

Ever the helmsman, President Roosevelt steered the country through choppy seas. His famous fireside chats, which began in May 1940, unified the American people as the president led them step by step through the difficult war years. Rationing his appearances to two or three a year, Roosevelt explained the conduct of the war to 65 million people with his characteristic flair. These radio talks, listeners agreed, brought the president into their living rooms and showed him to be a concerned and caring leader. His popularity was incredible: No other broadcasts of the time came close to FDR's 70 percent listenership.

In essence FDR was demonstrating incremental leadership, allowing his followers—the American people—enough time to grasp the strategies and risks of U.S. involvement in World War II. "We failed to see," Marshall said later, contrasting the military with the president, "that the leader in a democracy has to keep the people entertained. That may sound like the wrong word but it conveys the thought."

Marshall also had an extraordinary ability to inspire trust, a vital trait for leaders at every level. His followers often became worshipers. Marshall was able to put a human face on soldiering. He showed special concern for those who had to bear the heat of battle and was ferocious in his determination to ready his troops for the fight and equip them with the means to win. Marshall insisted that every soldier know and perform his job well, and he never forgot that the ultimate cost of victory was the loss of human life.

Marshall loved being a soldier. To him soldiering was all about loyalty and esprit de corps. "Make a point of extreme loyalty, in thought and deed, to your chiefs personally," he urged young officers going off to war. "In your efforts to carry out their plans or policies, the less you approve, the more energy you must direct to their accomplishment." He told a group of graduating officers at Fort Benning that success comes from "the previous reputation you have established for fairness, for that high-minded patriotic purpose, that quality of unswerving determination to carry through any military task assigned you."

True, Marshall could be ruthless when a soldier didn't measure up to his lofty standards. Fire-eating George Patton vowed he "would rather face the whole Nazi panzer army single-handed than be called to an interview with General Marshall." Marshall was neither warm nor familiar, and a grunt of appreciation was often the only compliment a subordinate could expect. Nevertheless, Marshall was, in his own way, a sensitive, caring leader, acutely aware of the personal toll soldiering could exact. "Please take me very seriously," he wrote one overly stressed young general. "You have wonderful qualities, but you are too conscientious. It's pretty hard for a leopard to change his spots, but you must [make] a deliberate effort to be quite casual."

A "virtually invisible gift" is how leadership expert John Gardner describes Marshall's trust-building skills. "The leader who can win a battle, dazzle an audience or smash electoral opposition has something the journalists and historians can write about. How many have ever written about the bonds of trust that . . . Marshall forged so quietly?"

The Greatest Sacrifice

Working tirelessly in the shadow of President Roosevelt, Marshall changed the course of history in 1943 when he convinced the British allies of the wisdom of mounting a cross-Channel invasion of Europe. Reluctantly Churchill agreed that an American commander, appointed by Roosevelt, should lead Overlord (code name for the invasion). Churchill recommended Marshall for the task, and rumors flew on both sides of the Atlantic that Marshall was slated for the job.

Make no mistake, Marshall desperately wanted the assignment of supreme commander of what would be the most memorable battle of the war. His entire army career had prepared him for this command. No one else deserved it more. And, given that he was 63, it probably represented his last chance for battlefield glory. Hence Marshall, and virtually every other Washington insider, felt the assignment was his for the asking.

Initially FDR leaned toward Marshall for the post, asking him to begin preparing a plan of attack, including selecting field commanders. In a letter to Pershing, Roosevelt had conceded that losing Marshall from the Combined Chiefs would be a hardship—but one the president initially felt obliged to make. "I want George to be the Pershing of the Second World War," FDR wrote, "and he cannot be that if we keep him here."

However, in time the president decided Marshall was indispensable in Washington. His prestige with Congress was "almost without precedent," columnist Ernest Lindley noted. "It is a staggering tribute to one man that he is regarded by so many diverse but competent judges as . . . the best equipped to administer the American Army, to represent it before Congress, and the public, [and] to represent it on the highest Allied strategy-making body." Roosevelt reasoned that the younger General Eisenhower had more battlefield experience, having shown his mettle as a commander in North Africa and the Mediterranean. FDR also doubted that Eisenhower had the ability to replace Marshall in Washington. Through Harry Hopkins FDR learned that Eisenhower preferred serving under Marshall on the Overlord campaign to returning to Washington to become the new chief of staff.

The matter came to a head in Cairo. The president was not prepared to offer Marshall the job of supreme commander unless he asked for it. And that, the shrewd Roosevelt reasoned, would probably not happen. Even in the historian Leonard Mosley's view, Marshall "would never beg a favor of anyone, not even the President of the United States—not for himself anyway."

The decision was made. Marshall would remain in Washington. "I feel I could not sleep at night with you out of the country," the president told him, which was probably little consolation. FDR then proceeded to meet Eisenhower in Tunis and inform him of Ike's forthcoming command of Overlord.

Marshall was bitterly disappointed by the announcement. Without saying a word to the president, Marshall disappeared from Egypt with two of his closest aides on an unscheduled 35,000-mile trip around the world—journeying back to Washington via Ceylon, Australia, and the Pacific. Marshall never displayed any other sign of pique. He never publicly questioned Roosevelt's choice, and he supported Eisenhower at every turn. Back in Washington, Marshall discussed the president's decision with Secretary of War Henry Stimson, who recalled that Marshall "showed his usual bigness about the whole darn thing."

Marshall transcended rank and office. He was the exemplary servant-leader whose power grew out of his rare moral authority (not unlike Gandhi and Martin Luther King). Always putting service before ego, Marshall was willing to do anything for his country, except compromise his principles. Losing command of Overlord disappointed Marshall greatly, yet he pressed on with the successful prosecution of the war. "It has not fallen to your lot to command the great armies," Churchill later consoled him. "You have had to create them, organize them, and inspire them. Under your guiding hand, the mighty and valiant formations which have swept across France and Germany were brought into being and perfected in an amazingly short space of time."

When Franklin Roosevelt died on April 12, 1945, Marshall wholeheartedly threw his support behind Harry S Truman, whose spunk he had come to admire over the years. After Marshall's brief retirement in 1947, President Truman recalled him three times to posts normally held by civilians: head of the mission to China, secretary of state, and secretary of defense. Despite Marshall's unsuccessful efforts to mediate the Chinese civil war, he was widely praised as the nation's No. 1 diplomat. "He was the most important military man in the Second World War," Truman said, in announcing Marshall's first cabinet appointment. "And he will become the most important secretary of state in the next decade. He has qualities that cannot be beaten. He is good at organization and as a judge of men. He is not an overbearing man. He gets along with people. And people trust him."

The American people do not, as a general rule, like or trust the military. But, as Truman knew, they revered General Marshall. While he was secretary of state, Marshall's contributions included the provision of aid to Greece and Turkey, the recognition of Israel, and the discussions that led to the establishment of the North American Treaty Organization (NATO). But even more important, Marshall first called for and then directed the recovery program in Western Europe. He challenged Americans to look beyond narrowly defined nationalism and to share their resources, energies, and values with the very nations that had recently been enemies. "Democratic principles do not flourish on empty stomachs," he reminded America. The European Recovery Program, known as the Marshall Plan, played the decisive role in the reconstruction of war-torn Europe. In the four years between 1948 and 1952, this extraordinary act of generosity channeled $13.3 billion in economic assistance to 16 European countries. The plan was, in Churchill's view, "the most unsordid act in history."

In 1949 Marshall resigned as secretary of state because of ill health. A year later, when he was nearly 70, Truman asked him to return to public service as secretary of defense. The Korean War had begun, and the United States desperately needed a coherent military strategy. In short order Marshall secured the United Nation's involvement in the conflict, while increasing U.S. troop strength and matériel production. The nation applauded Marshall's selfless and distinguished service, with one notable exception: Senator Joseph McCarthy. The infamous red-baiter labeled Marshall "a traitor," charging him with conspiring with FDR to keep American commanders uninformed about the imminence of the 1941 attack on Pearl Harbor; betraying Chiang Kai-shek and the Nationalist movement; and pursuing a pro-Soviet strategy in Europe. Perhaps even more painful to Marshall was the anemic defense of him by General, soon to be President, Eisenhower. For reasons still unexplained, Ike failed to denounce forcefully the vicious, right-wing attack on his former mentor. McCarthy's empty but insidious charges darkened Marshall's final years.

Marshall left public office for good on September 1, 1951. Even then he remained on the active-duty list as the highest-ranking general of the army, available for consultation with the government. In 1953 he became the first professional soldier to receive the Nobel Peace Prize for his contributions to the economic rehabilitation of postwar Europe and for his efforts to promote world peace and understanding.

George Marshall embodied the ideal of the citizen soldier. "The Noblest Roman of them all," Churchill called him. Never elected president, denied the opportunity to lead the deciding battle of the century, Marshall was, in many ways, the noblest co-leader of them all. He served his country, indeed the world, in war and peace, as few have, however exalted their rank.

Whether the job was building the modern American military or rebuilding postwar Europe, Marshall stayed focused on the task, never dwelling on what was in it for him. Duty, honor, and country always came before self. His simplicity and self-sacrifice make his achievements seem greater still.

George Catlett Marshall died on October 16, 1959, at Walter Reed Hospital in Washington. His burial instructions reflected his modest nature. "Bury me simply," he requested, "like any ordinary officer of the U.S. Army who has served his country honorably. No fuss. No elaborate ceremonials. Keep the service short; confine the guest list to the family. And above everything, do it quietly."

Marshall "was the greatest of the great in our time," declared his former boss, Harry Truman. "I sincerely hope that when it comes to my time to cross the great river, Marshall will place me on his staff, so that I may try to do for him what he did for me."

7

Bernice Pauahi Bishop

A Legacy Second to None

Bernice Pauahi Bishop, the last direct descendant of Hawaii's royal Kamchameha line, created America's wealthiest charity. She is shown with her husband, Charles Reed Bishop, in San Francisco in 1875. (Bishop Museum and Bradley & Rulofson, San Francisco)

7 | Bernice Pauahi Bishop

Who can find a virtuous woman, for her price is far above rubies . . . Her children rise up and call her blessed.
—PROVERBS 31:10, 28

"Coming to Kamehameha Schools gave me a sense of what it means to be Hawaiian," recalls Melissa Kallstrom, a graduate of the class of 1994. "Being Hawaiian is a way of life. Hawaiians think of other people first. Giving to others—that's the way I picture Hawaiians." A recent visit to the verdant, 500-acre campus at Kapalama Heights on the island of Oahu brought back fond memories of her early school days.

Because of her exceptional academic ability and part-Hawaiian ancestry, Kallstrom was admitted to Kamehameha Schools in the seventh grade. Her keen interest in ecology began as a freshman in the environmental club, *Hui Lama*. Later a five-day backpacking trip to Maui's Haleakala Crater turned Kallstrom's interest into commitment. "It taught me about God's creation," she remembered. "It taught me about working together, looking out for one another, and sharing the load."

These same virtues motivated Princess Bernice Pauahi Bishop, the last direct descendant of Hawaii's royal Kamehameha line. King Kamehameha I, one of the islands' most storied leaders, came to power in 1782 and succeeded in unifying Hawaii's warring kingdoms into a flourishing empire. However, during the princess's lifetime, the native population withered from almost 400,000 to 45,000 as a result of smallpox and other diseases introduced by Western explorers, missionaries, and merchants.

Bernice Pauahi Bishop believed that education offered the best hope for the Hawaiian race. Before her death in 1884, she placed more than 375,569 acres of her lands in a perpetual trust and created Kamehameha Schools as its sole beneficiary. Her will launched an institution that would give generations of young Hawaiians like Melissa Kallstrom the tools they needed not only to survive but to fulfill their dreams. The princess directed that students receive "a good education in the common English branches, and also instruction in morals and in such useful knowledge as may tend to make good and industrious men and women." To manage the trust, popularly known as the Bishop Estate, Princess Pauahi appointed five trustees, giving them full control over financial and educational matters.

Today Kamehameha Schools' lush hillside campus, with its commanding view of Honolulu Harbor, houses the nation's second largest private primary and secondary school in terms of enrollment. Its Hawaiian and part-Hawaiian student body numbers 4,400 from preschool through high school. Entrance is limited: Only one in eight applicants is admitted. More than 90 percent of Kamehameha's graduates go on to institutions of higher learning, including Harvard, Yale, Stanford, and Princeton. The school's 17,000 alums include prominent doctors, lawyers, engineers, business, and government leaders throughout the United States and the world.

Bishop Estate subsidizes about 94 percent of the cost of educating a Kamehameha student. It also awards a host of generous scholarships to current students and to alumni enrolled in undergraduate and graduate degree programs. The Bishop Estate's largesse is made possible by its enormous wealth. Thanks to Bernice Pauahi's generosity, the land-rich, cash-rich trust owns 367,509 acres of Hawaii land (or almost 9 percent of the State's total land area) as well as an impressive portfolio of U.S. and Pacific Rim holdings. The giant trust owns 11 percent of Goldman, Sachs & Co., the New York investment powerhouse; 4.1 percent of the upscale retailer, Saks Fifth Avenue; 300,000 acres of Michigan timberland; energy ventures in Texas; a partial interest in a Bermuda reinsurance company; an exclusive northern Virginia country club; and even a Chinese bank.

With annual revenues of more than $375 million, Bishop Estate officially reports net assets of approximately $5.7 billion, a figure many believe is grossly understated. A more realistic net asset figure may be perhaps as high as $10 billion—which makes Bishop one of the nation's wealthiest charities. If true, the 114-year-old educational trust possesses an endowment roughly equal to Harvard's.

Our objective is not to examine how a remote Hawaiian trust became Croesus-rich. Rather, it is to show how power sharing allowed a Polynesian princess to realize her unique vision for her people. As the ultimate partnership, marriage is an ideal prism through which to view co-leadership. Frequently marriage involves an unequal distribution of power, but, ideally at least, decision making is shared according to the unique needs and abilities of each partner. In the course of their 34-year marriage, Bernice Pauahi and her influential husband, Charles Reed Bishop, were devoted co-leaders who sometimes led and sometimes followed, but always worked together toward a noble goal.

Princess Pauahi's dream for Kamehameha Schools was realized in part through the foresight and business acumen of her husband, who served as one of Bishop Estate's original trustees. After her death, Bishop managed both the estate and the schools with skill and insight, keeping his wife's wishes firmly in mind. It was Bishop who established the trust's solid financial footing in the critical early years by leasing rather than selling the royal lands. He also dipped deeply into his own personal savings to begin construction of school buildings and to pay salaries. "Princess Pauahi clearly was the visionary," says current trustee Oswald Stender, "but Charles Reed Bishop was the implementer—the one who made the vision happen."

For her part Bernice Pauahi was a royal who bucked tradition to follow her heart and realize her dream. Against the wishes of her parents, the great-granddaughter of Kamehameha the Great rejected princely suitors in favor of Bishop, an upstart, immigrant *haole* (foreigner). Later she did the unthinkable and turned down the Hawaiian throne. To her ruling the island kingdom was secondary to preserving her marriage and crafting a better future for her race.

Hawaii Calls

About A.D. 400, the first voyagers arrived on Hawaii's shores after sailing for months in huge canoes propelled by sails made of the hala or pandanus plants. They migrated from the Marquesas and Tahiti far to the south. Together these enterprising explorers became the people known as Hawaiians. These early migrants had Hawaii to themselves for over a thousand years. In relative isolation they developed a highly structured society, which produced the greatest flowering of Polynesian culture. Powerful classes of chiefs and priests emerged, as did numerous internecine conflicts not unlike the feudal struggles in Europe. Except for a break at harvest time, year-round fighting between rival rulers was the norm.

Contact with the West was a colorful and oftentimes tragic chapter to the Hawaiian Islands. British Captain James Cook, searching for the Northwest Passage, a route through the icy seas above the American continent, landed in Hawaii at daybreak on January 20, 1778. Cook's "discovery" of the islands led to subsequent foreign contact. Able to preserve his culture but take what he wanted from the West, the remarkable Kamehameha I utilized European technology and weaponry to emerge as Hawaii's unifier and foremost leader.

After Cook's voyages to the islands, other European and American adventurers, trappers, and whalers regularly visited for fresh supplies. While there were sporadic attempts by the British and the French to construct spheres of influence in Hawaii, the American footprint was always dominant. Yankee whalers began wintering in Hawaii as early as 1819 (the year of Kamehameha the Great's death). Two decades later close to 500 American ships choked the bustling harbors of Honolulu and Lahaina.

Social change began to sweep through these once-isolated islands. Trade and commerce drew indigenous people away from the rural villages and into seaport towns. The land that had sustained the Hawaiian populace was often neglected. Worse yet, the native population fell prey to a bevy of Western diseases—cholera, measles, bubonic plague, leprosy, and venereal disease—to which they had no immunity.

Missionary families from Puritan New England arrived in 1820, bringing with them Christian values and Western customs. Kamehameha II already had broken the sacred *kapu* (taboo) system by eating with women. The Western-influenced monarch had also proclaimed the death of the Hawaiian gods, destroyed the power of native priests, and obliterated their *heiau* (temples).

As a result, Hawaiians experienced something of a religious void. A loss of faith in the old deities, an intense interest in the ways of foreigners, an avid desire to learn to read and write, and the need for spiritual identity made Christianity appealing for many Hawaiians. By the 1830s the island kingdom was well on its way toward becoming a Christian nation.

"The troubled thirties," is how Ralph Kuykendall, a prominent Hawaii historian, described the decade. Princess Bernice Pauahi Paki was born in these tumultuous times on December 19, 1831. The daughter of the High Chief Abner Paki and his wife, Konia, Pauahi was the great-granddaughter of Kamehameha I and a member of the ruling *alii* (royal class). As was the Hawaiian custom, soon after her birth Bernice Pauahi was taken to live with her *hanai* (adopted) mother, Kinau, who was the eldest daughter of Kamehameha and the highest royal at the time. With her husband, Kekuanaoa, a judge and the governor of Oahu, Kinau carefully watched over her adopted child and exposed her to the best of traditional culture and the privileges of royalty.

When the princess was growing up, Kauikeaouli (or Kamehameha III) succeeded his brother Liholiho. "Mine is the kingdom of education," the new king proudly proclaimed. Recognizing the importance of literacy for all Hawaiians, he encouraged the creation of more than 1,000 schools serving 50,000 students—about 40 percent of the total native population. He also commissioned two American missionaries, Amos Starr Cooke and his wife, Juliette Montague Cooke, to oversee the first formal school for young *alii*. The monarch further insisted that the language of instruction be English, thereby affording the kingdom's future leaders the opportunity to know and understand foreigners.

On June 13, 1839, the Cookes opened the Chiefs' Children's School to six children, including Princess Pauahi. Eventually six future kings and queens of the island kingdom would receive their education at the new boarding school. The no-nonsense Calvinist couple enforced a strict code of conduct. There was no fraternization between boys and girls. Students were responsible for feeding and caring for themselves and for doing assigned chores. *Kahu* (royal servants) were expelled from the school grounds, and, for the first time in their lives, young *alii* discovered the meaning of self-reliance.

By intention, Western ideals and values permeated the course of instruction. Like other missionaries, the Cookes came from antiroyalist New England and believed in individualism and egalitarianism. They often challenged the kingdom's time-honored tradition of elitism and extolled virtues of a more open society.

No doubt the adjustment process for the much-pampered princes and princesses was difficult. Although there are no records of formal report cards, the evidence clearly suggests that Bernice Pauahi was among the best and the brightest. She quickly mastered a variety of subjects, from chemistry to Euclid. The princess learned to read in English, "thereby acquiring a love for the best literature, and an appreciation of what constituted the best."

The delicate Pauahi was exceptionally beautiful as well. An early visitor to the school described her as a "slender, graceful child, with an exquisite figure. Her hands, always small and remarkable for their beauty, were perfectly formed by the manipulations of her nurses in babyhood, a custom that formerly prevailed among all Hawaiians of high rank. She had beautiful dark hair that fell in a cloud of lustrous, silken ringlets to her waist, and her skin, as in infancy, was fair."

As she matured, Princess Pauahi became known as "an interesting and brilliant conversationalist, ready to talk upon almost any topic, with distinguished men and women whom she met at the school and who enjoyed her hospitality in later years." While deeply Hawaiian, she was keen to meet and understand those outside her race. "She has always been more under foreign influence than most of the other pupils of her age," recalled Gorham D. Gilman, a friend and businessman.

Deeply in Love

Early in 1847 a young American from Glens Falls, New York, visited the Chiefs' Children's School. The slight, dark-haired man with a trim black beard and intense blue eyes was Charles Reed Bishop. Born in 1822, Bishop was orphaned in early childhood and reared by his grandparents. He left home at the age of 15 and, after holding several minor jobs, sailed (the preferred route) for Oregon in 1846 to seek his fortune. His ship, the *Henry,* was severely battered during the longest passage ever recorded around the Horn—231 days—and diverted to Honolulu Harbor for repairs. With no cash and meager academic credentials, Bishop took a dollar-a-day job posting ledgers for the kingdom's treasury. Captivated by the magic of what Mark Twain called "the loveliest fleet of islands that lies anchored in any ocean," Bishop became a naturalized subject in 1849. Shortly thereafter he was appointed collector general of customs.

Romance with a foreigner was the last thing on Pauahi's mind that summer night. At the time, she was betrothed to Prince Lot (later Kamehameha V), a choice made by her parents, Konia and Abner Paki, as well as the Royal Court. Had she married him, she would have been for life the highest political power in Hawaii. Yet the lovely princess, described by Queen Liliuokalani as "one of the most beautiful girls I ever saw," was smitten by the blue-eyed caller. With the Cookes's blessing, Pauahi began to see more and more of Bishop. And the two fell deeply in love.

Her parents were aghast when the 18-year-old announced her plans to reject a royal marriage for this humble *haole*. They threatened to disinherit her. But Bernice Pauahi had the iron will of the Kamehamehas. She proceeded to marry the 28-year-old Bishop in a simple ceremony on June 4, 1850, in the school's parlor. Much to her distress, her parents refused to attend the wedding, saying that Pauahi must now look to the Cookes "for all her *pono* [welfare]."

If the Pakis were concerned about Bishop's ability to support their daughter, their fears quickly subsided. In April 1853 Charles resigned his government position to form a business partnership with William A. Aldrich. Later the two opened Hawaii's first bank, the Bank of Bishop & Co., Ltd. (now First Hawaiian Bank) in a tiny waterfront office. In the early years, they concentrated on financing the lucrative whale oil and whalebone trade. However, with whaling clearly on the wane by 1860, the enterprising bankers shifted their attention to the burgeoning sugar industry.

The American Civil War was a bonanza for Hawaiian sugar and the Bishop Bank. "Prices zoomed so high that local planters could make money despite high tariffs at U.S. ports," writes Joseph G. Mullins. "By 1866, the Kingdom was exporting almost 18 million pounds of sugar, compared to 1.5 million pounds just six years earlier." However, the real boon to the industry came with the passage of the Reciprocity Treaty of 1876, which eliminated restrictive U.S. duties on all island products. This in turn increased the value of Hawaiian lands, which led to the more aggressive planting of sugar cane.

As King Sugar grew so, too, did the fortunes of Bishop and his bank. Because of his integrity and innate ability, everything he touched prospered. "There was no fuss, no sham, no double-dealing about him," Harold Kent noted. "His word could always be depended upon." Naturally Bishop's marriage to Princess Pauahi contributed substantially to his ability to do business and to the bank's reputation.

"Charles must have been pleased with the fact that his wife had an impeccable reputation that he could draw upon in establishing the bank's initial credibility," writes Hawaiian historian George H. S. Kanahele. "He may have been able eventually to achieve credibility on the basis of his own very solid image in the community, but Pauahi's status and *mana* (spiritual power or influence) . . . must have helped, although it is impossible to tell how much."

Clearly Bernice Pauahi's royal blood brought Bishop closer to the inner sanctum of the Hawaiian monarchy. As a result of his growing stature in commercial circles and his marriage to the beautiful great-granddaughter of Kamehameha I, Bishop was tapped for government service. In 1859 he was made a noble of the kingdom. He was also appointed to the Privy Council during the reigns of four kings and one queen. Throughout his life he served as a trusted adviser to royalty and managed many of their personal affairs. Thanks to Princess Pauahi, Bishop enjoyed *alii* status in every way except blood.

However, Bishop's forays into public service caused occasional conflicts with the Hawaiians, Mrs. Bishop included. In 1873 he had to make one of the toughest decisions of his life. For years the United States Navy had eyed the strategic potential of *Puuloa* Lagoon, or Pearl Harbor. Negotiations between the U.S. government and the Kingdom of Hawaii, represented by Foreign Minister Bishop, led to a special treaty of reciprocity conditional on Hawaii's ceding its sovereignty over Pearl Harbor. To Bishop and King Lunalilo, reciprocity offered the defenseless kingdom the military security of the United States without the more oppressive elements of annexation. On July 12, 1873, the king and Bishop publicly announced their support of the Pearl Harbor compact, urging prompt legislative approval.

The proposal was greeted with howls of protest. Dr. Kanahele reports that 1,500 Hawaiians rallied against ceding any island territory to a foreign power. Atypically for the times, the king was roundly criticized. Bishop, for his part, was reproached for turning the foreign office into a "real estate brokerage."

Over the years the native population had become increasingly concerned about the loss of their land to acquisitive non-Hawaiians. Prior to 1848 all Hawaiian land belonged to the king. However, under the *Great Mahele* (land division), the land was split three ways: one part went to the crown, one to the nobles, and one to the common people. Because Hawaiians had no tradition of private land ownership, their properties often fell into the hands of greedy outsiders.

By 1873 the Hawaiians had had enough. None of them, including Mrs. Bishop, wanted Pearl Harbor to be transferred to the United States. In Queen Emma's private correspondence, she noted that "Pauahi opposes cession of territory, whilst he [Bishop] favors [it]." Bishop later admitted: "[My wife] consoles me by saying that I ought to have known that the natives would not favor cession. Every chief in the country was opposed to it." In 1874 the Legislature rejected the treaty, only to see it pass two years later.

Although Bishop remained a loyal confidant to the monarchy, he was much more comfortable in business than in government. The Pearl Harbor controversy convinced him that politics could irreparably tarnish not only his commercial reputation, but his marriage as well. Mrs. Bishop's life was also becoming increasingly complicated. Early in their marriage, her duties were primarily domestic—maintaining their home and its staff of 30 attendants. Like many of the female *alii,* she was inflicted with *kapu* lap, meaning she could not bear children. Instead Pauahi focused her attention on social and cultural affairs. Distinguished visitors from Japan to England gathered at her Honolulu home for dinner, dances, receptions—or simply good conversation. No guest was ever turned away.

As would any true *alii,* Bernice Pauahi felt a special kinship for her people. The Hawaiian community held her in great esteem, and shouts of joy greeted her wherever she went. "It pleased me to see how much interested the natives were in Mrs. Bishop," said one family friend, "as I imagine Hawaiians were [with] all their *alii.* . . . They were curious as well as loyal, and she thoroughly enjoyed her life among them."

Princess Pauahi frequently received and counseled those in need and offered help to the troubled. And troubles abounded. By 1870 the

Hawaiian population had shrunk to 45,000. From 1850 to 1870 the non-Hawaiian community had ballooned sevenfold, to 14,000, primarily due to the influx of foreign plantation workers. Two decades later outsiders would outnumber Hawaiians. These sobering statistics steeled Mrs. Bishop's resolve to assist her blood brothers and sisters.

The opportunity to help her people came to Bernice Pauahi through inheritance. In 1855 her father, Paki, left her 5,780 acres on Oahu. Two years later Konia passed away, leaving her daughter an additional 10,231 acres on the islands of Oahu, Kauai, and Hawaii. This made the princess, at age 25, a major landowner. Twenty years later her holdings grew by another 9,557 acres (mostly on Hawaii) following the death of her aunt Akahi. However, these generous bequests paled in comparison with that of her cousin Princess Ruth Keelikolani. At her death in 1833, Keelikolani left Pauahi a mind-boggling 353,000 acres and other assets valued at approximately $500,000. In an instant Mrs. Bishop was the largest landowner and wealthiest woman in the Kingdom of Hawaii.

Royal Rejection

The last male in the Kamehameha line was Lot (Kamehameha V), the royal suitor Princess Pauahi had rejected years ago. On his deathbed the bachelor king offered her the ultimate gift: his throne.

In the early morning of December 10, 1872, a messenger summoned Mrs. Bishop to Lot's mansion. "I wish you to take my place, to be my successor," the king said to Pauahi, who was at his bedside. She replied: "No, no, not me. Don't think of me. I do not need it."

The king pressed on. But Mrs. Bishop again spurned the throne: "Oh, no, do not think of me. There are others." After considering the alternatives, Kamehameha V said no more on the subject and died about an hour later. His failure to name a successor resulted in the election of a king, as provided for in the kingdom's constitution.

A similar succession problem followed the death of the popular William Charles Lunalilo, who became the first elected monarch in 1873. After only a year in office, Prince Bill died of tuberculosis without naming an heir. This time, however, there is no evidence that the dying king asked Princess Pauahi to assume the throne. Nor is there any indication that Charles Reed Bishop, who headed Lunalilo's cabinet, suggested to the king that Mrs. Bishop be named royal successor. But a few scholars believe that Pauahi, who was on excellent terms with the king, may have had the crown for the asking.

Why then did this respected, even revered member of the royal family turn down her kingdom's overtures for the highest office? No one knows for sure. The answer may have been contained in Mrs. Bishop's letters and other memorabilia left in the care of her husband. Unfortunately they were destroyed during the great San Francisco earthquake of 1906.

Could she have led Hawaii? Although Princess Pauahi lacked government experience, she was born into a caste that had led her people for generations. And as her land holdings grew, so too did her executive responsibilities. After inheriting her father's properties, Pauahi initially depended heavily on *konohiki* (land managers), who looked after the general welfare of the parcels as well as the numerous tenant farmers. Eventually, however, she adopted a more hands-on management style, visiting her estates "frequently, sometimes remaining for months."

"Though she relied on *konohiki,* as landlord she had ultimate responsibility for management," writes George Kanahele, "She carried the main burden herself." While she turned to her husband on leasing matters, "she was far more familiar with her lands and people and the *konohiki* system than he was." By age 40 Bernice Pauahi was an experienced and proven *haku aina* (landlord) on an imposing scale.

In addition the princess understood the *haole* world far better than most members of the *alii.* Her English was impeccable, and, with Bishop's help, she had endeared herself to many in the non-Hawaiian community. Her home, *Haleakala,* was a favorite gathering spot for both locals and foreigners. Furthermore, she had begun to travel extensively within the United States, acutely aware of the benefits that overseas contacts might offer her people.

Despite her qualifications, Bernice Pauahi concluded that the throne was not for her. Most likely family concerns weighed heavily in her decision to turn down the royal scepter. Tensions were already building within the Bishop household over the best future course for the island kingdom.

Bishop had become increasingly concerned about the crown's ability to produce a generation of leaders capable of coping with the nation's rapidly changing environment. "Whichever way I turn, affairs look discouraging to me," he wrote. "Demoralization is going on among the Hawaiians, and they do not realize their own shame and danger." His solution? "The only safe thing . . . is Annexation to the United States under territorial form of government."

Princess Pauahi, however, remained a devout royalist. She staunchly defended *alii* rule and worried deeply about the further erosion of Hawaiian land, values, and culture. While she recognized the limitations of the monarchy, annexation to the United States or any foreign power was unthinkable.

Pauahi probably chose not to assume the throne because it would have endangered her happy marriage with Bishop. Bishop's Western-style commercial success inevitably conflicted with her deep-felt desire to preserve Hawaii's political and cultural identity. The princess reasoned that regal responsibilities would exacerbate these differences in the most public way—as later proved to be true in the ill-fated Pearl Harbor affair. "In short, her partnership with Charles was the most precious and enduring relationship she had," writes George Kanahele, "and she was not about to jeopardize it in exchange for the uncertainties of the crown."

We can speculate further that Bernice Pauahi may also have had visions of a more permanent, nonpolitical solution to the problems facing Hawaii's people. Having no children of her own, the princess began to think hard about the disposition of her massive fortune. In the recent past, other *alii* had created charitable trusts for various Hawaiian beneficiaries: King Lunalilo, a home for the poor, destitute, and infirm; Queen Emma, a hospital. Later Queen Kapiolani would establish separate refuges for Hawaiian mothers and female lepers, while Queen Liliuokalani funded a children's center, primarily for native sons and daughters.

After much careful thought, Pauahi concluded that education would best serve a people on the verge of racial extinction, cultural disintegration, and crippling poverty. Education, she believed, could reverse decades of neglect and restore a sense of dignity to the indigenous population. Her decision was to create a single-purpose trust that would help native Hawaiians become meaningful contributors to society.

In preparing her will, the princess sought the counsel of several trusted advisers, including her husband, who had served on the Board of Education for many years. But Bernice Pauahi Bishop was the architect; her imprint remains deeply etched in the resulting document. "It would have been totally out of character for her to let anyone else, including Charles, decide things for her." Kanahele notes. "As her life shows, she was entirely able to make large and important decisions in the best or worst circumstances. Now in her last days, making the most critical decisions of her life . . . she and she alone would decide."

With Charles's help Pauahi influenced the design of the Kamehameha Schools. Reportedly she insisted on separate institutions for boys and girls, with their curricula—from English language instruction to Christian teachings—mirroring her own early schooling. In the most explicit terms, she also reaffirmed her lifetime commitment to land preservation: "[The] trustees shall not sell any real estate . . . but continue and manage same, unless in their opinion a sale may be necessary for the establishment or maintenance of said schools, or for the best interest of my Estate."

In October 1883 Bernice Pauahi completed her brilliantly crafted 11-page will. She directed her legacy, the vast Kamehameha lands—one-ninth of all land in the islands—to one end: the creation and support in perpetuity of a coeducational school for Hawaiian children.

Aloha, Pauahi

Shortly after her fifty-second birthday, the princess began to experience the initial effects of the cancer that would claim her life. She died shortly after noon on a rainy Thursday, October 16, 1884. Within minutes of her passing, Hawaii wept. Government buildings were closed, the courts recessed, flags dropped to half-mast. Students were released from school and joined a multitude of mourners at the family home.

Funeral *mele* (or chants) were sung nonstop for 15 days until her burial on October 30. More than 900 people and 75 carriages led the long procession to Kawaiahao Church. The Royal Hawaiian Band played the "Pauahi March," and lengthy eulogies were offered.

"Princess Pauahi was thus a link between the old and the new, between the native and the foreign, in a sense which was not true of any other person," said one mourner. . . . "The Hawaiian race may yet develop noble characters, devoted and virtuous women, but the peculiar niche occupied by Bernice Pauahi Bishop is vacant and must ever remain so."

An ode to the Princess further proclaimed:
Long in our memory will thy virtues live,
Long in our hearts the thought of thee survive,
Ill can we spare thee, none can take thy place,
Thou last and noblest of a noble race.

From the hour of Pauahi's death, rain poured from the skies. But on the Sunday she was buried, the clouds lifted, the skies cleared, and all of Hawaii was drenched in brilliant tropical sunlight.

A grief-stricken Charles Reed Bishop immediately threw himself into making his wife's dream a reality. The task was formidable. Eighty-five percent of the properties ceded to the new trust were nonproductive. Worse yet, the estate's annual income was only $30,000; cash on hand, a paltry $18,000. Undeterred, Bishop reached into his own pockets to launch the Kamehameha School for Boys, which enrolled its first students in 1887, and the Girls' School, which opened seven years later. Every year he funneled more and more of his own money into the schools. By the time Bishop left Hawaii in March 1894, he had contributed approximately $2.5 million to the estate—an astronomical amount at the time.

Undoubtedly Hawaii's greatest philanthropist, Bishop also built the world-renowned Bernice Pauahi Bishop Museum as a memorial to his wife, primarily for the care and preservation of Hawaiian and Pacific Island artifacts, flora, and fauna. In addition he created a separate trust for its support. His generosity touched virtually every private school and hospital in the islands, the YMCA, American Relief Fund, the Kalaupapa leper colony, and a host of other institutions. When he moved to San Francisco, "he walked away from Hawaii with only the cash in his pocket and an agreement that the Charles R. Bishop Trust would pay him $6,000 per year if he needed it."

However, Bishop's commitment to his wife's epic vision went far beyond his personal largesse. For the rest of his life, the covisionary challenged the estate to live up to the lofty standards of Pauahi's will. He often chided the trustees for their extravagance. "I do not like to find fault," he wrote the board in 1895, "but I do wish to have all proposed improvements and changes well considered before spending the money. In short, I ask for real and constant economy." On another occasion he wrote: "If the Kamehameha Schools are to *endure* . . . the yearly expenditures must soon be brought down and kept *clearly within* the net income of the estate." Frequently he reminded the overseers of Mrs. Bishop's charge that the "trustees should do thorough work in regard to said schools," and he expressed his keen disappointment "that so many [trustees] should be unavoidably absent for a considerable time."

Consistent with Pauahi's wishes, Bishop demanded that the estate lands be preserved. "As a rule, I am strongly opposed to selling the lands of the estate of Mrs. Bishop," he wrote the board. "The Estate cannot have any better security than the real estate which it owns." Bishop also applauded Kamehameha's headmaster for "declining to admit a boy to the school who had no Hawaiian blood in his makeup . . . [It is] wise to prepare for and admit natives only."

During his remaining years, Bishop insisted that the schools concentrate on "character-building and preparation for the successful struggle with the conditions of life which [the Hawaiians] cannot avoid." At the age of 88, Bishop restated Princess Pauahi's belief in the value of hard work and high morals in the classroom. "Thoroughness in teaching both in the academic and in the manual branches should be kept up," he wrote, "and in discipline and moral influence, there should be no letting down."

These protestations aside, Bishop remained justifiably proud of the Kamehameha Schools. In a stirring Founder's Day address, he said: "Could the founder of these schools have looked into the future and realized the scenes here before us this day, I am sure it would have excited new hopes in her breast, as it does in my own."

After the overthrow of the Hawaiian monarchy in 1893 (which troubled him deeply) and with the assurance that Kamehameha Schools were safely launched, Bishop bid a fond aloha to the Hawaiian Islands. He was 72. Living at the Occidental Hotel in San Francisco, the astute businessman made another fortune in banking, estimated at $9 million. For all his wealth, he was painfully alone. He never remarried, nor did he ever return to Hawaii. Bishop died in Berkeley on June 7, 1917, at the age of 93. His ashes were returned to Honolulu and interred alongside the remains of his beloved wife in the Royal Mausoleum.

At a simple state funeral, an honor guard of cadets from the Kamehameha Schools accompanied the cortege. Leading the procession was the deposed Queen Liliuokalani, who had been his devoted friend. In the eulogy the Reverend H. H. Parker of Kawaiahao Church remarked: "If I should say anything about Mr. Bishop, I would talk to the young people of Hawaii, especially the young Hawaiians, of Mr. Bishop and the Princess, his wife, and their great life work for the youth of this land."

Each year on Bishop's birthday Kamehameha students visit the Royal Mausoleum and decorate his tomb with fragrant flowers and garlands of lei. On one occasion they offered the following tribute: "The Kamehameha students should well honor this great man for only through his wisdom and foresight were Princess Pauahi's lands saved from the destruction allotted to others of Hawaiian royalty who lacked the protection of a wise and good man to save their inheritance. Only because of him do present day Hawaiians reap the benefits of lands intended for their enjoyment by the Great Kamehameha."

Indeed it was Kamehameha I, who at the very end of his life said, "Tell my people that I have planted in the soil of our land the roots of a plan for their happiness. All that is now necessary is that you cultivate the ground so that there may be growth." Six decades later, his last living descendant, Bernice Pauahi Bishop, nourished the growth of his people by establishing the Kamehameha Schools in perpetuity. Along the way the beloved princess rejected the throne—first, to marry the man she loved and, later, to preserve their marriage. Ironically it was Pauahi's choice of a lifetime partner and co-leader—someone unlike herself in everything but their commitment to each other and the Hawaiian people—that made her vision an enduring reality.

Reverend J. A. Cruzan best summed up Bernice Pauahi's life. "The last and best of the Kamehamehas," he called her. "Refusing a crown, she lived that which she was—crowned. Refusing to rule her people, she did what was better, she served them."

8

Anne Sullivan Macy

The Miracle Worker

The Miracle Worker: Helen Keller (left) "hears" Anne Sullivan Macy by feeling the vibrations on her lips. Macy collaborated with Keller for nearly 50 years. (AP Wide World Photo)

8

Anne Sullivan Macy

The world is moved not only by the mighty
shoves of heroes, but also by the aggregate of
the tiny pushes of each honest worker.
—HELEN KELLER

Day in and day out Kim Powers juggles the responsibilities of being a wife and mother with the high-profile demands of her job anchoring *Kim's World,* an award-winning cable TV show in San Antonio, Texas. What makes Powers unusual is her determination in the face of extraordinary adversity.

As Powers told *Good Housekeeping* magazine in 1996, she was born deaf. Eleven years later she developed retinitis pigmentosa. In the course of time, her field of vision became narrower and narrower, until she was legally blind (her vision continues to deteriorate). But instead of giving up in the face of this second disability, Powers vowed that her life would be as rich as anyone else's.

Where a less courageous soul might have hidden from the world, Powers leaped into living rooms across the nation. As the title implies, *Kim's World* focuses on her life. One day's episode may show her skiing or bungee jumping. It also shows how she handles the more mundane exigencies of daily life, from cooking to child care. Subtitles make the program accessible to her hearing-impaired fans. A narrator speaks to the vision impaired.

What accounts for Powers's extraordinary success? "I try to ignore problems and just keep going," Powers, whose sign language is fast and fluent, told *Good Housekeeping.* "I want to help disabled people understand that they can learn to face the challenges, whatever they

143

may be. . . . Everyone has some kind of a disability. But it's only a disability if you focus on it instead of your abilities." Moreover, she signed, "I have a positive heart."

As impressive as Kim Powers's accomplishments are, they are not unprecedented. A century ago another young woman was freed from a prison of sensory deprivation by an extraordinary teacher named Anne Sullivan. The child—Helen Keller—would go on to become a world-famous crusader for the disabled. Her story would inspire millions. But more important, working together, these two remarkable women changed forever the way the Western world viewed the disabled and indeed the way the disabled viewed themselves.

The story of Helen Keller is bittersweet. As tragic as her condition was, her disability was the springboard for a life of extraordinary intensity and public service. It was through her beloved collaborator and co-leader, Anne Sullivan, that Helen Keller learned how to connect with the world, as well as how to influence it. The gifted, indefatigable Sullivan made Keller's liberation possible. Sullivan's guidance and companionship for nearly 50 years enabled Keller to emerge from barely imaginable isolation into a wondrous new world of understanding. Indeed the genius of the teacher was as remarkable as that of her valiant student.

Like the story of the two Bishops, Anne Sullivan's tale reveals co-leadership in its most human form. We begin by examining how an impoverished waif acquired the rare skills and insights needed to unlock the mind of an exceptional young woman. Widely different in background and personality, Sullivan and Keller made contributions together that would have been unimaginable for either of them independently. Theirs was a truly great partnership. But mutual dependence has its costs. In the course of unleashing Helen Keller's gifts, Sullivan sacrificed her marriage, her health, and her career.

As Helen Keller's fame grew, she became what we now refer to as a brand, one that she and her teacher nurtured and promoted with great, apparently innate entrepreneurial skill. Their purpose was a noble one—to improve the lives of the disabled everywhere. But they also depended on the Helen Keller enterprise that they had built together to support themselves. Their more genteel friends were shocked when Helen and her teacher used their remarkable shared experience as the basis of a successful vaudeville routine. The women had no such qualms. As co-leaders of the Helen Keller enterprise, the women realized they needed money, and they knew how to get it. Sharing a vision and deploying their complementary talents, they created meaning and value where once there had been only tragedy. Their symbiotic story continues to inspire to this day.

From the Depths of Despair

Anne Sullivan's childhood was the stuff of nightmares. She was born on April 14, 1866, in Feeding Hills, near Springfield, Massachusetts. Her poor Irish parents fled to America in the 1860s to escape the potato famine. Instead of warmth, comfort, and bounty, which they had hoped to find in America, Thomas and Alice Sullivan found harsh winters, hard times, and abject poverty. They were too poor to take Annie to a doctor, and, at age three, her neglected trachoma caused partial blindness. Incredibly her intemperate and ignorant father believed that all her sore eyes needed was a drop of water from the River Shannon and they would be well.

Annie was not the only member of the Sullivan clan who was sick. Her mother wasted away from disease and hunger and died of tuberculosis. Her five-year-old sister succumbed to a fever, and her younger brother, Jimmie, was afflicted with a tubercular hip.

Abandoned by their father, Annie, aged 10, and Jimmie, aged 7, were made wards of the state—in the squalor of the public almshouse at Tewksbury, near Boston. Its shabby buildings housed a pitiable group of social outcasts, many of them epileptics, syphilitics, street-walkers, drug addicts, the demented, the diseased—all the throwaways of nineteenth-century society. These were Anne's companions for most of five harrowing years. Death was a daily occurrence in this grim world.

Annie's only friend, her brother, Jimmie, died within the year. Afterward, Annie crept into the poorhouse's improvised mortuary and crouched all night beside the wasted, misshapen body of the only person in the world she loved. "Two [orderlies] separated us," she recalled. "They dragged me back to the ward and tried to put me in bed. But I kicked and scratched and bit them until they dropped me upon the floor, and left me there, a heap of pain beyond words. . . . I longed desperately to die." The next day she accompanied her brother's body to his grave. The priest was sick, so there was no funeral service. The memories of those dreadful years and of Jimmie's death remained with Sullivan all her life.

At last, a lively old former prostitute told Annie that there was a place where she might seek refuge and even learn to read—the Perkins School for the Blind based in Boston. The plucky 14-year-old took her case to Franklin B. Sanborn, chairman of the State Board of Charities, who was visiting the almshouse on an inspection tour. "Mr. Sanborn! Mr. Sanborn! I want to go to school," she pleaded, pulling at his coattails. Impressed by her spirit and tenacity, Sanborn arranged for Sullivan to attend Perkins.

The school, the first of its kind anywhere, had become famous four decades earlier, thanks to the work of Dr. Samuel Gridley Howe, a gallant and gifted physician whose place in American history was eclipsed by his wife, Julia Ward Howe, the author of "The Battle Hymn of the Republic." Under Dr. Howe's care, a deaf, blind, and mute child, Laura Bridgman, had learned to communicate with others, a pioneering achievement that Charles Dickens chronicled in his *American Notes*. "There she was before me," wrote Dickens, "built up, as it were, in a marble cell, impervious to any ray of light or particle of sound; with her poor white hand peeping through a chink in the wall, beckoning to some good man for help, that an immortal soul might be awakened."

"Long before I looked upon her, the help had come. Her face was radiant with intelligence and pleasure. . . . From this mournful ruin of such bereavement, there had slowly risen up this gentle, tender, guileless, grateful-hearted being."

Michael Anagnos, Dr. Howe's son-in-law and successor, welcomed Anne Sullivan to the Perkins School on October 3, 1880. When she arrived, with a coat but no toothbrush, she did not know how to spell or write her own name. But Sullivan was hungry, a wise child who knew that education would save her. She quickly learned to read Braille, smiling in recognition as her fingers flew across the eloquent bumps on the page.

While Sullivan was at Perkins, an acquaintance who was moved by her predicament and her pluck arranged for her to have surgery at the Massachusetts Eye and Ear Infirmary. "I can see the window," she cried afterwards. "And there's a tree outside. And the Charles River, too. I can see them. I can see them all!"

However, Annie's doctor warned her that she would never see perfectly and that she must always avoid overusing or straining her eyes. With her sight partially restored, Annie remained at Perkins as a student and a helper. There was no other place for her to go. There she spent many hours chatting with Laura Bridgman, who taught her the manual alphabet—a method of spelling words with fingers, a system brought from Europe where it was said to have been invented by Trappist monks to circumvent their vow of silence.

At age 20, now a lovely young woman, Anne Sullivan graduated as valedictorian from Perkins. "She was obliged to begin her education at the lowest and most elementary point," Headmaster Anagnos later wrote. "But she showed from the very start that she had in herself the force and capacity which insure success. . . . Miss Sullivan's talents are of the highest order." The school had done what it could. The rest was up to Annie.

Worry and self-doubt paralyzed the young graduate. "Here I was, twenty years old," she recalled, "and I realized that I didn't know a single subject thoroughly. I could not possibly teach and I had no urge to teach. I knew better than I had six years ago how abysmal my ignorance was."

Anagnos disagreed. Here was a young woman, toughened by experience, who had relatively good eyesight yet knew Braille and other techniques for teaching the blind. She also had sharp ears and yet knew sign language as well as the psychology of deafness. At that fateful moment in time, Anagnos received an unusual request from Captain Arthur H. Keller of Tuscumbia, Alabama.

Keller's letter described the plight of his daughter Helen. At 19 months, she had developed "acute congestion of stomach and brains," in the words of her doctors. Her high fever had passed quickly, but it left Helen completely blind and deaf. The few words the toddler had begun to use were soon lost. After years of seeking help for Helen, Captain Keller and his wife, Kate, consulted a Baltimore oculist who told them that Helen's eyes were beyond treatment. He urged them to visit Alexander Graham Bell, the famous inventor, scientist, and teacher of the deaf. In Washington Dr. Bell told the Kellers about the remarkable progress made by little Laura Bridgman and recommended that they contact Anagnos at Perkins. In an age when communication took weeks, not nanoseconds, the Kellers didn't even know if the school was still in business. But a few weeks later, a traveling harness

salesman assured the distraught couple of Perkins's continued existence and supplied them with its address. "Could the School recommend a governess for his daughter?" Captain Keller inquired, in a
letter to the headmaster.

Anagnos immediately thought of Sullivan, who accepted the
offer with considerable trepidation. Sullivan recognized her handi-
caps—her compressed education, her limited social graces, and, above
all, her faulty vision. And frankly Sullivan had hoped for a position
more exciting than looking after a deaf, blind, and speechless child in
the Alabama boondocks. Yet Captain Keller's offer, which included a
salary of $25 a month, was the best she had.

After accepting the job, Annie spent a month studying, in minute
detail, the record of Dr. Howe's training of Laura Bridgman. She also
took to heart Laura's advice not to show pity for Helen and to quash
any hint of disobedience. The blind girls at Perkins bought a doll as a
gift for Helen, and Laura herself made the doll's clothes. Their sole
request: that "doll" would be one of Helen's first words. Annie stashed
the gift in her trunk, packed her modest belongings and meager
teaching aids, and headed south.

Slaying the Phantom

Red-eyed from a recent operation and from crying with homesick-
ness, Sullivan arrived in sleepy Tuscumbia on March 3, 1887, a date
Keller came to cherish as her "soul's birthday." "Thank God someone's going to try to help the poor little thing," Helen's mother said
on meeting Sullivan. "Don't let anybody call her a poor little thing
any more," the neophyte teacher snapped.

Bringing the world to Helen would be difficult enough, Annie
knew, but first she had to convince the family that their pity was mis-
placed. The adult Helen concurred, describing pity as "the chief
stumbling block to the sightless. . . . A person who is severely impaired
never knows his hidden sources of strength until he is treated like a
normal human being and encouraged to shape his own life."

In truth, seven-year-old Helen had been treated differently from
her peers. She was a spoiled, willful, and stubborn little imp, revolting
against the dark and lonely world which robbed her of any meaningful human contact. Helen described herself as "a phantom living in a

no-world." Sullivan, perhaps seeing herself reflected in Helen, was determined not to break the child's spirit as she took on the formidable task of trying to tame and teach her. With infinite patience the inexperienced tutor began to prod her pupil to eat quietly at the table, to fold her napkin, to dress herself.

Despite some initial progress, the young girl's parents stymied Annie's work. "I very soon made up my mind that I could do nothing with Helen in the midst of the family," Sullivan wrote to Anagnos. With the Kellers' approval, she moved the child to a small cottage about a quarter of a mile from the main house. There she worked to discipline Helen and, at the same time, built a friendship that would last almost half a century.

Touching her fingers to Helen's hand, Sullivan would spell out words and then give Helen the named objects to touch. Bright and inquisitive, Helen was soon imitating the finger motions. On April 5, 1887, Helen discovered the universe. In a much-celebrated incident, Annie took Helen to the water pump that day and let the cold liquid spill over one of the child's hands and simultaneously spelled "w-a-t-e-r" in the other. In one thrilling moment, Helen had found the key to her kingdom. She realized that everything on this earth had a name.

"Suddenly I felt a misty consciousness of something forgotten," Keller later wrote, "and somehow the mystery of language was revealed to me. That living word awakened my soul, gave it light, hope, joy, set it free! There were barriers still, it is true, but barriers that could in time be swept away."

Helen beamed. Suddenly transported to a world of meaning, she thrust her little hand at Sullivan for more. Sullivan led Helen to other familiar objects for which Helen had no name. Sullivan spelled, "p-u-m-p," "t-r-e-l-l-i-s." Then Helen pounded on Sullivan, demanding to know her name. "T-e-a-c-h-e-r," Sullivan replied, spelling out for the first time the name Helen would always use to address her beloved mentor.

From then on Helen's curiosity was insatiable. In three weeks she knew 18 nouns and 3 verbs. By the end of August, she had mastered 625 words. She went on to read several forms of Braille, to write using thin rulers to hold her hand in alignment, and eventually to use a typewriter.

Under Sullivan's guidance the feral creature with the furious temper was transformed into a loving, inquisitive child. Before the incident at the water pump, Helen refused to be caressed. But the events of that day changed her forever. "Last night when I got in bed, Helen stole into my arms of her own accord and kissed me for the first time," Annie wrote to a friend. "I thought my heart would burst, so full was it of joy!" Similarly Helen later recalled her emotions of that same night: "It would have been difficult to find a happier child than I was as I lay in my bed at the close of that eventful day and lived over the joys it had brought me, and for the first time longed for a new day to come."

Instead of staying aloof from her student, as Dr. Howe had, Sullivan merged her life with Helen's. A child must be childlike, Sullivan believed, and to develop properly a young girl must be exposed to the world outside her disability. Sullivan thought that Laura Bridgman's training was only moderately successful because of her institutionalized existence at Perkins. Helen Keller, Sullivan resolved, would live a normal life.

"Hereafter there would be no set time for forcing Helen to sit at a little table learning special words or doing routine work," writes Helen Elmira Waite, author of *Valiant Companions,* a joint biography of Keller and Sullivan. "She would come and go and do and play without knowing she was doing something important. She would learn just by living!"

Sullivan introduced Helen to nature, teaching her, among other things, how to care for a variety of farm animals and household pets. "Touch everything as you would a flower," Sullivan taught, "lightly, tenderly; observe, observe, observe, just as you do my voice; and imitate with care."

"I learned how the sun and the rain make to grow out of the ground every tree that is pleasant to the sight and good for food, how birds build their nests and live and thrive from land to land, how the squirrel, the deer, the lion, and every other creature finds food and shelter," Helen remembered. "As my knowledge of things grew, I felt more and more the delight of the world I was in."

Yet some locals thought that Sullivan was pushing her young student too hard and that Helen was advancing at too rapid a pace. "We are bothered a great deal by people who . . . tell us that Helen is overdoing, that her mind is too active (these very people thought she had no mind at all a few months ago!)," Sullivan wrote of her critics. "They suggest many impossible and absurd remedies. But so far, nobody seems to have thought of chloroforming her, which is, I think, the only effective way of stopping the natural exercise of her faculties."

Naysayers aside, the high point of their first year together was Christmas, the first of which Helen was truly aware. The atmosphere around her was vibrant with anticipation, and the child tingled with the excitement of it all. The enticing smells and pleasant tastes—once mysterious—now were attached to words and, as a result, carried wonder-filled meaning.

On Christmas morning she spelled, "Merry Christmas" for the first time into the hands of her family. Among Helen's many presents that day was a Braille slate of her own. "I will write many letters and thank Santa Claus very much," she spelled out to her parents and younger sister, Mildred, who, thanks to Sullivan, now were proficient in the manual alphabet.

That first Christmas brought poignant memories for the Keller family. Helen's joyous face stood in sharp contrast to her stolid and self-ish behavior of previous years. The stoic Captain Keller was speechless, but he took Sullivan's hand and grasped it tightly in affection and grat-itude. Kate Keller was more emotional. "Miss Annie," she said softly, "I thank God every day of my life for sending you to us, but I never real-ized until this morning what a blessing you have been to us!"

Sullivan in turn developed a lifetime fondness for the Kellers. Her bond with Helen was infinitely more intense and complex, reflecting Sullivan's realization that their fates were intertwined. "Never did a teacher have more reason to be proud of a pupil," she informed Anagnos. "A sweeter or brighter child would be impossible to find." But to another friend, Sullivan revealed much more: "I want to say which is for your ears alone. Something within me tells me I shall succeed beyond my dreams. . . . I should think Helen's education [will] surpass in interest and wonder Dr. Howe's achievements. I know that she has remarkable powers, and I believe that I shall be able to develop and mold them."

To be sure Sullivan's self-confidence and her own achievements were growing rapidly. Helen's progress was so impressive that educators at home and abroad soon became aware that a truly great teacher was at work, greater perhaps than the fabled Samuel Howe. In the 1887 report of the Perkins School, Anagnos lauded Sullivan, comparing her achievements with Howe's. "In breadth of intellect, in opulence of mental power, in fertility of resource, in originality of device and in practical sagacity, she stands in the first rank," Anagnos boasted. "In view of all the circumstances, her achievements are little short of a miracle."

The portion of the Perkins report about Helen and her illustrious teacher was widely reprinted, reviewed, and quoted in magazines and newspapers. The story captured the imagination and hearts of people all over the United States and the world. From then on the little girl in Alabama and her Irish-American tutor were front-page news.

The Meaning of Shared Sacrifice

In March 1888 Anagnos, returning from Florida, visited the Kellers and invited Mrs. Keller to bring Annie and Helen to Perkins. Although awed by the young prodigy's progress, he was appalled at Sullivan's failing health. Back in Boston, Anagnos wrote to her: "I feel considerable anxiety about your overworking yourself, and I beg of you most earnestly, yes, I command you not to do more than is absolutely necessary between now and the first of June. . . . Remember that if you break down, you cannot be of service either to Helen or to yourself."

In Washington, D.C., Sullivan and Keller met with Alexander Graham Bell. Grilled about her teaching methods, Sullivan said she constantly tried new things. "Some of them work," she said. "Some don't." The famous inventor was astonished at Helen's progress. "Her achievement is without parallel in education," Bell exclaimed, vowing henceforth to assist both student and teacher.

After a heartwarming welcome at Perkins, including lengthy conversations with Laura Bridgman, Sullivan and Keller became guests of the school. Helen enrolled officially as a student the next year. Although Sullivan still had exclusive charge of her education, Helen took full advantage of the institution's unique range of facilities for the disabled. The shared reputation of the teacher and her remarkable student spread rapidly over the next several years, both in Boston and in the other cities they visited, often meeting famous people along the way. Wealthy friends—including "Sugar King" John Spaulding, Henry H. Rodgers of Standard Oil, literary critic Lawrence Hutton and his wife, Eleanor, and industrialist Andrew Carnegie—helped support the twosome, critical because Captain Keller had fallen on hard times and could no longer pay Sullivan.

Meanwhile Sullivan's vision began to worsen. She seriously considered ending her teaching of Helen but was convinced otherwise by Bell and another friend, writer Mark Twain. Both men felt that, despite Helen's growing self-reliance, she would continue to need her gifted teacher. After a brief leave of absence to rest her failing eyes, Sullivan rejoined Helen to begin the next important stage of her development.

"Do deaf children ever learn to talk?" Helen asked Sullivan. "Yes," she explained. "They do sometimes. . . . [But deaf children] can see their teacher's lips, so they can learn to read what other people are saying, and then learn to make their own teeth and lips go the right way." Undeterred, Helen announced that she was going to learn to talk with her mouth as most people did, instead of with her fingers like the deaf.

As a result, Sullivan sought the expert advice of Sarah Fuller, who headed Boston's Horace Mann School for the Deaf. After 11 lessons with Fuller, Helen learned to mumble words by feeling Sullivan's throat (sometimes Helen put her fingers so far inside Sullivan's throat that she gagged). At the age of 10, Keller managed her first full sentence, "I—am—not—dumb—now!" It became a kind of mantra, often repeated when she had an audience.

With Sullivan by her side, Helen improved her speaking and lip-reading skills at the Wright-Humason Oral School for the Deaf in New York City. Remarkably Helen learned to appreciate music, recognizing the distinctive vibrations of different instruments. She learned how to explore a sculpture with her fingers. Later she knew when her train was approaching St. Louis because she smelled its breweries miles away. She could distinguish a Catholic church from a Protestant one by the scent of incense. She could even tell when a house painter got on the bus she was riding.

Of all her amazing accomplishments, Helen Keller contended that learning to speak was by far the most difficult. It commanded all her Rock-of-Gibraltar strength and courage, plus Sullivan's patient help and encouragement. "But for Miss Sullivan's genius, untiring perseverance and devotion, I could not have progressed as far as I have toward natural speech," Helen wrote. "In the first place, I laboured night and day before I could be understood even by my most intimate friends; in the second place, I needed Miss Sullivan's assistance constantly in my efforts to articulate each sound clearly and to combine all sounds in a thousand ways."

"A new life came for me as I began to speak," Helen explained. "Speech gives my spirit wings. These wings for me are broken, but they help me more quickly to reach the minds of others." Helen quickly mastered enough natural speech to read his "In School Days" to poet John Greenleaf Whittier, but her speech never sounded truly natural to her lifelong regret.

As Helen advanced through adolescence, she committed herself to reaching the minds of other disabled people. But first she needed a first-rate university education. Already the deaf-blind girl had mastered Greek, Latin, German, and French. However, her ambitious decision to attend Radcliffe College became the news event of the day.

Aided by Mark Twain's fund-raising efforts, Helen entered Radcliffe in 1900 at the age of 20. Sullivan sat next to her in class, repeating the lectures to her using the manual alphabet. Because few of Helen's required readings were available in Braille, Sullivan spent five or six exhausting hours a day translating course assignments for her. Finally an ophthalmologist warned Sullivan to rest her eyes or run the risk of permanent blindness. Fortunately a young friend versed in the manual alphabet stepped in as Helen's temporary tutor.

Sullivan's health problems worsened during Helen's senior year, when the teacher developed a painful limp. After a thorough examination, an eminent Boston surgeon told her that she needed surgery at once. But Sullivan balked. She did not want to jeopardize Helen's scheduled graduation. The doctor was adamant. "Miss Sullivan, your health is more important to Helen Keller than her education," he told Sullivan. Reluctantly she agreed to the operation. Because of lack of funds, the surgery was performed successfully in an improvised operating room in the apartment she shared with Helen.

In 1904 Helen Adams Keller graduated *cum laude* and also received a citation for excellence in English letters. Everyone recognized the tall, serious, and dignified Keller as she strode on stage to accept her Radcliffe degree, the first deaf-blind person ever to graduate from college. "Who is that woman with her?" people in the audience asked of the tiny woman who stood next to Helen. Most assumed the black-clad woman was simply an aide.

Although few of the attendees appreciated her accomplishments, several graduates expressed indignation that Sullivan had not been recognized officially during the ceremonies. Some thought Sullivan, too, should have been awarded a degree. As for Helen, she recalled, "the best part of my success was having her by my side. . . . [She] kept me steadfast to my purpose."

Expanding the Co-Leadership Circle

After Helen's graduation, she and her partner and soul mate settled on seven acres of land in Wrentham, not far from Boston, where they lived for the first time in a home of their own. The property had been purchased some months earlier with a bequest from John Spaulding. A year later Sullivan married writer and literary critic John Albert Macy, who had edited Keller's first best-selling book, *The Story of My Life.* The threesome seemed to live together happily, as Sullivan, Macy and Helen went to work on articles and books, each in their own field.

"I wish I could engrave upon these pages the picture in my fingers that I cherish of those two friends," Keller wrote of her new life in *Midstream,* a story of her adult years. "My teacher with her queenly mind and heart, strong and true, going direct to the core of the subject under discussion, her delight in beauty, her enthusiasm for large service and heroic qualities. Her husband with his brotherly tenderness, his fine sensibilities, his keen sense of humour, and his curious combination of judicial severity and smiling tolerance. Since I was out of active life, they both strove to keep my [life] pleasant and interesting."

In truth Sullivan's decision to marry John Macy was, in part, born out of her concern for Helen's future. At 39, Sullivan was 11 years his senior, and her primary loyalty—she repeatedly informed Macy—would always be to her female companion. Sullivan was confident that, in the event of her death, her husband would succeed her as Helen's mentor and guardian.

For a time the arrangement worked. Helen continued to write and, with Sullivan, embarked on a series of lecture tours, where she spoke on the problems of the disabled, particularly the blind. When she first spoke in public, Helen was self-conscious about her voice, but with Sullivan at her side to explain and interpret, Helen's nervousness soon evaporated as she encountered warm and sympathetic audiences across the country. Macy, for his part, aided Helen in her writing while pursuing his own career as a literary critic and, for a while, as associate editor of *Youth's Companion*. But serious strains developed in the marriage, and in 1912 Macy moved to Schenectady, New York, to assist the city's Socialist mayor. From time to time, Macy returned to Wrentham, but feeling increasingly left out of Sullivan's life, he separated from her in 1914. The couple did not divorce, and Macy, Sullivan, and Keller remained friends until Macy's death from a stroke in 1932.

The separation sapped much of the joy from Sullivan's life, as did the tiresome demands of the lecture circuit. On tour in Bath, Maine, Sullivan became desperately ill with no one to look after her but Helen—and no one to look after Helen. Sullivan called on all her reserves and managed to summon the hotel manager. A few days later, the women stumbled back to Wrentham. Worried about Sullivan's ill health, Helen wrote to her friend and benefactor, Andrew Carnegie, for assistance. He provided Helen with a modest pension, but it was not enough to cover the living expenses of two disabled women. In 1914 Helen hired Polly Thompson, a young Scottish woman, to serve as the pair's assistant. Thompson would remain with Keller for the next 45 years.

Now with three mouths to feed, Helen, Sullivan, and Thompson embarked on another hectic, transcontinental lecture tour. The crowds had eyes only for Helen—at least initially. "Without Annie's skillful translations of her speech and her fascinating demonstrations of how Helen had been taught, the audiences probably would have lost interest," writer Helen Elmira Waite observed. "Annie had a marvelous speaking voice and a delightful stage presence."

Frightened by their lack of funds and Sullivan's deteriorating health, Helen accepted a proposition to appear in a film dramatizing her life. The prospects of making a stupendous sum of money thrilled her as she, Anne, and Polly entrained for Hollywood in 1918. As it turned out, the movie, *Deliverance,* was a major flop at the box office, forcing student and teacher to try yet another medium: vaudeville. In a 20-minute act, Keller and Sullivan demonstrated how Helen had been taught to communicate and how she learned to live in the outside world. The show, staged in noisy tents to boisterous crowds, disturbed some of Helen's friends. But it was a financial success. For the first time in her life, the deaf and blind woman was supporting not only herself but her two partners.

The live-theater performances lasted off and on for four years, interrupted by Sullivan's worsening eyesight and respiratory problems. Finally, at age 43, Keller was able to devote herself exclusively to her life's work—aiding those living in what she described firsthand as "darkness, silence, sickness, or sorrow." In 1923 she was hired by the American Foundation for the Blind and, for the balance of her life, concentrated on writing, lecturing, and lobbying for legislation for talking books and pensions for the blind. By now Helen's companion and colleague Polly Thompson had assumed the primary role of guide and interpreter, while Sullivan remained an invaluable counselor.

Sullivan's vitality and vision were deteriorating rapidly. Hoping to reinvigorate her health, Keller and Thompson organized, in 1930, the first of three consecutive summer sojourns in the British Isles. But Sullivan's condition worsened, and the moodiness and melancholy to which she was prone grew more intense. By the spring of 1935, she was totally blind. In a dramatic reversal of roles, Keller obtained a leave of absence from the Foundation to care for her beloved teacher. In the 50 years in which Sullivan's eyes had served her well enough, she had forgotten all the ways of blindness. She had to learn Braille all over again. But this time Helen became teacher, helping Sullivan remaster the language system she had neglected.

A few weeks before Sullivan's death, Helen pleaded: "Teacher, you must get well. Without you, Helen would be nothing." "That would mean," Anne Sullivan replied sadly, "that I have failed."

Sullivan's lifelong ambition was to liberate Helen's mind. Like a good parent, Sullivan wanted Helen to be free, even of her. Emancipating this brilliant woman became Sullivan's mission, a cause worthy of all her labor and sacrifice.

In October 1936, at age 70, Sullivan died of heart disease in their Forest Hills home. Her funeral was conducted by Harry Emerson

Fosdick at New York's Park Avenue Presbyterian Church. When the services were over and the procession was filing down the aisle, Keller walked with Thompson at her side. Tears streamed down Polly's cheeks. That prompted a gesture from Helen—a quick flutter of her birdlike hands. *She* was trying to comfort Polly.

Sullivan's body was cremated and her remains interred in Washington's National Cathedral. Left in the competent hands of Thompson, Helen sailed to Scotland to grieve and recover. "Teacher's departure so disorganized my life that many months passed before I could reorientate myself," she wrote. "I was so conscious of her soul as a separate being that I did not cling to her physical part—her earthly garment, as she had clung to the body of her little brother, and I cannot say that she seemed to live on in me. She was lent to me from the Lord so that I might develop my own personality through darkness and silence."

In the succeeding years, Keller emerged as one of the world's great humanitarians. Her achievements are legendary. Feted by presidents, royalty, and other luminaries, she fought for the blind around the world. "If you really want to help the blind, you must realize that they are just as you would be if you had to live in the dark," she told her audiences. "They have the same feelings that you have. They crave the same things—work, play, food, and pleasure. You have heard how a new life started for me when one little word from another touched the darkness of my mind. Help my comrades to awaken as I have awakened to the sunshine and beauty of life!"

Helen Keller's alert and searching mind became an instrument by which the world was able to know and understand the needs and potential of the disabled. Her efforts led to better care, training, and employment. Through her writings and lectures, she inspired many and in turn received the world's highest honors. She became one of the most influential women of all time. Keller died of heart disease in 1968, less than a month before her eighty-eighth birthday. Her ashes rest next to Sullivan's and Thompson's at the National Cathedral.

Her Other Self

"What a blind deaf person needs," Sullivan once said, "is not a teacher but another self." For all her fame, Helen Keller never forgot her other self, her first and greatest teacher—the other half who made her whole. She never forgot Sullivan's role in their precious partnership. For years Keller grappled with the challenge of writing Sullivan's biography. At first too grief-stricken to undertake the task, she was finally able to piece together the story of Sullivan's life. However, while visiting the war-blinded in Europe in 1946, Keller learned that her house had burned to the ground and, with it, her three-quarters-finished manuscript.

Ordinary mortals would have given in to despair. Not Annie Sullivan's star pupil. Sullivan had taught Keller many things, including never to give up. Over the next 10 years, Helen slaved away on a borrowed typewriter. She wrote as steadily as she could, although frequently interrupted by yet another assignment on behalf of the deaf and blind. In 1955 *Teacher* was published to enthusiastic reviews—a glowing tribute to both an inspired educator and a remarkable collaboration.

Only toward the end of Sullivan's life did this brilliant co-leader begin to receive the recognition she deserved. In 1931 she and Keller were both granted honorary degrees by Philadelphia's Temple University; in 1933 they were made honorary fellows of the Educational Institute of Scotland; and in 1936 the Roosevelt Memorial Foundation awarded them its medals for "co-operative achievement of heroic character and far-reaching significance." Since Sullivan's death, her story has been retold in *Teacher* and many other books and dramatized in William Gibson's popular Broadway play and the film based on it, *The Miracle Worker*.

Sullivan and Keller were often thought of by their contemporaries as Geminis. However, in many respects they were very different. Sullivan's personality reflected her tragic early years in the Tewksbury poorhouse. She approached the world with a chip on her shoulder and assumed everyone was ready to knock it off. Sullivan had a kind of split personality. "On one hand she overflowed with insight and self-understanding, with love and solicitude and a desire to serve," Joseph P. Lash writes in *Helen and Teacher*. "On another level, she was beset with fears and terrors, riven with resentments, hating, as she says, both herself and others."

"A porcupine of principle," Keller called her. "In her best moods, she enveloped everyone with her sympathy. . . . [But] she was too apt to assume an aggressive attitude in argument. . . . She could be inflexible and proud, and it was a point of honor with her to pound her arguments into those who differed from her instead of trying to win them over with tact." Embarrassingly forthright, Annie did not suffer fools gladly. "It was a lifelong struggle for her to be kind to dull people," Keller observed. "Their incessant chatter irritated her like a menagerie, and she wanted intensely to escape."

No group triggered Sullivan's caustic tongue and incendiary temper more than society's upper crust. The powerful Boston Brahmins often saw fit to ostracize her, while warmly embracing young Miss Keller. On numerous occasions the Boston elite held Sullivan's Irish roots and early impoverishment against her. Once at a party for her famous student, Sullivan grabbed Helen and stormed out when the hypersensitive teacher felt she was being dismissed as a servant. "It was not easy for a young woman of my humble origin and limited education to defend herself," Sullivan wrote. "[The Brahmins] were convinced I was a vulgar upstart. . . . As a matter of fact, I was always uncomfortable, and consequently painfully aggressive when I was with them."

If class antagonism and pessimism characterized Sullivan, Helen Keller was, at heart, an affectionate woman raised in an upper middle-class Southern home. Unlike her impetuous co-leader, Helen accepted the world with love and kindness. "One always viewed the world 'through a glass darkly,' while the other, though sightless, surrounded it with sunshine and gaiety," Lash writes, contrasting the women.

Helen's essay entitled "Optimism" denounced the pity usually directed at the disabled in her day. No Pollyanna, Helen knew that optimism could make people dangerously blind to genuine evil. But she thought pessimism was worse. Pessimism, she argued, "kills the instinct that urges men to struggle against poverty, ignorance and crime and dries up all the fountains of joy in the world."

Sullivan always sought to buffer Helen from those who might dispirit her. She told Keller nothing of her early poverty, illness, and degradation until she was 64 and Helen was 50. Nor did Sullivan ever tell her charge that, for many years, Captain Keller had been unable to pay her salary. The heroic co-leader who opened Helen Keller's eyes to many things kept her in the dark about others.

The women differed in other ways as well. Although they both supported the Socialist party, Sullivan—unlike Helen—opposed women's suffrage. Nor did Sullivan, who had abandoned Catholicism, share Keller's passion for Protestantism. "The more we talked, the less we thought alike, except in our desire of good and our intense longing for intelligence as a universal attribute of mankind," Helen wrote. "She counted among my God-given privileges the right to express my views on politics, economics, and religious topics and to hear what others said with equal frankness."

Sharing Power And Credit

During their life together, observers often wondered whether Sullivan *was* Helen Keller. "The answer is not simple," writes Nella Braddy Henney, author of the definitive biography of Sullivan. "During the creative years neither could have done without the other." According to one member of the Keller family, "No one can judge how much Helen owes to her [the] originality and suggestion of ideals. Certainly, it is the great mind of Miss Sullivan that absorbed, digested and fed Helen's mind and heart until she was independent. . . ."

Like a good partner, Sullivan was always willing to cede the spotlight to the more famous Helen. "The genius is hers, but much of the drudgery is mine," Sullivan declared modestly. Others, though, questioned Helen's intellectual prowess. She is not a "brilliant genius," said John Macy, who knew both women as well as anyone. "Many women have keener minds and a deeper capacity for scholarship." But, he added: "Her heart is noble. The world has yet to see a finer spirit, a loftier and more steadfast will to do the best."

Certainly Sullivan shaped Helen's education and her later achievements. That someone as profoundly disadvantaged in terms of communication as Helen became a world-famous communicator reflects Sullivan's eloquence as well as her pedagogical gifts. Helen was the first to acknowledge this. "It was an exceptional advantage to study English literature with a word artist at my side," Keller wrote. "There was an artistic quality about Teacher that cannot be overemphasized."

On the lecture circuit, Sullivan "had a natural gift for public speaking," Helen noted. "Her part on the program became the principal one, and I was happy to see that her precious light—her work—could no longer be hidden under a bushel. Over and over, I heard people say that Annie Sullivan was a fascinating woman and that there was an irresistible sparkle in her repartee."

People everywhere marveled at Helen's courage and many came to love her. Oliver Wendell Holmes and Edward Everett Hale became lifelong friends. Mark Twain called her "the greatest woman since Joan of Arc." Alexander Graham Bell, Henry Ford, and Andrew Carnegie were immensely impressed by her contributions. The famed sculptor Jo Davidson remarked: "We are all good when we are with Helen."

Would the genius of Helen Keller have unfolded were it not for Anne Sullivan, her tireless and gifted other self? Many close to both women thought not. Bell, in particular, was always an outspoken admirer of Sullivan's innovative teaching techniques. He believed they should be shared with the world, contending that "Helen's remarkable achievements are as much due to the genius of her teacher, as to her own brilliant mind." In a letter to Sullivan, Bell predicted that her teaching methods "will become a standard. The principles that guided you in the early education of Helen are of the greatest importance to all teachers."

Mark Twain, too, fully realized the importance of Sullivan's work and the largeness of her character. Cynical though he was, Twain found only virtue in her. Although many people had eyes only for Helen, he saw Sullivan as an exceptional and caring person in her own right. Twain praised her "brilliancy, penetration, wisdom, character, and the fine literary competences of her pen."

Another person quick to appreciate Sullivan was Dr. Maria Montessori. The Italian pioneer in early childhood education described Sullivan as the "the creator of a soul." In San Francisco during the Pan-American Exposition, where both educators received awards, Montessori was asked to comment on Sullivan's work. "I have been called a pioneer," Montessori said. Pointing to Sullivan, she declared, "There is your pioneer!"

Albert Einstein also heaped praise on Sullivan. "Your work, Mrs. Macy, has interested me more than any other achievement in modern education," he said. "Not only did you impart language to Helen Keller, you unfolded her personality, and such work has in it an element of the superhuman."

Many have speculated on what Sullivan might have accomplished with her life had she never met Helen. "My own life," Sullivan once said, "is so interwoven with my Helen's life that I can't separate myself from her." Helen, though, had a different view of how Sullivan's life might have been. "She could have lived her own life, and had a better chance of happiness," Helen wrote. "Her power of clear, audacious thought and the splendour of her unselfish soul might have made her a leader among the women of her day. The freshness and lucidity of her writing would have won distinction. But she has closed these doors to herself and refused to consider anything that would take her away from me. She delights in the silence that wraps her life in mine. . . ."

Others believe that, for all her talents, Annie's precarious self-confidence, possessive perfectionism, and volatile mood swings would have limited her success without Helen. Only her selfless devotion to Helen made Sullivan's own achievements possible, in this view. Yet throughout her career, enticing offers came her way, which she invariably rejected to remain with Helen.

"If you had your life to live over again, would you follow the same path?" Sullivan was asked. "Would I be a teacher?" she answered. "We do not, I think, choose our destiny. It chooses us."

Although the pair's roles evolved and shifted in the course of almost 50 years together, to Helen, Anne Sullivan was always Teacher. Helen Keller always acknowledged that her extraordinary life was as much Sullivan's creation as her own. "How much of my delight in all beautiful things is innate and how much is due to her influence, I can never tell," Keller wrote. "I feel that her being is inseparable from my own, and that the footsteps of my life are in hers. All the best of me belongs to her—there is not a talent, or an aspiration or a joy in me that has not been awakened by her loving touch. . . . People think Teacher has left me, but she is with me all the time."

9 | Al Gore

Hail to the Co-Chief

Pledge of Allegiance: Co-leader Al Gore (left) reinvented the vice presidency with the help of Bill Clinton. But in aspiring to the Oval Office, Gore must distance himself from the boss. (Stephen Crowley / NYT Pictures)

9 | Al Gore

> . . . the most insignificant office that ever
> the invention of man contrived or his
> imagination conceived.
>
> —JOHN ADAMS, on the Vice Presidency

"Once there were two brothers," goes the old Washington saw. "One ran away to sea, the other was elected vice president. Neither of them was heard from again."

Throughout history America's official co-leader has received little respect. The job only Rodney Dangerfield could love has been the subject of perpetual ridicule. With few exceptions the vice presidency has resembled what C. S. Lewis called "shadowlands," places of disappointment and faded dreams.

America's first No. 2, John Adams, did not foresee what an often frustrating and ineffectual position the vice presidency would turn out to be. Adams envisioned the newly created position as one of genuine co-leadership, a role of great importance in a democracy with an unprecedented commitment to the sharing of power. However, when the grim realities of the office set in, Adams wrote his wife, Abigail, that the job was truly "insignificant." To be fair Adams might have had more success as vice president if he had less obvious disdain for the president, George Washington, whom Adams judged "too illiterate, unread, unlearned for his station and reputation."

The vice presidency has been a running gag for years, indeed for centuries. Daniel Webster, when offered the vice presidential nomination in 1847, replied: "I do not propose to be buried until I am really dead." Earlier Benjamin Franklin called America's No. 2 "his superfluous excellency." In 1912 the office of vice president was so poorly regarded that 3.5 million Americans voted for a dead man: James Schoolcraft Sherman.

The popular view of the vice presidency as an institutionalized mockery was reflected in the musical satire *Of Thee I Sing,* which won a Pulitzer Prize for drama in 1932. Written by George S. Kaufman and Morrie Rysind, with lyrics by George and Ira Gershwin, the play featured fictional Vice President Alexander Throttlebottom. After his election, the bored and bumbling Throttlebottom devotes most of his time to feeding pigeons in the park. So despised is he by the president that he has to join a tour group to be admitted to the White House.

If the vice presidency has long been regarded as a place where unlucky politicians go to be forgotten, it need not be. Indeed the nation's forty-fifth vice president, Albert J. Gore, Jr., has reinvented the office and become the most effective and influential No. 2 in modern U.S. history. We will look at how Gore restored the office to one of genuine co-leadership, but, first, a bit of history.

Perks Without Power

The shadowlands that surround and often shroud the vice presidency are, in part, constitutionally imposed. The VP's only legislated duty is to preside over the Senate and to vote in the event of a tie in that body. The real power of the post is unleashed only if the president dies, resigns, is impeached, or becomes incapacitated. "I am nothing, but I may be everything," said John Adams. Nine vice presidents were catapulted into the Oval Office by the death of a president; one VP, Gerald Ford, ascended because President Nixon resigned. The fact that the vice president is waiting in the wings to replace the president may go far to explain the traditional strain between them. "It is, after all, disconcerting to have at one's side a man whose life's ambition will be achieved by one's death," observed Henry Kissinger.

The do-nothing image of the vice presidency may have become a self-fulfilling prophecy, discouraging most first-rate candidates. "No truly great leader would ever seek the vice presidency," writes political humorist and historian Steve Tally. "It is their lack of conviction that makes their ambition so bland."

Yet several vice presidents were anything but bland. Aaron Burr committed murder while in office; although to be fair he was acquitted after killing Alexander Hamilton in a duel. President Ulysses S. Grant had two vice presidents, Schuyler "Smiler" Colfax and Henry Wilson, who were tainted by the Credit Mobilier scandal when the Union Pacific Railroad was being built and graft went transcontinental. Nixon's VP, Spiro T. Agnew, resigned in disgrace in 1973 after a felony plea bargain for bribery, only to be convicted later of tax evasion. Two vice presidents, Burr and John Breckinridge (at age 36, the youngest to hold the office), were charged with treason, and two more, John Calhoun and John Tyler, probably could have been.

Though not feloniously inclined, several seconds in command behaved unusually in office. As vice president, Calvin Coolidge ate lunch alone every day. Thomas Marshall, Woodrow Wilson's second, is known chiefly (if at all) for his high opinion of the efficacy of a good five-cent cigar. Lincoln's vice president, Hannibal Hamlin, chose to sit out the Civil War in the safety and anonymity of his Maine farm and in the galley of a Coast Guard ship not far from shore. FDR's VP, John Nance Garner, remembered for striking a glass-of-bourbon "blow for liberty" in his office every morning at 10 A.M., proclaimed that the vice presidency was not worth "a warm pitcher of spit." VP Richard Nixon became the first politician to receive a review in *Variety* after his famous "Checkers" speech. Nixon got uniformly bad reviews from President Dwight Eisenhower, who on being asked about his vice president's accomplishments responded, "Well, if you can give me a week, I might think of one."

If the vice president too often gets no respect, the job does promise a big house, big office, and relatively big bucks. Since 1974, America's official No. 2 has resided in a government-provided mansion, which formerly quartered the Chief of Naval Operations. Built in 1893, the often renovated Queen Anne–style house has 12 rooms and 6 bathrooms and is nestled on a 12-acre estate complete with swimming pool and putting green. Overseeing the handsome property are several Navy stewards, who serve as butlers, plus a coterie of gardeners, cleaners, and helpers. Not being able to move into this "bigger house and somebody to do the laundry" was Senator Alan Simpson's only regret in being spurned as George Bush's running mate in 1988.

And indeed the vice president travels in a chauffeur-driven limousine to his well-appointed White House office just 18 steps down the blue-carpeted hallway to the rear door of the Oval Office. Like the president, the second in command has an official song: "Hail Columbia," which traditionally greets all vice presidents, who also receive a 19-gun salute. First-class transport—land, sea, and *Air Force Two*—shuttles the VP to a variety of official functions, from state funerals to tree plantings. And while Bill Gates won't die of envy, the vice president is fairly compensated. In 1789 James Madison approved the first VP salary of $5,000 a year. Today the gross compensation stands at $182,500, plus $10,000 for expenses, $90,000 for entertainment, and $324,000 for support of the vice presidential mansion.

Clearly America's second in command lives a pretty good life, marred only by the office's notorious lack of real clout. "I've got all the perks," Vice President Ford once lamented, "but power? Power is what I left on Capitol Hill."

Former president—and former vice president—Lyndon Baines Johnson once observed, "Power is where power goes." He assumed that his congressional clout would follow him to the vice presidency. He was wrong. LBJ liked to tell how his chauffeur had advised him not to leave his powerful post in the Senate to become vice president—and how, much to his regret, he had not taken this advice. Johnson often likened his role to that of a neutered "cut dog."

Ironically most former VPs who go on to become president, including LBJ, refuse to expand the duties of their own vice presidents. Many go out of their way to marginalize, even demean, their seconds in command. One would have expected Harry Truman, for example, to have removed the shackles from his vice president, Alben W. Barkley. Truman knew how frustrating the job could be even before he got it. Asked to become Franklin D. Roosevelt's running mate in 1944, Truman said, "Look at all the Vice Presidents in history. Where are they? They were about as useful as a cow's fifth teat."

When President Roosevelt died on April 12, 1945, Truman was thrust into the country's highest office. But his 82-day stint as Roosevelt's No. 2 had left Truman ill prepared for national leadership. FDR's staffers had isolated him from the decision-making process, and the few cabinet meetings he did attend dealt with little of real importance. At one of the most perilous moments in the country's history, Truman lacked the insider savvy he would have had if the ailing FDR had been willing to share power. "[Truman] had only the faintest idea [of] what a President was supposed to do," writes Columbia History Professor Alan Brinkley. "He had no important allies in Washington. He had only the barest information about the issues before him. He had not even been told about the Government's most important secret: the construction of the atomic bomb. Into these untested hands fell some of the gravest decisions ever to face an American leader."

Fortunately Truman (and the nation) survived—no thanks to his vice presidential experience. And yet Truman was no more willing to make Barkley a genuine co-leader than his own boss had been. From the get-go Barkley sensed that Truman would handcuff him. Thus Barkley began his 1948 vice presidential acceptance speech: "Inasmuch as I am about to enter upon the discharge of the duties of an office that requires four years of silence, I will be brief in my acknowledgement."

At times, Barkley provided President Truman with a useful link to Congress, and the VP was included in most Cabinet meetings and, by law, those of the National Security Council. But his role in the White House was insignificant. According to Steve Tally, Barkley compared himself to a catcher in a night baseball game after the lights had been turned off. He never knew what the pitcher was going to do next. Barkley's most memorable accomplishment wasn't even his. His young grandchild couldn't pronounce Barkley's office and cooed the term *veep* for America's No. 2.

But the cruelest former VP—bar none—was LBJ. When asked to identify the ideal traits in a running mate, the earthy Johnson said: "I want *loyalty*. I want [someone] to kiss my ass in Macy's window at high noon." In describing LBJ's choice of Hubert Humphrey, one senator remarked that Johnson didn't want a vice president, he wanted "a trained seal."

"It would soon become clear that Johnson had no intention of protecting Humphrey from that special misery he had suffered as Vice-President, but rather intended to pass it on in even greater doses," David Halberstam writes in his Pulitzer Prize–winner, *The Best and The Brightest*. "Rarely would a high public official undergo the humiliation and virtual emasculation that Humphrey underwent as Vice-President."

Co-leaders, Humphrey quickly discovered, depend on the generosity of the Chief Executive for any meaningful duties. And those assignments can be withdrawn at a moment's notice. As Humphrey later put it: "He who giveth can taketh away and often does."

Only two months before taking office, Humphrey delivered a major speech on educational reform in New York, suggesting that he was the administration's point man on education. A few days later, LBJ called him on the carpet and, in the most vitriolic language, reminded him that the president *alone* set national policy. Lest Humphrey miss the point, Johnson then told the White House press corps: "Boys, I've just reminded Hubert that I've got his balls in my pocket."

Humphrey suffered many such reminders. Johnson informed his No. 2 that all yachting excursions would require presidential approval. Johnson also made Humphrey beg for access to *Air Force Two*. Worse yet, Humphrey had to submit a travel request to the White House every time he wanted to leave town.

In his memoirs Humphrey described the frustrations of his tenure in the nation's second highest office. "It's like being trapped in the middle of a blizzard with no one to even offer you a match to keep you warm—that's the vice presidency," he wrote. "You are trapped, vulnerable, and alone."

Reinventing Government

How did Al Gore manage to interrupt this venerable cycle of vice presidential impotence and despair? Unlike many of his predecessors, Gore had a realistic notion of exactly what he was getting into. For starters Gore received good counsel on the subject from his father, Albert Gore, Sr., one of the most powerful and influential members of Congress. The senior Gore had served 18 years in the Senate when he was nominated for the vice presidency at the Democratic Convention in 1956, and he offered his son many useful suggestions on how to restore prestige to the institution. In addition the younger Gore sought the advice of Walter Mondale, who had made some headway in expanding the vice president's responsibilities under an amenable Jimmy Carter. It was Mondale who told Gore to locate his command post close to the Oval Office, to meet weekly with the president over lunch, and to try to link his staff with Clinton's. Clinton agreed to each request before Gore accepted his party's nomination.

During three lengthy negotiating sessions, Gore reminded Clinton of his publicly announced criteria for the nation's top co-leader. In Clinton's own words, the vice president should be someone "who really understood what had happened to ordinary Americans in the last twelve years, someone who was committed to making government work again for average hardworking American families . . . who would complement me and my own experiences, knowledge, and understanding to our common endeavor. And above all, [someone] who would be ready, should something happen to me, to immediately assume the office of the President of the United States."

With Gore on the team, Clinton issued a joint manifesto, *Putting People First*. And, working together, the talented pair began to rehabilitate what had long been the largely ornamental office of vice president. In the process Gore emerged as the president's most influential adviser and chief co-leader.

Chemistry counts in any co-leadership team. From the start Clinton and Gore became close allies as did their families. Similar in background and age, the men obviously enjoy each other's company. "He's not only the President of our country, he's my friend," Gore says of his chief. The president reciprocates: "We have a partnership and we're personal friends and we trust each other enough to be candid." Perhaps only the presidential partnerships of Jackson–Van Buren, Polk–Dallas, and McKinley–Hobart got along as famously.

Part of Gore's clout in the White House results from his willingness to dissent with the boss. Gore has grit. Recognizing Bill Clinton's tendency to flip-flop, the vice president has insisted on numerous occasions that the administration stick to its principles, and do so decisively. Despite lack of support from the armed forces and the general public, Gore pressed the president to lift the ban on homosexuals in the military. More hawkish than Clinton, Gore, a Vietnam War vet, also pushed for greater use of force in Haiti and for a more aggressive military presence in both Bosnia-Herzegovina and the Persian Gulf. When the Republican Congress seized the initiative in submitting a balanced-budget package, the vice president—against the wishes of then Chief of Staff Leon Panetta and aide George Stephanopoulos—urged that the White House offer a compromise plan. According to the *Wall Street Journal,* Gore insisted that it was imperative that the president stand *for* something—not just *against* the Republicans. Eventually Clinton agreed, and later he presented an alternative package that increased spending for education and training at the cost of deep cuts in energy, transportation, and housing—cuts that would have been unthinkable in previous Democratic White Houses. Although Gore is always prepared to speak truth to power, in the best tradition of co-leaders, he is also careful about how he presents a contrary opinion to the president. "I always keep my advice to him private," Gore says, "and I will continue to follow that rule."

Obviously the assertive vice president has not always swayed the mercurial Clinton—on gays in the military, for instance. Nonetheless, Gore has won the respect of Oval Office insiders for his tough-mindedness. "He doesn't pull rank; he makes an argument," says ex–White House adviser Stephanopoulos. Nor does the brainy VP brood when his position does not prevail.

Unlike many of his predecessors, Gore has a profound sense of the co-leader's role. "The Vice President must recognize that he is, in fact, a subordinate," writes Joel K. Goldstein, author of *The Modern American Vice Presidency.* "This in itself will not assure him the confidence of the Chief Executive. But failure to behave in such a fashion will almost surely result in ostracism."

Al Gore understands this and seems to enjoy his role as No. 2. "I have always felt it really and truly a privilege to be able to serve in the exact position in which I'm now serving," he says, "and to define it in the way I define it." In particular he is careful not to upstage Clinton. "Al Gore has all the qualities of being a very strong leader," said Richard W. Riley, the secretary of education. "But he's the *Vice* President. He's not trying to be the President as Vice President. That's why they get along so well together."

If there is anything that truly defines America's co-chief, it's Gore's desire to be a team player. Besides knowing his place, Gore wants to make things happen. Yet getting things done is not always easy in an administration that sometimes looks more like "The Amateur Hour" than Camelot. For the better part of Clinton's first term, the White House suffered one setback after another as the new administration learned the painful lesson that Washington is not Little Rock. But the Clinton White House is a learning environment, and the administration's early fumbling slowly gave way to a more measured approach to national and international issues. Behind the scenes, Gore's many tasks included translating complicated policy issues into easily grasped political messages.

One of the first things a wise co-leader must do is size up his or her No. 1. As vice president, Gore found himself dealing with a talented, articulate, intelligent boss who could also be, in the words of one Washington observer, "an undisciplined, fumbling, obtuse, defensive, and self-justifying rogue."

Virtually everyone who knows Clinton describes him as a paradox. He "is essentially sunny yet capable of black cloudbursts of thundering rage," observed Todd S. Purdum while covering the White House for the *New York Times*. "In a real sense, his strengths are his weaknesses, his enthusiasms are his undoings, and most of the traits that make him appealing can make him appalling in the flash of an eye." To former aide Stephanopoulos, the rakish president is a kaleidoscope—one who changes with every twist and turn. Those twists and turns were displayed publicly during the Monica Lewinsky sex scandal.

Great co-leadership teams often consist of people with different but complementary gifts. Anything but mercurial, Gore is a disciplined, systematic thinker who brings much to the presidential decision-making process. True, Gore spent most of his early days delivering speeches on less than provocative subjects: the National Performance Review, reinventing government, corporate welfare, world population growth, and the overhaul of telecommunications law. But over time Gore has broadened his policy portfolio. With the best cyberspiel in politics, he is the nation's leading technology-policy wonk. He is credited with crafting the term *information superhighway*. Gore urged the White House to support a V-chip to block violence on television programming, to bar taxation of electronic commerce, and to require the telecommunications industry to wire all schools and libraries to the Internet by 2000. He also helped Clinton snare the support of Silicon Valley during the 1992 and 1996 campaigns. For several years the unabashed technology enthusiast has been meeting regularly with Gore-techs, high-tech executives who share his belief that technology drives the New Economy. Regulars include venture capitalist John Doerr and Marc Andreessen of Netscape Communications Corp.

The tech-savvy VP, who thrives on daily doses of e-mail, has also been the administration's prime mover on the environment. The former reporter's book, *Earth in the Balance,* linking family and ecological dysfunction, sold more than 500,000 copies. Among his accomplishments in this arena: Gore brought the Big Three automobile companies together in an attempt to build an environmentally clean car; he insisted on stricter carbon monoxide emission standards on autos; and he pressured the State Department to commit to making environmental concerns a diplomatic priority.

As part of his co-leadership pact with Clinton, Gore has assumed primary responsibility for certain areas of national concern, including technology, the environment, free trade, and welfare reform. With the president's blessing, essential for such a division of labor, Gore has shaped high-profile issues "any politician would love to own," says Carter Eskew, a longtime adviser to the Democrats. What's more, the vice president has played political hardball when it was needed. In the famous 1993 debate on the North American Free Trade Agreement, he flattened the feisty Texas billionaire H. Ross Perot. During the 1996 campaign, Gore worked some of the nation's toughest terrain— touring poor urban neighborhoods and deeply entrenched GOP strongholds in the rural South. He didn't hesitate to take swipes at Speaker Newt Gingrich and the Republicans. Not known for his barbed rhetoric, Gore told voters: "Speaker Gingrich talking about the truth is a little bit like [flamboyant basketball star] Dennis Rodman talking about hair care."

The vice president has also been active in the administration's appointment process. It was Gore who urged Clinton to withdraw Lani Guinier's nomination as head of the Justice Department's Civil Rights Division. Conversely he lobbied hard for Carol M. Browner to oversee the Environmental Protection Agency. Gore recommended William Perry for secretary of defense and a prep school buddy, Reed Hundt, for chair of the Federal Communications Commission. Gore pushed for Mickey Kantor as commerce secretary (only two days after the funeral of his predecessor, Ronald H. Brown.) In addition Gore urged that Charlene Barshefsky take over from Kantor as trade representative, for Franklin D. Raines to be named director of the Office of Management and Budget, for Andrew Cuomo to run the Department of Housing and Urban Development, and for Richard Holbrooke to serve as U.S. representative to the United Nations. Gore's role in the administration was bolstered further by the rise of several of his closest aides. Gore's chief of staff, Jack Quinn, moved on to become White House counsel. So, too, did Peter Knight, the VP's talented fund-raiser. Robert Squier, Gore's longtime media adviser, shifted over to the 1996 Clinton campaign, only to return to assist the vice president after the president's reelection.

From policy making to personnel, Gore has had more impact on President Clinton's decision making than anyone else in Washington. A true co-leader, Gore has become one of the most influential VPs in modern times. "The Vice President goes to almost every meeting the President has and is free to go to any meeting he desires," Stephanopoulos said. "And before any big decision is made, the President always wants to know: 'What does Al think?' " Gore's standing with the president, says another senior White House adviser, "is unparalleled. He has access, trust, respect, continued influence . . . on every issue."

Clinton for his part recognizes the many contributions his able co-leader has made. "Based on everything I've been able to read or learn from others," Clinton says, "he has a larger role substantively and more influence than any Vice President. Ever. . . . The American people will never know, at least not until I write my memoirs, all the magnificent things Al Gore has done for them as Vice President." Richard L. Berke, who covers national politics for the *New York Times,* agrees: "Albert A. Gore Jr. has given the office of Vice President its most consequential place in history. He is now regarded as a natural in the job, as the ideal No. 2."

Surviving the Washington scene requires special skills. "The best way to stay out of trouble is to stay out of sight," President Kennedy once remarked. To survive in the Beltway, co-leaders often labor in obscurity. However, some chief executives have used their deputies as high-profile foils and lightning rods for the public's dissatisfaction. President Nixon unleashed his vice president, Spiro Agnew, to attack the administration's media and war critics. Agnew, in effect, became "Nixon's Nixon," says author David Halberstam.

"Nixon told me the press will pick on either the President or the Vice President," recalls former Bush VP Dan Quayle. "When Nixon was VP, Eisenhower was popular. So Nixon got picked on. Bush was popular, so I got picked on. Clinton's never been popular, so they leave Gore alone." Quayle's advice for Gore: "Stick with Clinton."

Whenever possible Vice President Gore judiciously avoids the limelight. He positions himself either off-camera or one step behind President Clinton. In the view of observers, Gore's loyalty and lack of self-promotion, despite his personal ambition, is his greatest strength.

Avoiding the Quayle Paradox

In politics or business, every successful co-leader must defer to the boss. From all accounts George Bush, as Ronald Reagan's vice president, did this scrupulously. He bent to the president's wishes, supporting all his domestic and foreign policies. Unswerving in his allegiance to Reagan, Bush was "a typical second banana, one step to the side and two steps behind," said Donald Rumsfeld, chairman of Gilead Sciences, Inc., and former secretary of defense in the Ford administration.

Eventually Bush succeeded in convincing voters that he was a kinder, gentler version of Reagan. On becoming one of 14 VPs to succeed to the presidency, Bush was finally able to forge an identity separate from Reagan's. Ironically Bush's bold choice of a much younger running mate, Dan Quayle, may have contributed to the Republican's presidential defeat in 1992. Many Americans viewed Quayle as a bit of a lightweight. He might have remained simply anonymous if he hadn't had a gift for misspeaking worthy of Yogi Berra. A motherlode of material for late-night comedians, Quayle's verbal fumbles could fill a large briefcase. As embarrassed as he must have been by his many gaffes, the likable but hapless vice president once said, good naturedly: "I stand by all my misstatements!" But the fact that a man who can't spell "potato" was a heartbeat away from the presidency triggered warning bells in the populace. Most people gave Quayle relatively high marks for his performance as vice president but low marks as Bush's heir apparent. What political scientists termed "the Quayle paradox" suggests that the public does not necessarily see the vice presidency as a springboard to the presidency.

To Gore's credit he has defied the paradox. But is he presidential timber? "That is one of the great questions of American politics," says Washington observer David R. Gergen. The odds are against Gore. Only 4 of the nation's 45 VPs were elected to the presidency at the end of their vice presidential terms: John Adams in 1796, Thomas Jefferson in 1800, Martin Van Buren in 1836, and George Bush in 1988.

President Clinton clearly wants Gore to succeed him. Some have even described the president as Gore's de facto campaign manager. According to former White House strategist Dick Morris, President Clinton has said: "I just want you to know that I will work ceaselessly, ceaselessly, to be sure that Al Gore is the presidential nominee of the Democratic Party in 2000, without a primary if at all possible."

Ironically Gore's challenge, like Bush's before him, will be to distance himself from a supportive but wounded president. If Gore is to win in 2000, he must continue to be seen as loyal but avoid being seen as a clone of a president whose integrity has been called into serious question. No easy task, because Clinton and Gore are similar in age, ideology, regional ties—and twangs. And so Gore's conundrum: How to be a faithful No. 2 while striving for the No. 1 slot?

In large part Gore's presidential prospects will depend on his ability to convince the public that he has the right stuff for the top job, despite his notorious lack of charisma. Two years ago *Time* magazine named Gore one of the 25 most influential Americans. But now he must convince voters that he deserves the ultimate promotion. "Under the best circumstances, the transition from sitting No. 2 to candidate for No. 1 is one of the most dicey in politics," says David Broder, political columnist for the *Washington Post*. "It requires shedding the subservience, the cheerleading and the emphasis on loyalty to the head man that popular psychology requires of the deputy, and the gradual unveiling of the qualities of vision, assertiveness, and independence that Americans crave in our presidents."

Thus Gore's transformation from a highly accomplished co-leader to a serious presidential candidate poses special challenges. Like VPs before him, he is joined at the hip, at least in the public's mind, with the president he serves. When the president is Bill Clinton, that's both a plus and a minus. For example, the Clinton-Gore team continues to call for a leaner, somewhat more limited government, but one still capable of compassion for social wrongs. For many voters the two New Democrats symbolize the 1960s—from civil rights to feminism. For those conservative voters, that was when America went wrong. For others the New Democrats look too much like the old Republicans. Both groups could back a candidate other than Gore.

Another boulder in the road is the economy. Should boom turn to bust, the vice president's candidacy would no doubt be jeopardized. He could also be blindsided in his quest for the presidency by a quarrelsome and increasingly partisan Congress. Congressional gridlock continues to keep him from doing big things. Others wonder whether the vice president can shuck his Beltway-insider image. In this antipolitical age, more and more Americans are searching for fresh faces. Born into politics, Gore bears little resemblance to the maverick outsider who promises dramatic change. Despite his willingness to poke fun at his woodenness, Gore's lack of spontaneity makes it difficult for many to warm up to him.

Gore has also made some mistakes, seemingly minor in comparison to Clinton's. Having long benefited from a reputation for integrity, Gore was widely criticized for his "solicitor in chief" role in raising funds for the 1996 Clinton-Gore reelection campaign. Although some argued that Gore was only a fringe player in the affair, Donorgate soiled Gore's previously spotless image and could hurt his chances for the presidency.

Assuming these hurdles can be overcome, Gore must still demonstrate to the American people that the lessons he learned as No. 2 uniquely qualify him for the nation's highest office. Despite the limitations of the vice presidency, the office does provide incumbents with an insider's perspective of how domestic and foreign policy is made and implemented. Richard Nixon once claimed that, unlike the House and Senate, "in the vice presidency you have an opportunity to see the whole operation of government and participate in its decisions." Gore will have to convince voters that they will benefit from his eight years of proximity to the Oval Office: namely that he has received a superb, college-of-one education on how to be president. As important, Gore will also have to remind the voting public of his own impressive list of accomplishments, including top-level visits to the former Soviet republics, China, South Africa, and the Middle

East. "Unlike other Vice Presidents who had to tag on to the President's coattails," says his former chief of staff, Jack Quinn, "Al Gore *will* have a real track record."

As the 2000 presidential race draws closer, Gore will have to shift out of vice presidential mode and prove himself of presidential stature. Facing tough tests is nothing new for Gore. In 1988 he lost the campaign to become the Democratic presidential candidate. A few months later, then Senator Gore saw his life change dramatically. On April 3, 1989, he and his family attended the Baltimore Orioles season opener. Leaving Memorial Stadium, son Albert, then six years old, was struck by a car while crossing the street. Gore and his wife, Tipper, watched in horror as their son was thrown 30 feet into the air and then skidded another 20 feet along the pavement after he hit the ground. For weeks the Gores maintained a constant vigil at his hospital bedside. Slowly Albert III recovered; today he shows no ill effects of the accident. But the incident transformed the Senator from Tennessee: "I was, in a sense, vulnerable to the change that sought me out in the middle of my life and gave me a new sense of urgency about those things I value the most," he recalled. In the future nothing would come before family, even politics.

After observing the stresses of the presidency firsthand, Al Gore knows that being the first president of the twenty-first century could be a bed of thorns, not roses. The office that Warren G. Harding likened to "a prison" has disappointed many of its incumbents. Thomas Jefferson said that the two happiest days of his life were the day he took office and the day he left it. John Quincy Adams moaned: "Make no mistake about it. The four most miserable years of my life were my four years in the presidency." And Franklin Pierce lamented, "After the White House, what is there to do but drink?"

If Al Gore becomes president, chances are the strains of "Hail to the Chief" will not go to his head. His two-term stint as the nation's chief co-leader has allowed him both to see the pitfalls of being No. 1 and to realize how important a contribution a strong No. 2— empowered by a sympathetic president—can make. More than any vice president in modern history, he has carved out an expanded role for future VPs. Gore may not be able to do the macarena, but he has already left a legacy any chief executive would be proud of.

10 | Bill Guthridge

Invisible but Invaluable

Into the Spotlight: After serving North Carolina basketball coach Dean Smith for parts of four decades, Bill Guthridge (left) emerged from the shadowlands. In 1997 he replaced the legendary Smith and led the Tar Heels to a top ranking. (Bob Donnan)

10

Bill Guthridge

The outstanding characteristic of the
relationship between the superior and his
subordinates is his dependence upon them
for the satisfaction of his needs.

—DOUGLAS MCGREGOR, Management Theorist and

Author of *The Human Side of Enterprise*

Little recognition, lots of overtime, not a lot of money. Hardly the most compelling job description. But that describes the typical college assistant coach. "Assistant coaches are invisible, but invaluable men and women," writes Frank Blackman of the *San Francisco Examiner.* "Mostly young, they are attendants-in-waiting to the king, the head coach who hired them." Their job is to watch, to make mental notes, to be prepared—and, above all, to stay under cover.

Across the nation coaching co-leaders walk in the shadows of their superiors. For 30 years Bill Guthridge sat at the right hand of University of North Carolina basketball mentor Dean Smith, the game's all-time winningest coach. Highly respected, the quiet, unassuming aide was basketball's quintessential co-leader. He helped coach more victories than any other assistant in the country, and his tenure as an assistant coach was the game's longest. Over the years Guthridge assisted in building a stellar 97.3 percent graduation rate for the UNC program. He also helped Smith win almost 80 percent of his games. There was a postseason tournament every year: 11 appearances in the National Collegiate Athletic Association's Final Four, including

2 championships and 3 runner-up placings, and the National Invitation Tournament title in 1971. Plus 1976's Olympic gold medal.

Bill Guthridge was the invisible member of one of college athletics' most successful partnerships. And that's the way he liked it. The 60-year-old Guthridge seemed to have put aside any thoughts of running his own show. "Chapel Hill offers an excellent situation, and I enjoy it. I can't see going someplace else since I'm extremely happy in my present job," he told us.

Being Dean Smith's loyal aide-de-camp represented all the upward mobility the unassuming Guthridge needed or wanted. His continued willingness to play a supporting role made him seem a flawed man to some, an enigma in a profession of ceaseless self-promotion and constant job-hopping. Earlier in his career, rival coaches unkindly labeled him "Tonto," "Little John," and "Robin."

Coaches are presumed to live on a career ladder, climbing as they work, always seeking a better job, until they reach the top rung of success. Fresh-faced graduate assistants vie to become assistant coaches, assistants to become lead assistants (or associate coaches), lead assistants to become head coaches who then go on to positions at more powerful schools. Those head coaches in turn move to professional sports. But in shaping his long and distinguished career, Bill Guthridge climbed off the ladder.

Not that there weren't ample opportunities to advance. Over the years Guthridge seriously considered leaving Chapel Hill several times for head coaching jobs at major universities—Colorado, Auburn, Louisiana State, even archrival Duke. In 1978 he actually accepted the top slot at Penn State, thanks to the hard sell of one of his heroes, football coach Joe Paterno. However, two days later an apologetic Guthridge informed the Nittany Lions of his decision to withdraw, thereby terminating one of the briefest head coaching assignments in collegiate history.

"The more I thought about it, the more I realized, 'I have a great job at Carolina.' I realized there was no better program than what we had, mainly because of Dean," Guthridge recalled. "Everybody has an ego. But I decided I didn't need to be a head coach to fulfill it. I was fully able to satisfy my ego with the success the team has." From then on he would accept no more job interviews. Until Smith retired in 1997, Guthridge was perfectly content to retire as a Carolina assistant coach.

Learning the Craft of Coaching

Coaches are usually former stars who understand greatness in their bones or former benchwarmers who understand the intellectual nuances of the game. William Wallace Guthridge is the latter. If coaching were to be his chosen profession, he would have to learn how to recruit, motivate, and mold taller, more talented athletes than he had ever been in new and different ways. To help in his professional education, Guthridge would turn to head coaches Fred "Tex" Winter and Dean Smith, both, like Guthridge, former gym rats with limited playing skills who became two of college basketball's leading innovators.

Guthridge was born during the depression in the railroad town of Parsons, in southeastern Kansas. His parents, Wallace and Betty, were educators of solid Midwestern stock who instilled in him a strong sense of discipline. At age 5, Bill discovered basketball as the mascot of the local Pratt Junior College team. His job was to sit at the end of the bench and throw balls to the players. It was then that he decided that coaching was his future. "I always liked athletics," Guthridge recalls. "They were my very special interest. And I always wanted to be a coach."

After a bout of polio in which he escaped paralysis, Bill went on to play hoops at Parsons High School for Harold Johnson, who, with brother Gene, is credited with the first zone defense and fast-break offense. Following a year at junior college, the undersized guard enrolled at Kansas State University "because I knew my chances of playing would be better there." Coached by the legendary Tex Winter, who is still active as an assistant coach of the NBA's Chicago Bulls, KSU won the Big Eight championship in each of Guthridge's seasons. During Guthridge's sophomore year, the Wildcats went to the NCAA Final Four, only to lose to Seattle University. "I wasn't a star," Guthridge admits. "I very seldom started and was more the seventh-man type."

After graduating in 1960 with a degree in mathematics, Guthridge coached at Kansas's Scott City High School. In 1962 he returned to his alma mater as an assistant under Coach Winter. During his five years on staff, Guthridge helped lead the Wildcats to a 93–43 record, a pair of Big Eight Conference crowns, and the 1964 Final Four. As a

KSU aide, he was coaching in the Puerto Rican League in the summer of 1967 when Dean Smith called him about an opening on the North Carolina staff.

Guthridge and Smith go way back—to the Kansas flats, actually. Older by six years, Dean grew up in Emporia, the son of a high school teacher and coach. He attended Kansas University and worked his way onto the basketball team, although, like Guthridge, he wasn't much of a player. Guthridge remembers driving 40 miles with his parents to watch Smith's KU team play on a friend's television set. Later, as a high school sophomore, Guthridge met Smith after a game in Lawrence. The men's relationship grew when Smith started dating Guthridge's sister, a fellow student at Kansas. "I knew Bill's family," says Smith. "My mother knew his grandfather. . . . He was academically very bright and very personable." Always on the prowl for talent, Smith was also acutely aware of Tex Winter's glowing endorsement of his young protégé.

Although Puerto Rico wanted Guthridge to coach its Olympic team, the Carolina offer seemed too good to refuse. As successful co-leaders always do, Guthridge knew there was something valuable for him in the assistant's job. He would be getting paid to learn from one of the profession's best: Dean Smith. "At the time, like probably everybody else, I wanted to be a head coach, and I thought [UNC] would be a great experience," Guthridge recalls. "After all, I figured I'd have the Tex Winter background and the Dean Smith background." So in the fall of 1967 he moved to Chapel Hill to begin a partnership that would make the Tar Heels one of collegiate basketball's most durable powerhouses.

Silent Partners

Smith's choice of Guthridge paid off. In his first six years, he served as the Tar Heels' freshman coach. His teams finished with a 72–25 record, and he directed the development of such future professional stars as Michael Jordan, Bobby Jones, Mitch Kupchak, Sam Perkins, and Walter Davis.

Forget making strategy: Assistant coaches labor in the trenches. They must find happiness in day-to-day operations, in the small things. Working 16-hour days, they are the ultimate company men and women—doing whatever it takes to allow the head coach to concentrate on coaching. "The job of the assistant is to take the pressure off the head guy and do the little things," Guthridge advises every young coach. "Those who aren't prepared to get stuck into the detail should choose another calling."

Although there was no doubt as to who was boss, head coach Smith had the confidence to share power as well as labor. "Coach Gut," as Guthridge is known, was involved in every aspect of coaching—teaching, motivating, on-bench decision making, and recruiting. "Coach Smith allows me enough input so I feel I'm an important part of the program," Guthridge said while still Smith's assistant. "I can make just about any decision I want to make." But, Guthridge noted: "Come game time, Coach Smith assumed command. He had everybody's undivided attention. Unlike football where there's an offensive and defensive coordinator, in basketball, the head coach directed everything."

Although Guthridge always respectfully referred to "Coach Smith," never "Dean," when talking to the team or the press, Guthridge was no Mr. Milquetoast. As good co-leaders do, Smith respected Guthridge for the unique skills and experience he brought to the team. Smith always considered his counsel in the course of a game. "I might suggest playing a certain offense or defense," Guthridge explained, "or I might say that so and so needs a break. Or maybe somebody on the other team isn't playing good defense—and we can take advantage of it in a certain way. I'll look for anything that might help the flow of the game." But in the end, Guthridge said: "Coach Smith took some of my ideas and threw others away. He made all the decisions about what we should do."

The so-called One Voice strategy was an important element in UNC's phenomenal success. Smith might tap his fellow coaches throughout a game, but during timeouts or at half time, the head coach took charge—no ifs, ands, or buts. "There needs to be one voice and, thank goodness, Coach Smith was the one voice," Guthridge said. "And there was none better in the business." In pregame or postgame interviews, any quotes about the team or individual players came from Dean Smith. Why? "Here again, we might be saying essentially the same thing to the media," Guthridge explained, "but I might say it in a slightly different way and the desired message gets garbled. We didn't want that to happen."

Guthridge, for his part, was the ultimate co-leader: satisfied in his roles as counselor to Smith, adviser and surrogate parent to players, scout, and frequent banquet speaker. "There was tremendous variety in my job," he said, beaming. "I never felt like I was stagnating. And in this business, that's crucial."

As the team's No. 2, Coach Gut did a little bit of everything that the head coach does, while specializing in shooting instruction. To him missing free throws or three-point shots should be crimes punishable by hard time. On the practice floor, when it came to shooting, all the Carolina coaches contributed, but Guthridge's was the One Voice. "I was the only one who talks with players about their technique," he said. "In coaches' meetings, we all discussed it and all decided what is the best thing for this shooter or that shooter. But in the end, I'd work with him on it. The reason is that shooting was a lot like a golf swing. It's very delicate. So you don't want four different people suggesting to a player that he work on four different things."

With Guthridge's guidance, the Tar Heels consistently swished more than 50 percent of their shots and achieved some of the nation's top marks for field goals. Giving pointers to Carolina's tall timber was another Guthridge specialty. He worked individually with Tar Heel front-court players prior to each practice session. Over the years he tutored a galaxy of UNC big men: Bob McAdoo, Mitch Kupchak, Sam Perkins, Brad Daugherty, Eric Montross, and Rasheed Wallace.

"I think Coach Guthridge has influenced every player that's gone through the program," said Bobby Jones, a former college and professional star. "He's a perfect extension of Coach Smith. They both have the same basic values."

Smith gave his staunch sidekick much of the credit for helping develop the players—short and tall—who kept UNC at the pinnacle of college basketball for three decades. "Bill made tremendous contributions to our program," Smith said. "He's one of the greatest coaches in college basketball, and you'll notice I didn't say assistant coaches."

Paying Attention to Detail

For decades success to the gray-haired, bespectacled Guthridge meant doing whatever it took to lift the tremendous load off Dean Smith so the team could thrive. "Over the years, Coach Smith's

workload had increased tenfold," Guthridge recalled. "He needed
assistance with the tons of mail that crossed his desk, the infinite
requests for information, the speaking engagements, the appearances,
and much more. I tried to help him with the little things, because
there was no one better to deal with big things than Dean."

To this day attention to detail comes easily to the fastidious
Guthridge. He dresses as neatly and conservatively as an accountant.
Amid the swirl, noise, and hoopla of college basketball, he is a quiet,
precise presence. For him bringing order out of chaos is what it's all
about. Uncertainty unnerves him. He is unapologetic about prefer-
ring strict routines to the ambiguities of daily life.

Rain or shine, the trim Guthridge begins his day with a three- to
five-mile run at the same measured pace. Working from his spotless
desk, he takes up the multiple tasks of UNC basketball—reviewing
videotapes of high school prospects, planning practices, working with
players or academic advisers on class schedules. At precisely noon, he
jumps into his loaned Pontiac Bonneville and motors to the same
Chinese restaurant at the Eastgate Shopping Center for his usual
sweet-and-sour chicken. At road games, he always buys a Diet Coke
and a box of popcorn first thing. Then, like clockwork, he climbs to a
remote spot high above the basketball court to scope out the away-
game arena.

We first caught up with Guthridge, the Administrator, during the
three-week Carolina Basketball Camp in 1996, when close to 1,500
players and several hundred coaches descended on the UNC campus.
With little fanfare he oversaw the massive undertaking with the skill
of a seasoned battlefield commander. An army of school buses transported the campers to and from 17 gyms in and around Chapel Hill
and nearby Durham. Cafeterias produced prodigious amounts of
healthy foods for the budding hoopsters, and UNC dorms were
commandeered so the exhausted youngsters could bed down at the
end of the day. All this—with very few hiccups.

"Bill's philosophy is that if you take care of the little things, you
never have big problems," explained Ken Miller, the former coach at
Chapel Hill High, a veteran counselor at the camp, and a longtime
Guthridge admirer.

Naturally the continuing success of North Carolina basketball has
made the school a cradle for coaches. Over the years several assistants

have moved on to run their own programs. Ken Rosemond left to become head coach at Georgia. Larry Brown, the Philadelphia 76ers' top gun, joined the New Orleans franchise of the now defunct American Basketball Association. John Lotz went to the University of Florida, while Roy Williams became the headman at Kansas. Eddie Folger, now the No. 1 at South Carolina, left to coach Wichita State and later Vanderbilt. Ex–Tar Heel Randy Wiel is now rebuilding the Middle Tennessee State program, Buzz Peterson directs Appalachian State, and Jeff Lebo oversees Tennessee Tech.

Yet Guthridge opted not to strike out on his own. Why? He had the wisdom to know that it's always great to *get* the top job, but not necessarily great actually doing it. "Too many assistants simply don't know what they're getting into," he said. He cites the case of former Seattle SuperSonics' assistant coach Tim Grgurich.

When Grgurich accepted the head coaching job at the University of Nevada at Las Vegas in 1994, he sounded like a man who would have worked for free. At age 50, the longtime No. 2 took a pay cut from his $320,000-a-year salary in the National Basketball Association to resuscitate a faltering, scandal-tinged college program. Grgurich's appointment was welcome news to many Runnin' Rebel fans, who felt betrayed by predecessor Rollie Massimino's pomposity and subpar 36–21 record. The UNLV faithful remembered Grgurich as the lead assistant to the infamous, towel-chomping Jerry Tarkanian, who founded the program 22 seasons earlier and blasted Duke 103–73 to win the 1990 national championship. Unfortunately Tark the Shark also caught the attention of the NCAA's infractions committee— leading to his ouster and Massimino's subsequent appointment.

The return of Tarkanian's deputy was greeted warmly by UNLV's supporters. But the pressure to get the Rebels back on the winning track got to Grgurich, who had to be treated for exhaustion and depression before leaving the job. Eventually he returned to the NBA as an assistant coach.

If Bill Guthridge needed other evidence of the pitfalls of ascending to the No. 1 job, he could turn to his Carolina colleague John Lotz. In 1972 Lotz left the security of his eight-year apprenticeship with Dean Smith to become the head coach at Florida. In his rookie season, he was named Southeastern Conference Coach of the Year, an honor he earned again in 1977. But a mediocre record forced the likable Lotz to resign only 11 games into the 1979–1980 season. He has been out of coaching ever since and is now in his eighteenth year as an assistant athletic director at UNC.

Of course, co-leadership is not for everyone. Deputies must be comfortable working in the shadows of their higher-profile superiors. "The head coach should get the credit," Guthridge believes. "He's responsible for the program. He alone gets blamed when things go wrong. And he's the one who gets fired, too."

Guthridge's decision to remain a lieutenant said a lot about him, but it also says much about his special relationship with Dean Smith. "To remain supportive to a personality that is so visible and so powerful and to stay in that position year after year—through all the basketball camps and all the recruiting trips—is a tribute to Bill's real sense of his own identity," said Bishop McDuffie, headmaster of the Laurinburg (North Carolina) Institute and a student manager of the Tar Heels in the 1970s. "[Guthridge] knows that every head man needs a second fiddler," wrote David Perlmutt of the *Charlotte Observer*. "And I think he's content to know he's one of the nation's best second fiddlers."

The Winningest Coach

The fact that Dean Smith, collegiate basketball's greatest virtuoso, was playing first fiddle was the clincher in Guthridge's decision to stay. College hoops' winningest coach led UNC to the top of the fiercely competitive Atlantic Coast Conference on 17 occasions and won the ACC Tournament 13 times. Fifty of his charges went on to play professionally in the National Basketball Association or the American Basketball Association. North Carolina, in fact, had more men drafted in the first round of the NBA than any other school. Smith also placed at least one member on each of the last eight U.S. Olympic teams. Four Tar Heels played on the 1976 gold-medal squad, coached by Smith, Guthridge, and Georgetown Coach John Thompson.

Smith-coached teams were characterized by their unselfish play, great teamwork, and tenacious defense. Although the Tar Heels specialized in a fast-breaking offense, they were also comfortable in a more disciplined style of attack. His squads were well known for their innovations, among them the run-and-jump defense, the point zone, team huddles at the foul line, the scramble defense, multiple screens against zone defenses, and the famous four-corners offense.

"Dean is one of the most organized and brilliant minds that I've ever met in basketball," said Georgetown's Thompson. "He has shared ideas and thoughts and philosophies with me that people just don't share . . . I will always be grateful and respect him for that." "The Michelangelo of coaching," Arizona's Lute Olson called him. The "Wizard of Westwood," former UCLA Coach John Wooden, agreed: "In my opinion, he's the best teacher of basketball I've ever seen."

Guthridge's deep feelings for Smith sometimes border on reverence. The shy, mild-mannered assistant would occasionally lose his cool, particularly if his chief were under attack. "Let someone cross Coach Smith and watch out," said Milwaukee Bucks mentor George Karl. "Coach Guthridge will be right there."

Former Maryland coach Lefty Driesell, who now directs Georgia State University, ran afoul of Bill's feisty side a decade or so ago. After a tough, last-second loss to North Carolina, Driesell unintentionally failed to shake Smith's hand. Guthridge immediately berated Driesell for his poor sportsmanship. Later both sides apologized over the well-publicized incident.

As towering a talent as Smith is, Guthridge was clearly a significant factor in both the team's and Smith's success. "Coach Guthridge is a pillar there," said Middle Tennessee's Randy Wiel. "I cannot imagine Coach Smith without Coach Guthridge at his side."

Chemistry helps. "Dean Smith has been the ultimate boss," Guthridge said. "I couldn't and probably wouldn't have done this for anybody else." The Smith-Guthridge combo survived because of their similar backgrounds, beliefs, and values. Their heartland upbringing helped two owlish math majors from eastern Kansas to form one of the most successful partnerships in collegiate basketball. Guthridge can't recall any serious spats with Smith. "I'm sure I must have second-guessed him somewhere along the way," he said, "but I honestly can't remember where or when. We think a lot alike. Our philosophies are virtually the same." "But," he said, touching on one of the keys to effective co-leadership, "Dean appreciated that I wasn't a yes-man."

Both men credit their close friend, the late Dr. Earl Somers, a Chapel Hill psychiatrist, for improving their communications skills and facilitating their personal and professional bond. Guthridge cited Smith's uncanny intuition for their simpatico: "Dean has great understanding of people. Oftentimes he could tell if I was having a problem before I'd realize it. And then we'd sit down and talk about it."

Assistant coaches are routinely underpaid, a fact that has caused them to protest and even sue. Not at North Carolina. "Coach Smith has always taken care of me and my family with the summer basketball camps and other things," Guthridge said. "He very much looks after us. His generosity is one of the keys to his success." Speculation was that Guthridge made more money as a UNC aide than he would as a head coach elsewhere. "I'm in a situation where I'm paid more than I'm worth," he said modestly. "If you're the No. 2 man and you're getting paid well, it's much easier to stay put."

Coach Smith, for his part, believes that their common backgrounds, similar personalities, and the passage of time accounted for their unmatched staying power. "By staying here, [Bill] has certainly given great stability to our program," Smith said. "Obviously, it was also very pleasant for me having the same guy to work with all these years."

"Guthridge and Smith built more than a strong working relationship," observed Bill Cole, who has covered Tar Heel basketball for the *Winston-Salem Journal* for 25 years. "They forged a very special bond. Coach Smith gave Bill far more responsibility than any other head coach I've covered." The twosome formed an unbeatable team. "If Dean Smith [is] the father of Carolina basketball," wrote Lee Pace, a local sports authority, "then Guthridge [is] the kindly old great uncle, the kind who endears himself to all those around him."

Over the years North Carolina's student-athletes were the principal beneficiaries of Guthridge's skillful but humane co-leadership. Guthridge conducts himself more like a vicar than like the slick, glib coaches who are the current norm in collegiate athletics. Honesty is perhaps his defining quality. "The man has no curve balls," says former Tar Heel player and current assistant coach Dave Hanners.

George Karl credits Guthridge even more than Smith with leading him into coaching. "[Guthridge] put the idea into my head when he was recruiting me in high school," Karl recalls. "I had never even considered it until then. To me and those who played, Bill Guthridge is as much North Carolina basketball as Dean Smith is. People can't believe it, but it's like one big, close family. And that's initiated by Dean and Bill."

No less than Smith, the low-profile Guthridge demanded excellence from his players, on and off the court. For years he's had a jar labeled "Excuses" on his desk. "I'm a bottom line kind of guy," he explains. "If someone has an excuse, they can put it right in there. If a player didn't go to class or was late to practice, I'm sure they have a reason, but . . . that's where the reasons go." The Excuses jar is usually empty.

One of Guthridge's special strengths is that he recognizes that college coaching is 90 percent human development, 10 percent X's and O's. "What I always liked was that he was never cynical, or insulting," George Karl recalls. "[He] was always positive . . . throughout college basketball and the pros, he has everyone's respect."

Michael Jordan, America's leading sports celebrity and an ex-Tar Heel, remembers Guthridge's frequent visits to the school's infirmary when Jordan came down with tonsillitis his freshman year. Scott Williams, now with the Philadelphia 76ers, has sad memories of Guthridge's sensitivity. On the team's first day of practice during Williams's sophomore year, he was informed by Smith and Guthridge that his father had committed suicide after murdering his estranged wife, Scott's mother. Sensing trouble in the family, Bill had flown to the West Coast a few weeks earlier to counsel the troubled parent— but to no avail. Guthridge represented the university at the funeral services in Los Angeles and, to this day, remains a confidant of Williams.

In assessing his co-leadership role, Guthridge said: "There are always some negatives to it. Sometimes there are things you like and things you don't. But I've had a great run—the good far outweighs the bad."

Guthridge's special bond to Smith and Tar Heel basketball were two of the three factors that rooted him to the University of North Carolina. The other is the contentment that he, his wife, and three children have found in Chapel Hill. Touted by artist William Meade Prince as "the Southern part of Heaven," the town casts a magical spell on anyone who comes to experience its unique blend of cosmopolitan living and Southern hospitality. Rich in history and steeped in tradition, the community of 50,000-plus people has become a magnet for newcomers from around the country and the world. Along with nearby Durham and Raleigh, Chapel Hill anchors North Carolina's famous Research Triangle Park, host to 130 companies, with some 92,000 employees, devoted primarily to research and development.

Chartered in 1789, the University of North Carolina is the nation's oldest state university. Today roughly 24,500 students are enrolled in its 13 colleges and schools, offering instruction in more than 100 fields. The Carolina campus, long considered one of America's most beautiful, coexists peacefully with a community described as "the perfect college town" by Richard Moll in *The Public Ivys*.

It is understandable, therefore, that the Guthridges remain content to spend their days in this idyllic Southern setting. "When you say the University of North Carolina and Chapel Hill to people at home and abroad," Guthridge says, "folks are truly impressed. They say, 'Oh, you're from North Carolina,' or 'You're from Chapel Hill.' That means an awful lot to us."

In an era of galloping egos, especially in his profession, Guthridge has put quality of life before conventional notions of success. He doesn't want to leave North Carolina to be a head coach just for the sake of being a head coach. He has weighed ambition against the status quo and found ambition wanting—as more and more gifted adjutants do. He has a good life, a happy family, a wonderful working environment, and the respect of his peers. It looked like he would be an exemplary No. 2 forever.

In effect Guthridge downshifted before the term became popular. "[Guthridge] doesn't need to be head coach," wrote Sam Donnellon, an area sports wag. "He has bent his goals around his life, and not the reverse. He has measured achievement by his own standards." Guthridge demonstrated that a supporting role can be as rewarding as a traditional leadership role. "Happiness is enjoying going to work each day and going home with a smile each night," he said. "That's why I'll be happy in my present situation for the rest of my life."

Looking ahead, Guthridge saw his life as inextricably linked to his boss's. "Coach Smith will probably outlast me," he told us in 1996. "I think he's one of those coaches like an Adolph Rupp or a Phog Allen or a Bear Bryant, some of those great figures in college sports who reach retirement age and just keep going and going." Guthridge said he would continue to aid and support Smith indefinitely.

Changing of the Guard

However, the Dean Smith era came to an abrupt end on October 9, 1997. The King of Hoops made the shocking announcement that he was stepping down to a packed conference room in the 21,572-seat Dean Dome (officially the Dean E. Smith Center). While the Tar Heels huddled closely offstage, Smith fought back the tears and explained that he had lost his drive to compete. The little things, "the out-of-season things," prompted him to quit just nine days before the start of fall practice.

His players were somber and saddened that Smith had decided to retire so suddenly. "I'm in shock. I still can't believe it," said point guard Ed Cota, reflecting the sentiment of both players and fans. The previous day Smith had broken the news to the team in the locker room. He left as he started to cry. Then players began to sob.

Not surprising was that Smith's job was given to Guthridge, who had served a longer apprenticeship than Prince Charles. Smith's handpicked successor accepted his new assignment with characteristic modesty. "It was never my goal to be the head coach at the University of North Carolina," he said at his first press conference. "This isn't quite the way that I would have envisioned this whole scenario through the years. . . . I was hoping that Dean and I would ride into the sunset together in five or six years. But that obviously isn't going to work out."

Guthridge's promotion assured continuity of the tried-and-true Carolina style and met with the overwhelming approval of the returning players. "You're losing Coach Smith," said All-America candidate Antawn Jamison, "but Coach Guthridge is the only person who can come close to him. . . . It's like you're losing your father, but he's being replaced by your uncle."

The transition from Dad Dean to Uncle Bill was expected to go smoothly. Guthridge inherited a skilled, veteran team, ranked in the top five by most pundits. He understood the Smith system—in many respects better than the legend himself. But the transition from the shadowlands to one of collegiate sports' most visible jobs is never easy.

"It's very weird," Guthridge said. "At one time I went from a promising, young assistant to veteran, longtime assistant. Now I'm an old, rookie coach."

In assuming the leadership mantle he once assiduously avoided, the new head coach inevitably invited comparisons with his predecessor, a living sports icon. But Guthridge wasn't overly troubled by being mentioned in the same breath as Dean Smith. "It's a very tough situation to follow the greatest coach of all time," Guthridge said. "I know I will never live up to all he's done. But I am excited about the opportunity and I'll do all I can to uphold the tradition. I think we'll be successful."

Coach Gut was given a five-year contract, considered long term in college athletics. But there were doubts he would coach all five years. Some predicted he would hold the job only until *his* favored co-leader, nine-year assistant Phil Ford, was up to the task. "My sources tell me that Guthridge does the job as long as he wants, as a way of grooming Phil Ford," said ESPN/ABC television analyst Dick Vitale. However, Guthridge quickly squelched such rumors. "I'm not taking it as a bridge to anything. I'm taking it as a long-term commitment. I don't know how long it will be. I'll probably have a better idea after this season." Then with a twinkle he said, "I might not like it."

But like it he did. The rookie steward answered the challenge, guiding the Tar Heels to a No. 1 ranking, a shot at the finals, and, in the process, became the first first-year coach in the history of the Atlantic Coast Conference to be named Coach of the Year. Finishing with a 34–4 record, Guthridge captured more victories than any other rookie Division I coach. Three national organizations named him the top coach in the country.

Like many of the cases we have studied, the Tar Heels' succession was seamless. North Carolina didn't miss a beat when the legendary Smith retired. Predictably the always self-effacing Guthridge gave much of the credit to his players and the rest of the coaching staff: "They were great—so supportive, so hard-working," he said. In truth the former assistant proved himself to be a remarkably poised head coach. "It was eerie how confident Coach Guthridge was," said assistant coach Dave Hanners. "It was as if Coach Smith was still here."

Asked how his coaching style differed from his predecessor's, Guthridge replied: "We don't differ in any way. I believe completely in what Dean Smith taught, and our goal this year is to build on what we were doing last year." The players, too, sensed that Smith and Guthridge were one. "Every rule Coach Smith set down is still here," said star forward Jamison. "Nothing at all has changed except for the coach. And you really can't tell we have a new coach."

Give Smith his due. Lots of chief executives have great difficulty letting go; some don't want their replacements to succeed. "Not Dean," says Guthridge. "He's been a great ex-coach—staying out of the action, but always being willing to listen and, when asked, offer suggestions."

Naturally the "old, rookie coach" had to make some adjustments, including an unlisted phone number. But on game days he still managed to munch his pregame popcorn, albeit in the bowels of the auditorium to avoid the media's hounding. In assessing his new role, Guthridge confessed, "I haven't done a very good job of delegating a lot of the detail things I used to do—and I could have done a better job defining the duties of my assistants." However, he promised to address these shortcomings over the summer and "to get better organized."

Finally the big question: "Which role—leader or co-leader—do you prefer?" Without hesitating, he answered: "No. 2!" The lack of privacy, he said, makes the No. 1 job less appealing. "Besides," he said, undoubtedly with tongue in cheek, "it's a whole lot easier making suggestions than making decisions."

11

Amy Tucker

Hoop Dreams

Hoop Dreams: Stanford's Silent Assistant, Amy Tucker
(right), has supported Tara VanDerveer for 15 years. In
1996 Tucker filled in for the legendary head coach, leading
Stanford to a third national ranking. (Rod Searcey)

11

Amy Tucker

It is said that it is far more difficult to hold
and maintain leadership than it is to attain
it. . . . We are apt to forget that we are only
one of a team, that in unity there is strength.
—SAMUEL JONES TILDEN, Nineteenth-Century Lawyer
and Public Official

For years Amy Tucker patiently suffered the curse of the understudy: She knew all the lines, she just never got to play the part. But in April 1995 Stanford women's basketball coach Tara VanDerveer opted to lead the 1996 USA Olympic Team, and Tucker no longer had to watch from the wings. Promoted to interim head coach, Tucker was suddenly the star, not the faithful lieutenant. While the temporary change of command put both women on something of an emotional roller coaster, it also offers a vivid illustration of how both organizations and individuals can benefit from a strong co-leadership culture.

The Stanford Stand-In

Stanford is unlike most collegiate sports programs in that its women often steal the headlines from the men—nowhere more so than in basketball, where the university has always been in the vanguard. In 1886 the school made history by meeting the University of California in the first documented intercollegiate game for women. During the last decade, the VanDerveer-led Lady Cardinal has become one of the nation's elite programs, with teams that have won much more consistently than the men. Hanging high from the rafters at the south

203

end of the school's Maples Pavilion are 12 banners marking the sisters' past successes. They document the Stanford women's dynasty, which now includes five Final Four appearances in the last decade and two national titles. The male hoopsters made just two visits to the NCAA finals, winning the championship in 1942.

But aren't women simply easier to coach? That's the contention of some pundits. "Men have this macho thing going on," says Teresa Edwards, the veteran guard who played in her fourth Olympics in 1996. "Women have a much better comfort zone with each other than men do." Perhaps the stepchild status that still confronts women's sports may contribute to team unity. Vince Goo, who coaches the University of Hawaii's successful women's basketball program, thinks the idea makes sense. "Women *are* more coachable than men," he argues. "They're more open and more receptive to teaching and criticism."

Women's sports, at this stage in its evolution, is usually under less pressure to generate significant revenues. As a result, the pressure to win year after year may be less. "Women's athletics aren't quite like men's programs," says Candace Putnam, a sportswriter for the *San Jose Mercury News.* "If a coach has a losing season, they're not immediately shown the door." However, on The Farm, as Stanford is known, fans take their hoops seriously.

Stanford's legendary Tara VanDerveer developed her basketball talents on her next-door neighbor's driveway. They had a hoop; she had a ball. When there was no girls' basketball program at her junior high school in upstate New York, she volunteered to be the school mascot so she could get in the gym and watch the boys practice. Later she perfected her skills at Indiana University, where she was a starting guard for three years. But even as a player, it was the X's and O's of the game that fascinated her, VanDerveer admits. After two years of graduate school at Ohio State, she accepted a position at the University of Idaho, one of the country's first full-time head coaching opportunities in women's basketball. She compiled a 42–14 record there, then led Ohio State to a five-season, 110–37 mark. In 1986 VanDerveer began her successful reign in Palo Alto.

During her first decade on The Farm, she led the Lady Cardinal to two NCAA championships (1990 and 1992), four Final Four appearances (1990–1992, 1995), eight NCAA tournaments (1988–

1995) and six Pacific-10 Conference titles (1989–1993, 1995). In the process, she compiled a 251–62 career record at Stanford and served as mentor to six previous USA Basketball teams. It was this incredible string of victories that prompted her selection as coach of the USA National Team. Understandably Coach VanDerveer found it difficult to walk away from Stanford, even temporarily. "An agonizing decision," she called it. However, with the university's full support, she took a one-year sabbatical to accept the challenge of leading the Red, White, and Blue. She would do everything possible to guide Team USA to Olympic gold in Atlanta.

No one was better qualified to replace the highly respected coach than Amy Tucker, her loyal assistant and co-leader. For 3 seasons at Ohio State and 10 at Stanford, the last 5 as associate head coach, Tucker had displayed her extraordinary gifts as a recruiter. Her crops of incoming student-athletes were consistently ranked in the nation's top echelon. Besides being regarded as one of the country's best recruiters, Tucker was respected as an excellent floor coach with an outstanding technical mind. Therefore, VanDerveer felt comfortable relinquishing temporary control of the Cardinal program to her talented junior partner.

"Amy and I have been coaching together for a long time," VanDerveer said when Tucker's interim appointment was announced. "She knows my style and knows what I want. By the same token, she'll be able to impart her own way of doing things. . . . She knows our team not only in terms of personnel, but in terms of personality. . . . [Amy] will be as dedicated as any in continuing the strong commitment here at Stanford. . . . I'm very confident that she'll do a great job."

Creating a Winning Team

The daughter of a career Air Force officer, Amy Tucker was a basketball phenom in Springboro, Ohio, south of Dayton. As a high school senior, she set scoring records in the state championship and attracted the attention of several big-time programs, including Texas, Tennessee, and Louisiana Tech. But when Woody Hayes, the legendary football coach, made a personal pitch for Ohio State, Tucker knew she wanted to be a Buckeye. She went on to lead her OSU squad in scoring for two seasons, finishing as the school's second all-time leading scorer. She also established a Buckeye career record for games played with 123. Tucker played forward for VanDerveer in 1981– 1982, then served as a graduate assistant and assistant coach under her. When VanDerveer accepted the Stanford position, Tucker decided to follow.

During their 10-year relationship in Palo Alto, Tucker toiled tirelessly but ceded the spotlight to her longtime mentor. Tucker's ability to thrive in another's shadow made her a classic co-leader in the Bill Guthridge mold. But VanDerveer's one-year absence from The Farm gave Tucker what she described as "the opportunity of a lifetime."

The 1995–1996 season was Amy Tucker's year of living dangerously. With the Final Four stalwarts of the previous season graduated, she had to wonder if she could continue the Lady Cardinal legacy. Cynics asked if this was the end of Stanford's national prominence in women's hoops. In the press and elsewhere, Tucker's mostly untested Cardinal team was being cast in the unaccustomed role of underdog instead of the frontrunner. In fact most observers picked either Washington or Oregon State to unseat Stanford for the Pac-10 title.

"I definitely felt a lot of pressure going in, because of the personnel losses we had [four key players as well as VanDerveer] and the high expectations of the program," Tucker admitted. "I thought it was possible we'd win 22 or 23 games. I knew we could get to the 'Sweet 16' [the 16 best teams in the country] and probably be in a regional final, but I wasn't looking past that."

Indeed Tucker confronted her most serious challenge not on the court but in the arena of campus politics. Her appointment triggered a major brouhaha on campus. Two other Stanford assistants, Julie Plank—who reportedly believed she should have gotten the job— and Carolyn Jenkins, quit in protest. Tucker suddenly had a worrisome lack of bench strength in her coaching staff. With Stanford women's basketball now down three coaches, she needed bodies— fast. Counseled by VanDerveer, the athletic department decided that two heads would be better than one and hired Marianne Stanley on an interim basis to co-coach the Lady Cardinal with Tucker.

Many in the basketball world wondered whether the unique arrangement would work. Some thought the joint venture between Tucker, a quiet Ohioan, and Stanley, an outgoing Philadelphian, was destined to fail.

Tucker has long been known as an outstanding judge of talent, the prime mover in recruiting most of the team's exceptional athletes. But her manner is shy, and, at times, she is muted almost to the point of invisibility. Skeptics wondered whether she would be tough enough not only to replace the high-profile, sometimes high-volume, VanDerveer but also to temper the equally demanding Stanley. Tucker, whose 13-year coaching career had been spent as VanDerveer's Silent Assistant, as she was called, might be in over her head. The talented Stanley had been a highly successful head coach for 16 years—at Old Dominion (one NCAA and two AIAW national titles), Pennsylvania, and the University of Southern California. She had earned four conference Coach of the Year honors. She won national Coach of the Year kudos in 1979 and had coached 10 different U.S. teams in international competition.

There was another complication. Marianne Stanley had been out of coaching for two years. In 1993 she was fired by USC after filing a multimillion-dollar sex discrimination lawsuit against the school over a salary imbalance with the men's coach. (Later the suit was dismissed twice in federal court.) After leaving USC, she floundered. Nobody would hire her. Stanley estimates that she applied for more than 100 coaching jobs. "Men's and women's, Divisions I, II, and III," she says. Stanley received a few interviews, but no offers. She was untouchable. To make ends meet, Stanley did whatever she could: stripping furniture, cataloging books, and, with VanDerveer's help, promoting Lady Cardinal basketball.

Nevertheless, Stanford made the courageous hire. The university decided that bringing such an experienced coach on board would do more than just rehabilitate Stanley's career. Her formidable presence offered the best prospects for a winning season and—maybe, just maybe—another trip to the NCAA finals.

"It made sense in this situation because both Amy and Marianne had worked with Tara," Cheryl Levick, Stanford's associate athletic director, recalls. "Amy's strength was knowing Tara's coaching strategy, the athletes knew her and she knew the Stanford system. Marianne brought in head-coaching leadership."

Co–head coach Stanley, for her part, saw the Cardinal opportunity as the road to redemption. "It's a high-profile situation that I can't wait to tackle," she said. "I realize this is a temporary position for me. . . . Perhaps afterward I can go on to a similar situation of my own." As for the new alliance with Tucker, Stanley said: "I'm looking forward to working with Amy Tucker. I have great respect for her ability as a coach, [and] I think we'll work very well together this season at Stanford."

To be sure the university fully appreciated the pitfalls of job sharing. But, in fact, the unusual compact was not a truly dual leadership assignment. At Levick's insistence, Tucker was the undisputed No. 1. However, given Stanley's record of accomplishment, she was designated co–head coach instead of an assistant. During the season, Tucker ran the team and reported directly to Levick. "I call the time-outs, I talk in the huddles," Amy said at the time. "I'd been at Stanford for 11 years, so I have a good idea of how we do things. . . . I know what Tara wants." Stanley scouted Cardinal opponents, coached perimeter players, and, when asked, counseled Tucker.

Stanford's co-leadership team worked, albeit slowly. With three seniors gone from the previous year's Final Four squad, Tucker and Stanley began to rebuild their team around 10 talented, but unproven underclasswomen. One thing was clear: The interim co-coaches were not about to tinker with VanDerveer's winning formula. The playbook would pretty much stay the same. "To try to put my stamp on [the program] would have been foolish," Tucker said. "The system has worked."

In preseason practice the challenges of orchestrating new players and new coaches took its toll. Unlike the high-volume VanDerveer, Tucker is much more low-key. From the get-go she had to establish a firmer coaching voice. "When I have something to say, people know they need to be quiet," Tucker said. "I've had to become tougher on people. Anytime you're in charge of playing time you have a different relationship with the players. You're not buddy-buddy anymore."

Stanley observed her co-leader's metamorphosis. "Amy wasn't timid about stepping up, and she's put her own style—her own stamp—on what it is to be the head coach at Stanford," Stanley told Dick Rockne of the *Seattle Times*. "I think it's been a real learning experience for the players—a good one. I think they've come to appreciate that, even though she has been seen in the past as a recruiter and second fiddle, that she is a very competent strategist."

Having experienced both, Tucker was struck by the dramatic difference between being No. 1 and being No. 2. "Although I'd watched

Tara for many years, being a head coach is something you really can't prepare yourself for. As the No. 1, you must always be on. On the court, off the court, everywhere—you're constantly under a microscope. Assistants simply don't have that level of responsibility."

Tucker was surprised how much the top job demanded of her. "It's been a huge adjustment. Sometimes I miss my old job but I know I'll eventually be getting it back. . . . Before, I never felt responsible for how someone played on the floor. Now I do. I feel totally accountable about how our team plays every game, even how they practice."

As the season started, the adrenaline rushed a little faster than usual around Palo Alto. At first blush, the naysayers seemed right. The Lady Cardinal opened its year on a November afternoon in Amherst, Massachusetts, with a devastating loss: unranked University of Massachusetts 65, eighth-ranked Stanford 56.

"You could just see the wheels coming off the cart really quickly," VanDerveer explained to reporter Rockne. "It was really hard to see them lose. It was painful to see someone else take over something you've worked so hard at." The Stanford hoopsters could easily have collapsed—using VanDerveer's absence as an excuse for losing. Instead the Cardinal team regrouped after some soul-searching up and down the ranks.

Two days after the UMass loss, Stanford held Providence scoreless for the first 10 minutes of the second half in an 81–58 victory. "That was a defining time for this team," VanDerveer told the *Charlotte Observer*. "They had to accept the challenge, not just blow it off and say Tara's gone and we've had this coaching change. The team had plenty of excuses. To its credit, it didn't use any of them."

For Amy Tucker the team's breakthrough came three weeks later with its blowout victory, 90–72, over top-ranked Tennessee at jam-packed Maples Pavilion. "That game gave our squad a lot of confidence and our fans a lot of confidence," she says. "We knew: 'Hey, we're going to be all right. We're going to make it through the season without Tara.' "

As the season wore on, the Lady Cardinal lost just two games (the other, 71–65 at Texas Tech). Players seemed to develop a special bond that some of their predecessors did not have, while showing the grit and determination that is a hallmark of Lady Cardinal basketball.

Unlike VanDerveer and Stanley, who are louder and tougher, Tucker is a mellow leader. Her openness and velvet glove soon won the respect of Stanford players.

"We wondered how it would be under Amy," junior guard Jamila Wideman said at the time, "but she brings a lot of special qualities to the position. She has been able to maintain a lot of what she brought up as an assistant. She's someone we can trust. From the beginning, she kept the lines of communication open with the players."

Putting her own imprint on the tried-and-true VanDerveer system, Tucker allowed the Cardinal to run more, taking advantage of the open-court skills of Wideman and All-American forward Kate Starbird. The looser, more spontaneous squad silenced the doubters by finishing the Pac-10 season undefeated and winning the conference crown. Stanford then gained admission to the Final Four, the quartet of best women's basketball teams in the country, for the fifth time in the 1990s. Although the Lady Cardinal lost to Georgia, the eventual runner-up to Tennessee, the dynasty of Stanford's women remained intact.

And the Winner Is . . .

The Lady Cardinal's remarkable accomplishments in 1995–1996 resulted in a win-win-win situation for all three coaches. When Marianne Stanley's contract expired in April 1996, the University of California at Berkeley tapped the clever, but controversial coach to oversee its women's basketball program. Cal is normally loath to follow Stanford in anything. But the Bears' dismal 7–20 season and dwindling attendance (an average of 961 fans a game) prompted the change of heart.

Stanley claims that her brief respite as a Cardinal "allowed [me] to be a second banana and gain a unique perspective of the challenges of being next-in-command." A head coach at age 23, she had leapfrogged the traditional career ladder—graduate assistant, assistant coach, associate head coach. Her Stanford stint, she believes, has made her a better coach at Cal.

For Tara VanDerveer it was a tremendously challenging hiatus. Gold medal. Gold medal. Gold medal. That was the mantra USA Basketball officials kept repeating as they tried to convince themselves that America's women hoopsters could regain Olympic gold. They made it crystal clear that anything less would be unacceptable. "It was explained to me by C. M. Newton, who is president of USA Basketball, that this is not about bronze, this is not about silver, this is about gold," VanDerveer recalls.

From day one she took her new responsibilities seriously. "I am extremely focused on doing the very best job I can for this team," she said at the time. "When you are representing your country, it is not something you want to mess up." Everybody wants to win, but America's women had extra incentive. The U.S. team had finished a disappointing third in the 1992 Barcelona Olympics. Since the '96 Games would be on American soil, U.S. coaches and players were especially loath to disappoint the fans.

With the weight of titanic expectations on her shoulders, VanDerveer gathered her players together at the U.S. Olympic Training Center in Colorado Springs. The initial workouts were brutal: two-mile runs in thin air, at 30 degrees, with sharp winds cutting through their skimpy gear. Next came body-banging scrimmages, weightlifting, and more running. But boot camp, VanDerveer-style, solidified the squad. She then took her hardened hoopsters on 14 months of global barnstorming. After 51 games and a physically and emotionally exhausting tour that covered more than 10,000 miles—from Siberia to the Great Barrier Reef, VanDerveer's players arrived in Atlanta undefeated. Before a prime-time television audience and a raucous crowd of nearly 33,000, perhaps the best women's team the United States has put on an Olympic court soundly defeated Brazil 111–87 to win its first gold medal since the 1988 Games. "They took care of business," VanDerveer said.

Indisputably the history-making team propelled U.S. women's basketball to new levels of popularity. Many considered the American girls of summer to be the real Dream Team. They were a sister act worth standing in line for.

Despite her Olympic responsibilities, VanDerveer was never far away from Stanford in spirit. She attended a dozen Cardinal games during the course of the year and became known as the Distant Assistant. As the season progressed, she had to cut the umbilical cord. "I'm not like a parent now," she said. "I'm not spanking them." I don't have to be critical. I just pat them on the backs and say, 'Hey, that's great. Keep it up.' "

During her year-long absence, VanDerveer discovered an array of fresh challenges beyond Stanford, including the prospect of coaching in two fledgling women's professional leagues. "This year has opened up a whole different world of basketball to me," she said. "Now I see there are a lot of options, and I will look at things in the future a different way."

Coaching the USA National Team also afforded her large blocks of unstructured time, a rarity in college sports. With her newfound freedom, VanDerveer became a fitness fanatic, religiously working out daily. "I'm in the best shape I've ever been in my life," she announced. Back at Stanford, she would have to make time for student-related issues. Tougher yet, she would have to find a way to return gracefully to a program, which, in her absence, went unbeaten in the Pac-10 and reached the coveted Final Four.

Her reaction to the team's success? "I'm ecstatic," she said. "I'm so proud of them and really proud of the job Amy Tucker did. She's one of the best coaches in collegiate basketball. It's obvious there are different ways to do things. Amy didn't try to be me. She was herself. Next year, I can only be myself. It's a win–win situation."

So on Monday, August 5, 1996, it was back to work—parenting once again. The gold medal safely secured, VanDerveer returned to The Farm, stepping back into the job that Tucker had done so ably with Stanley at her side. "If it wasn't such a special place, if it wasn't something I really loved, I think it would be very hard [to return]," VanDerveer said. "It would be like, 'What could there be after this?'"

Winning creates its own complications. Perhaps the returning head coach would have the biggest adjustment of the new season. In 1995 the team definitely warmed up to low-key Tucker's open, unobtrusive style. The flinty, disciplined VanDerveer would have to regain her players' trust and confidence. Could she put Olympic glory behind her and rekindle the glow of the Cardinal's winning tradition?

"It's likely," predicted Dwight Chapin of the *San Francisco Examiner,* "she'll approach her return to Stanford the same way [she arrived], slowly and carefully re-establishing her relationships with her team and staff. And she'll be faced with a whole new set of expectations." Clearly the athletic department did not contemplate any reentry problems. "It will be a quick adjustment, maybe a week," women's athletic director Levick reckoned. "Tara will be a little stricter than

Amy was. The athletes will know the heat's been turned up. But I really don't anticipate a big transition problem."

In any case VanDerveer was prepared for the challenge. "Think of next year—they went undefeated in the Pac-10," she said. "Coming off of that, let alone a national championship, is very tough. It's a lot of work. You have to be realistic. It is a lot easier to build a program than maintain it."

Amy Tucker, too, has had to adjust. "It was really a strange year for everybody—the transition—it was a funny feeling," she recalls. "But it went as well or better than anyone expected. I think no one enjoyed our success more than Tara."

Tucker, for her part, saw her stock soar as a head coaching candidate. After the '95 season, she was named UPI national Co-Coach of the Year (with Stanley) and Pac-10 Conference Co-Coach of the Year (also with Stanley). She was one of five finalists for the Naismith national Coach of the Year award. Any program prowling for a new head coach was bound to consider the Silent Assistant.

"I'm not looking for a job," Tucker said. "But I'd certainly talk to people if they're interested. If it happens, it happens. But I'm very happy at Stanford."

Aware that Tucker was being wooed, the Cardinal top brass signed her in the spring of 1996 to a lucrative three-year contract to remain as associate head coach. "Stanford has been my home for the past 11 years, and I would find it very hard to leave. Once you work at Stanford, once you work at the top even as an assistant, it's hard to have something of your own at the bottom," she said. "I've often told people how I feel that Tara VanDerveer has the best job in the country. But at the same time, I feel I've got the second best. Being associated with this program and its great players and working with Tara is so much better than having my own [head coaching] job."

Stanford's Special Appeal

For Amy Tucker the lure of Northern California and one of the world's great universities is a major factor in her willingness to return to assistant coaching. At the hub of the vital and diverse Bay Area, Stanford sits an hour's drive south of San Francisco and just north of Silicon Valley, an area dotted with computer and high-technology firms largely spawned by the university's faculty and graduates. Students and scholars enjoy one of the most beautiful academic settings in the country. The Farm covers 8,180 acres (almost 13 square miles) of grassy fields, eucalyptus groves, and rolling hills that were the generous legacy of Leland and Jane Stanford more than 100 years ago.

By any measure, Stanford's faculty, which numbers approximately 1,300, is one of the most distinguished in the world. At last count, it includes 12 Nobel Laureates, six Pulitzer Prize winners, 15 MacArthur ("genius") Fellows, 19 National Medal of Science winners, and 92 members of the National Academy of Sciences. As triumphant as Van-Derveer's return was, it was dwarfed by the enormous excitement that gripped the campus at the same time when Stanford researchers, in collaboration with NASA scientists, discovered evidence that life existed on Mars more than 3.6 billion years ago.

Like the faculty, the Cardinal student body represents the best and the brightest. Approximately eight students applied to Stanford for every place in the 1997–1998 freshman class, which included First Daughter Chelsea Clinton. Nearly 90 percent of graduating seniors attend graduate or professional schools. The university is also an athletic powerhouse. Stanford has won 53 NCAA team championships and 197 individual NCAA titles since 1980, the most in the nation. In the 1996 Olympics, its athletes earned 16 gold medals, 1 silver, and 1 bronze.

Unlike most Division I schools, Stanford refuses to compromise its academic standards for incoming athletes. Recently entering women basketball players had a 3.68 composite grade point average, with SAT scores just under 1100. Fewer than a dozen high school prospects qualify academically and athletically each year. The team's graduation rate approached 90 percent. By every indicator, Cardinal coaches in all sports are blessed with a pool of extremely bright and talented young men and women.

"Our players are not your normal student-athletes." Tucker boasts. "They're very special. They come to Stanford well prepared. They're high-achievers. So there is absolutely no baby-sitting around here."

Some of her peers jealously contend that Tucker may be "too cozy" at Stanford. In truth, the same could be said of almost anyone associated with this extraordinary institution. Business School Professor George Parker explains the reluctance of "almost any sane person" to leave The Farm. "First, there's the image factor, the reputational dimension," he says. "Anybody who's part of the Stanford scene takes enormous pride in being part of a great and prestigious university. For most of us, anyplace else would be a step backward. Second, there's the reality. Stanford is, in fact, populated with truly exceptional people at all levels: students, faculty, administrators, coaches—you name it. Finally, there's geography. To leave the Bay Area—its weather, physical beauty, economic, and cultural vitality—would be gut wrenching for lots and lots of people. Taken together, these factors make dyed-in-the-wool Stanford-types deeply rooted to the place."

Amy Tucker cherishes those roots. She appreciates the Stanford mystique. Anything but immobile, she could have almost any coaching job in the country. But it would take a rare opportunity indeed for her to abandon Palo Alto. "I can't see Amy stepping down and coaching a different style of kid," says associate athletic director Levick. "She strongly believes in the Stanford model and the kind of kids we bring in. She loves and works well with the athlete who is highly driven, strong academically and strong athletically."

If and when Tucker packs her bags, it most likely will be for the handful of universities with comparable academic standards and an equally strong commitment to gender equity in sports. Speaking realistically, few schools meet these criteria. "Let's face it," Cal's Marianne Stanley says. "Stanford University is one of a relatively few model [women's] programs in the country. Being second-in-command there is certainly much more rewarding than being top banana at 75 percent of the other schools."

"In America's culture, we're taught to be top bananas," she adds. "But lots of people can find great joy and comfort in the No. 2 role. When you find a special niche and you enjoy it, why change? I think Amy Tucker may very well find that she's better suited and happier in that role. In any case, she's extremely well respected. She's probably had as much of an impact on Stanford women's basketball as anyone."

As the 1996–1997 season began, Tucker soldiered on—happily—on The Farm. She was probably the only basketball coach who took a team to the Final Four one season and then wound up an assistant coach the next season.

To no one's great surprise, the reunited tandem of VanDerveer and Tucker produced another gaudy record (33–2). The Lady Cardinal finished third nationally behind Tennessee and Old Dominion University. Fighting Olympic year burnout, her father's cancer, her mother's broken leg, and a slew of team injuries, VanDerveer turned in one of her best coaching performances and, like Tucker the year before, was named the Pac-10 Conference Coach of the Year. In March 1997 she quashed rumors that she would be leaving The Farm to coach in the professional leagues—inking a three-year contract with a two-year option to renew. "I have always thought it's a real privilege to work at Stanford," she said at the time.

With her Cinderella year over, Amy Tucker had to scoot down the Cardinal bench. How did she readjust to being No. 2? "Initially, it was maybe a little harder than I expected," she admits. "But I was prepared for it." No doubt her healthy ego and strong sense of self helped. As for her working relationship with VanDerveer, co-leader Tucker said it has never been better. "I think the off-year made us both better coaches and, on balance, a better staff."

For the time being, Tucker's hoop dreams remain confined to The Farm. Since 1996 she has spurned several head coaching offers at other universities, including her alma mater, Ohio State. Her next move, she predicts, will probably be "to the next level, to professional basketball. We'll just have to wait and see." Some day the allure of again being head coach may cause a change of heart. For now Tucker's happy doing work she loves in tandem with a great team and a partner she respects.

12

Dr. Watson and Sherlock Holmes

Fiction's Most Famous Pair

Crime Fighters: The classic team of Dr. Watson (left; Nigel Bruce) and Sherlock Holmes (Basil Rathbone). (Springer/Corbis-Bettmann)

12 | Dr. Watson and Sherlock Holmes

*What should I call the fellow? First it was
Sherringford Holmes, then it was Sherlock
Holmes. He could not tell his own exploits,
so he must have a commonplace comrade
as a foil . . . a drab, quiet name for this
unostentatious man. Watson would do.*

—SIR ARTHUR CONAN DOYLE

"Which of you is Holmes?" the desperate visitor asked. "I am Sherlock Holmes, and this is my friend and colleague, Dr. Watson." So
begins another introduction of one of the great partnerships in crime
fiction. The tall, thin, angular detective and his short, rotund companion are two of the most vivid characters in English literature. In the
tradition of James Boswell and Dr. Samuel Johnson, Mr. Pickwick and
Sam Weller, Sancho Panza and Don Quixote, Sir Arthur Conan
Doyle's immortal pair are contrasts in everything but their utter com-
patibility.

After a century, the brilliant investigator and his good-hearted aide
continue to enjoy an uncanny life beyond the printed page. The Baker
Street Irregulars in New York, the London-based Sherlock Holmes
Society, and the Japan Sherlock Holmes Club pursue Holmesiana
with a cultist fervor. Similar groups exist on every continent.

The figure in the deerstalker cap and the Inverness cape, smoking
a meerschaum pipe, and repeating "Elementary, my dear Watson," is
familiar to us all. Unfortunately his co-hero Watson was ill served in
subsequent movie, television, and radio versions, which portrayed
Watson as a blustery buffoon. "The fuddy-duddy of them all," one

critic said of these foolish versions of Watson. But Sir Arthur knew full well that his tales depended on creating a credible relationship between those two diverse, yet complementary characters. Doyle, a doctor-turned-writer like Watson, insisted there could be no Sherlock Holmes without a serious and coequal Dr. Watson. The complex symbiotic relationship between the fictional men is largely responsible for the thrillers' remarkable durability. And through his tantalizing fiction, Doyle not only achieved literary greatness, he also offered important insights into co-leadership that apply to real life as well.

Fiction or Prescriptions

Arthur Conan Doyle was born in Edinburgh on May 22, 1859, the son of Irish Catholics who had immigrated to Protestant Scotland. At his mother's urging, he entered the University of Edinburgh in 1876 to study medicine. In 1879 his first story, "The Mystery of the Sasassa Valley," was published in *Chambers Journal*, and the struggling medical student "first learned that shillings might be earned in other ways than by filling phials."

While at university, Doyle met a tall, hawk-nosed teacher named Dr. Joseph Bell. The self-effacing surgeon had incredible diagnostic powers that mesmerized Doyle and the other students. Later Doyle would appropriate Bell's scalpel-sharp mind and uncanny intuitive flair for Sherlock Holmes.

"In one of his best cases," Doyle recalled, "Dr. Bell said to a civilian patient:
'Well, my man, you've served in the army.'
'Aye, Sir.'
'Not long discharged?'
'No, Sir.'
'A Highland regiment?'
'Aye, Sir.'
'A non-commissioned officer.'
'Aye, Sir.'
'stationed at Barbados.'
'Aye, Sir.'
'You see, gentlemen,' [Bell explained], 'the man was a respectful man but did not remove his hat. They do not in the army, but he

would have learned civilian ways had he been long discharged. He has an air of authority and he is obviously Scottish. As to Barbados, his complaint is elephantiasis, which is West Indian and not British.' "

An inveterate note-taker, Doyle studied and recorded in minute detail Bell's numerous examples of diagnosis and reasoning. Some years later Doyle confessed to his former teacher: "It is to you that I owe Sherlock Holmes."

In 1882 Dr. Doyle opened a medical practice in Southsea, a suburb of Portsmouth, England. It was not a success. The most the young physician ever earned was a piddling £300 a year. Ironically the long intervals between patients gave him the opportunity to pursue his literary interests. In no time he was writing more fiction than prescriptions.

As his literary skills matured, Doyle decided to write a serious thriller. An insatiable reader, he greatly admired the pioneering detective fiction of Edgar Allan Poe, especially his master sleuth, Monsieur Dupin. Using Poe's "The Gold Bug" and "The Murders in the Rue Morgue" as models, Doyle set out to create his own cerebral detective hero—a man whose intelligence was so superior that he could solve mysteries of such profundity that ordinary men thought them supernatural. Doyle's former mentor, Dr. Bell, seemed the perfect model. "I thought of my old teacher, Joe Bell, of his eagle face, of his curious ways, of his eerie trick of spotting details," Doyle recalled. "If he were a detective, he would surely reduce this fascinating but unorganized business to something nearer an exact science. I would try [to] get this effect."

Doyle decided to surround his uncannily perceptive sleuth with solid English men and women typical of the mid-Victorian period—from Scotland Yard bobbies to cabdrivers and wenches, from middle-class businessmen and shopkeepers to haughty aristocrats. Instead of using initials to identify his characters as Poe often did, Doyle gave them names, often combinations of actual names of people he knew. He dubbed his detective Sherlock Holmes.

Mindful of Don Quixote's companion, Sancho Panza, Doyle wanted a sidekick and foil for Sherlock Holmes, "a commonplace comrade . . . an educated man of action who could both join in the exploits and narrate them." The narrator would be a doctor like Doyle himself. He would also be the person through whom the average reader could see a superman working and yet remain comfortable. Unlike Holmes, but like the rest of us, Watson could see a clue and yet miss its meaning. Originally Doyle called Holmes's partner Ormond Sacker, but he finally settled on John H. Watson, M.D. "And so I had my puppets," the writer recalled.

With his inspired duo in place, Doyle began outlining *A Study in Scarlet,* the first of 60 tales featuring the world's most celebrated detective and his faithful friend. Doyle wrote in the tiny study at the top of his somewhat shabby house. Occasionally patients found their way to his door, and breathless messengers summoned him to make an emergency house call. But such interruptions were rare. Doyle had remarkable powers of concentration and could put pen to paper anywhere and under any circumstance. He churned short stories out in a few days; books in a matter of weeks. His high-velocity writing was grounded in copious research, including unfaltering attention to detail. His swiftness may also have resulted from his customary method of working backwards from the solution. The Conan Doyle formula always began with the outcome of the crime first; then he developed the remainder of the story, always working artfully to conceal the explanation from his readers until the last pages.

Sherlock Holmes's popularity was boosted in 1891 with the appearance of a six-story series in *The Strand.* The magazine's circulation soared to a half million, and Doyle suddenly didn't have to practice medicine any more. Now well-heeled, Doyle was seized by the ambition that develops so often in best-selling authors. He wanted to abandon thrillers for serious literature. Weary of publishers' deadlines and cranking out mysteries, which he regarded as "a lower stratum of literary achievement," Doyle decided to get rid of his now legendary detective once and for all.

In "The Adventure of the Final Problem," Doyle encounters Professor James Moriarty, "the Napoleon of crime," whom the Great Sleuth describes as "the organizer of half that is evil and of nearly all that is undetected in this great city." The plot takes the archrivals to Switzerland where the evil Moriarty apparently throws Holmes over the 300-foot-high Reichenbach Falls.

Doyle was out of the country when "The Final Problem" appeared in *The Strand.* It soon became clear that the public was not ready to let Holmes die. More than 20,000 readers canceled their subscriptions to *The Strand*. Some fans were so dismayed they wore black mourning bands. Others sent Doyle hate mail, including one woman whose indignant letter began, "You brute!" In his autobiography the author writes: "I was amazed at the concern expressed by the public. They say that a man is never properly appreciated until he is dead, and the general protest against my summary execution of Holmes taught me how many and how numerous were his friends."

Back from the Dead

Doyle had little choice but to resurrect Holmes. He wrote 20 more adventures featuring Holmes and Watson over the next 22 years. In 1927 Doyle penned his last Holmes tale, "The Adventures of Shoscombe Old Place." He wrote in many genres, from mysteries to historical novels to science fiction to ballads. But the tales featuring Holmes and Watson are his enduring legacy. Sherlock Holmes paved the way for generations of eccentric crime busters, including Agatha Christie's Hercule Poirot, Dorothy L. Sayer's Lord Peter Wimsey, Earl Derr Bigger's Charlie Chan, Erle Stanley Gardner's Perry Mason, and Raymond Chandler's Philip Marlowe. In no small part because of Doyle, suspense became one of the most popular genres in history.

One of the things mystery fiction does superbly is to reflect society at a given moment. Doyle was incomparable in recreating Victorian England. His vivid portrayal of late nineteenth-century London—foggy nights, gas lamps, and hansom cabs—transports readers to a well-ordered world where, in the words of one writer, "it is always 1895." Another observer wrote: "[Doyle] got his dialogue marvelously right, swiftly economical without any feeling of thinness or austerity, illuminating character in a hundred tiny touches." Doyle was also a master of narrative, telling his readers what they needed to know just when they needed to know it. And Doyle understood, as few writers have, the power of a good story. No matter how fast one gallops through a Sherlock Holmes whodunit, one reads the last chapter at a crawl, hoping it will never end.

In 40 years of writing fiction, Doyle created more than 800 characters. He had a genius for hitting on just the right name (think of Dr. Grimesby Roylott, Bartholomew Sholto, "Holy" Peters, and Charles Augustus Milverton, as well as Holmes and Watson). And he understood that mystery fans love to see their characters develop and grow in a series of stories or novels, a truth demonstrated again and again on modern best-seller lists.

Dr. Watson is as credible a character as Holmes is fantastic. Obviously one of Watson's functions is to forge a link between the mundane reality of the reader and the esoteric skills and bizarre habits of Sherlock Holmes. Doyle made Watson so believable that a large segment of the public actually thought he was the author of the Holmes stories. In Holmes and Watson, Doyle believed he invented the "series character." In his view recurrent characters were a labor-saving device for readers. They allowed his audiences to devote their full attention to unraveling the puzzle at the story's heart.

The Two Doyles

Like Dr. Jekyll and Mr. Hyde, Dr. Watson and Sherlock Holmes are really different aspects of the same person—namely Arthur Conan Doyle. "I am afraid that in my own personality, I rather represent . . . Dr. Watson," Doyle readily admitted. "But the psychologists tell us that we really are very multiplex people; that we are like a bundle of faggots, or rather a rope with many strands, and that sometimes in the most commonplace rope there may be one single strand which, if you only isolate it, produces unexpected effects. There may [also] be represented in my being some strand of Sherlock."

Both characters were projections of the author, who demonstrated multiple personalities: a born poet who studied and practiced medicine, a patriot who frequently criticized his government, an optimist prone to bouts of depression, a rational man who favored spiritualism. "Containing within himself both Sherlock Holmes and Dr. Watson, he was gifted with the double vision that pervades his fiction," write biographers George Grella and Philip Dematteis.

As Doyle himself noted, there are many obvious parallels between Drs. Doyle and Watson. Both were outdoorsmen and "as brown as a nut." Both played billiards and rugby expertly. Both men loved dogs, and each kept a bull pup. Both enjoyed sea stories and were only casual in their practice of medicine. They were practical and sensible, outwardly genial, and in touch with everyday England. Both men were courageous, but overly romantic and somewhat gullible. Like

Doyle, Watson was patriotic, faithful to his friends and to his wife. Modest and self-effacing, both men were headstrong and capable of being rash.

The resemblances between Doyle and Holmes are equally clear. Giants in their respective fields, both men had enormous presence as well as human failings, including vanity and various prejudices. Both men liked boxing and Turkish baths, were chivalrous toward women, practiced mysticism, liked to wear disguises, were indifferent to untidy surroundings, read voraciously, were formidably intelligent, and cared little about money. Both Doyle and Holmes liked to work in solitude, in old dressing gowns. Both engaged in chemistry experiments, smoked pipes incessantly, and compiled voluminous scrapbooks. They shared the same banker, and each kept a magnifying glass on his desk and, in a drawer, a revolver. Each was a brilliant amateur criminologist who influenced subsequent generations of police officers. And in 1902 both were offered knighthoods: Holmes declined, Doyle reluctantly accepted.

Amazingly Doyle apparently matched Holmes in powers of diagnosis and reasoning. Doyle's son Adrian reported that his father could sit in a café and determine from the hats, coats, shoes, umbrellas, and walking sticks of those who came in virtually their whole life stories. Lady Conan Doyle corroborated this assessment: "The public does not realise that my husband had the Sherlock Holmes brain, and that sometimes he privately . . . was able, through his remarkable powers of deduction and inference, to locate missing people whose relatives had given them up as lost or murdered."

Doyle conceived Holmes and Watson as very different halves of a successful whole—in short, as classic co-leaders. The down-to-earth Dr. Watson was the perfect counterpoint and complement to the sometimes dominating genius of Sherlock Holmes. "Watson is predictable, where Holmes is unconventional," writes Don Richards Cox. "Holmes is cerebral, where Watson is physical; Watson is disciplined, while Holmes indulges his many whims." Watson exudes humanity, while Holmes is as coldly logical and above the tug of human emotions as *Star Trek*'s Mr. Spock. Each brings different assets to their partnership, allowing both to succeed where one might fail, not unlike such real-life co-leaders as Intel's brilliant but prickly Andy Grove and less volatile but no less talented Craig Barrett.

Mutual respect—one of the hallmarks of genuine co-leadership—
is key to the bond between Holmes and Watson. "For this to succeed,
Watson has to be a person one can visualise sharing lodgings with
Holmes over many years," literary historian Michael Pointer points
out. "He must be able to tolerate Holmes, with all his idiosyncrasies,
and *be* tolerable to Holmes." It is hard to imagine Holmes putting up
for one minute with the Watson played by Nigel Bruce—a pretentious ninny—in the movie and TV series starring Basil Rathbone.

Through the Watson of Doyle's tales, Sherlock Holmes is revealed
as something more than a heartless genius. Watson points out the
chinks in Holmes's character—his vanity, his indulgence in cocaine,
his complete contempt for fools. But in an almost parental way, Watson soft-pedals his partner's less attractive features. Doyle gives Watson
a difficult role to play. He must make us like the Great Sleuth—clearly
no easy task.

"Except yourself, I have none," Holmes says to his Baker Street
buddy. In fact several Sherlockian actors despised the prissy detective.
"I came to the conclusion . . . that there was nothing lovable about
Holmes," Basil Rathbone remarked. William Gillette, the first to play
Holmes on stage, lamented: "I want to make money on Holmes
quick, so as to be through with it!" Another actor termed the detec-
tive "an insufferable prig." Even Doyle admitted disliking Holmes.
But the author was clearly fond of Holmes's friend and colleague. In
"The Abbey Grange," Holmes decides to let the villain off, saying:
"Watson, you are a British jury, and I never met a man who was more
eminently fitted to represent one"—high praise for a loyal lieutenant
that reflects Doyle's own patriotism.

As the counterweight to the master detective, dependable, trustworthy Watson connects the razor-sharp Holmes to the ordinary
world, repeatedly calling attention to the human needs of the characters. "The incarnation of the *vox populi*," one reviewer called Watson.
As any dedicated co-leader would, Watson also expressed concerns
over his partner's health, indignantly reminding him of the evils of
cocaine. "Count the cost!" he warned Holmes. "Remember that I
speak not only as one comrade to another but as a medical man to
one for whose constitution he is to some extent answerable."

Watson also serves as a useful sounding board in the course of
solving various mysteries. In one instance the detective informs Wat-

son: "I shall enumerate them to you, for nothing clears up a case so much as stating it to another person." In a backhanded way, the sharp-witted sleuth concedes that Watson actually helps him: "When I said that you stimulated me, I meant, to be frank, that in noting your fallacies I was occasionally guided towards the truth." However, Sherlock Holmes wouldn't be Sherlock if he didn't regularly rebuke his dutiful right-hand man. In "The Adventures of the Solitary Cyclist," he tells Watson: "You have done remarkably badly!" In another case Holmes complains, "I cannot at the moment recall any possible blunder which you have omitted."

Only rarely does Holmes praise his "ideal helpmate." In the famous *Hound of the Baskervilles,* Holmes says, "Really, Watson, you excel yourself . . . I am bound to say that in all the accounts which you have been so good as to give of my own small achievements you have habitually underrated your own abilities. It may be that you are not yourself luminous, but you are a conductor of light." But Holmes knows that Watson is crucial to their shared success. "I am lost without my Boswell," Holmes confesses. "I will do nothing without my trusted comrade and biographer at my elbow."

Watson knows how important he is to their enterprise. But like other great co-leaders, he has the ego strength to let Holmes have the glory. In one of the final episodes, Dr. Watson reveals his role in the relationship. He says, with characteristic modesty: "As an institution, I was like the violin, the shag tobacco, the old black pipe, the index books. . . . But apart from this I had uses. I was a whetstone for his mind. I stimulated him. He liked to think aloud in my presence. . . . If I irritated him by a certain methodical slowness in my mentality, that irritation served only to make his own flame-like intuitions and impressions flash up more vividly and swiftly. Such was my humble role in our alliance."

■

Best-selling author P. D. James once observed that suspense writers are among the few to tell a story "that affirms the sanctity of individual life." In battling supervillian Moriarty, Holmes and Watson join together in an epic struggle against all that's evil in their world. Both men devote their considerable talents to the cause of truth and justice and to the protection of innocent victims of foul play. Just as real-life co-leaders complement and compensate for each other, this fictional odd couple forms a single, all but invincible crime-fighting team.

In "His Last Bow," the clairvoyant Holmes anticipates the pending Great War and the tremendous changes it will bring:

" 'There is an east wind coming, Watson,' says the detective.

'I think not, Holmes. It is very warm,' the doctor replies.

'Good old Watson! You are one fixed point in a changing age.' "

Foreseeing the dire end of Edwardian England, the great but troubled sleuth is comforted to have a good friend and colleague at his side. Whether the task is chasing Moriarty through a foggy London night or making an organization succeed, leadership can be lonely as well as arduous. Holmes knows that solutions always come faster with good old Watson on the case.

13 | Clash of the Titans

13

Clash of the Titans

Half of the harm that is done in this world
is due to people who want to feel important
. . . They do not mean to do harm. . . .
They are absorbed in the endless struggle
to think well of themselves.

—T. S. ELIOT, "The Cocktail Party"

Most people feel comfortable playing the co-leader. However, some strong-willed people reject subservience in any form. For instance it is hard to perceive Donald Trump, George Steinbrenner, or Leona Helmsley finding happiness laboring in the trenches. Being a co-leader is not part of their psychological makeup.

Often the most imperious CEOs are reluctant to identify their heirs apparent. For years J. Peter Grace (W.R. Grace & Co.), William S. Paley (CBS Inc), and Armand Hammer (Occidental Petroleum Corp.) had infamous revolving doors for anyone who aspired to replace them. Despite the evidence to the contrary, some high-powered executives seem to believe they will live forever. As they age, remaining in the fray seems to renew and rejuvenate them. The current crop of Fortune 500 companies whose bosses haven't publicly designated a No. 2 includes Coca-Cola, IBM, J. P. Morgan & Co., and Walt Disney Company.

As we shall see, being a co-leader can have a downside. Although the pay has jumped dramatically in the last decade, executive recruiters report considerable difficulty in filling these assignments. Too many people get burned taking these jobs. As we have seen, not every

231

leader wants strong, independent thinkers on the team. Many bigwigs refuse to share the limelight. Disney chairman and CEO Michael D. Eisner is apparently reluctant to share power. That characteristic is often cited as being behind the high-profile departures of former Disney studio chief Jeffrey Katzenberg, TV honcho Richard Frank, chief financial officer Stephen F. Bollenbach, and president Michael Ovitz.

Hollywood types, in particular, "cloak themselves in relationships and accessorize with ego," according to Los Angeles–based writer Deanna Kizis. "Thus they feud—a lot. They feud for power. They feud for security. Sometimes they even feud for fun. The only time they don't feud is when there's money to be made."

When superagent Michael Ovitz, who had done his share of feuding, agreed to join Disney as president in August 1995, industry heads turned. Could the feared and manipulative power broker, who had built Creative Artists Agency from zip to undisputed No. 1, subordinate himself to the brilliant but abrasive Michael Eisner? Was Disney's demanding CEO, who had undergone quadruple bypass surgery in 1994, really ready to give his faithful friend genuine responsibility, including a chance at being Eisner's successor? The answer was a resounding "No!"

After a tumultuous 14-month partnership, the two Mikes failed to make co-leadership magic in the Magic Kingdom. Although Eisner repeatedly said he believed the two strong-willed men could work together, they never formed a real team. The tenuous pairing finally collapsed with Ovitz's abrupt departure in December 1996. Despite protestations to the contrary, Eisner seems to view the entertainment giant as a one-man show—his show. He would not cede authority. "While Mr. Eisner sometimes pays lip service to the notion of having 'partners' to help run Disney's massive empire," the *Wall Street Journal* reported, "he doesn't actually want top-notch lieutenants determined to assert themselves." In Eisner's Disney there was room for only one superstar, and it wasn't Mickey Mouse.

Ovitz's exit from Disney was not only expensive (the original estimated cost was a staggering $90 million in cash and stock options), but it also exacerbated investor concerns about the organization's bench strength. "The succession issue rises anew here and creates a heightened degree of strategic uncertainty," said SG Cowen Securities analyst Harold L. Vogel. "Wall Street doesn't like uncertainty about these things. It's obviously such a large company with such global diversity that it needs a strategy and succession plan."

Of course, egos run amok are nothing new in Hollywood. Divorce has split many great partnerships. Gilbert and Sullivan, Abbott and Costello, Marge and Gower Champion, Dean Martin and Jerry Lewis, and the Marx Brothers all crashed and burned at the pinnacles of their careers because of personality differences. Man's inability to get along often transcends economic logic. Fueled by ego, warring partners routinely forget that their collective talents far outstrip their individual abilities and that their professional fortunes are married together.

Of course, egos drive people in every occupation. Power-hungry bosses may seem out of place in a business environment that emphasizes teamwork and collaboration, but organizational lone wolves remain a fact of life. Many strong personalities resist any diminution in power. As Mao Tse-tung put it: "Beauty lies at the *top* of the mountain." For China's Chairman Mao, it was No. 1 or nothing. Others readily admit co-leadership isn't for them. Like Eisner, they go a step further and seem determined to drive away any adjunct who begins to look too strong.

Why are some executives so good at power sharing, while others fail? Largely it is a matter of attitude and commitment on the part of those in charge. Think you're ready for a topflight co-leader? Executives who feel they want to create strong symbiotic relationships should ask themselves the following questions.

1. Can you overcome the superman complex? Or are you too self-centered? Do you typically emphasize others' strengths and contributions, and not your own? Is your heart really in teaming up with another high-powered talent, or would you rather run the organization on your own?
2. Do your core values and philosophies mesh with your prospective partner's? How's the chemistry between the two of you?
3. Can you share the limelight, even in small ways, with your co-leader? Or will you insist on being out front on every issue?
4. Are you prepared to split command with your new alter ego? Are you willing to delegate many important responsibilities to him or

her? Can you really cut yourself loose from day-to-day affairs and cede responsibility for them to someone else?

5. Does your prospective co-leader have skills that truly complement yours? Or do they simply reinforce your own strengths or biases? Where's the added value in taking on a partner?

6. Do you consider your second in command successor material? Are you fully prepared to lay out a specific career path that leads him or her to the corner office, *your* office? Do you have the patience to mentor your No. 2 personally and professionally?

7. What loyalty demands will you make on your new chief lieutenant? How will you evaluate his or her allegiance to the board of directors and other key constituencies?

8. Is the rest of the enterprise prepared to accept a strong co-leader? What's been the organization's history with other senior executives? Will you fight for the new co-leader's success? What role will the board of directors play in the co-leadership equation?

9. Are you prepared to hear dissenting opinions? Can you tolerate constructive criticism from your top executive, or have you come to like the softballing that is the norm of far too many subordinates? Will you listen and respond positively to things you need to know but may not want to know?

10. The ultimate test: trading places. Could you reverse roles with your new co-leader? How highly do you value his or her abilities? Is there a high degree of trust and mutual respect?

If you answered yes to these questions, you are probably ready to recruit a first-rate co-leader or have already done so. If many of your answers were no's, you are probably not ready to share power. In fact co-leadership is not always easy to achieve, as the following stories illustrate.

Dealing with the Deity Complex

The Dallas Cowboys, the self-proclaimed "America's Team," is the most loved and hated franchise in pro football. Fans around the country gloat over its wins and losses. In 1989 the nation watched as Jerry Jones, the Cowboys' egotistical owner, hired his first coach for the recently acquired franchise, the egomaniacal Jimmy Johnson. Five years later they got an acrimonious professional divorce—leaving onlookers to wonder how two guys could win two straight Super Bowls and be on top of the world and still not be able to get along.

Owner Jones grew up dirt-poor but, through a series of high-stake deals in oil, gas drilling, and real estate, built a fortune. In 1989 he spent a large chunk of it, $140 million, to buy the losing Dallas team and its increasingly empty stadium. Jones quickly became the most hated man in Texas when he fired legendary Dallas coach Tom Landry. Angry Cowboys fans began calling Jones "Jethro," suggesting that he might be rich, but he acted like a Beverly Hillbilly.

Ignoring his critics, Jones then shocked the pro football world by hiring Jimmy Johnson from the University of Miami. Roommates and teammates in college, Jones and Johnson, who had no National Football League experience, had common roots in Arkansas and were alleged to be best buddies. Their long-standing relationship and similar ages held out the promise of a marriage made in heaven.

The honeymoon was brief. In Johnson's first season in Dallas, his record was 1–15, only a bit less humiliating than the 0–10 performance that launched his career—as defensive coach of the Picayune (Mississippi) High School Maroon Tide in 1966. Johnson was unapologetic: "At times people looked at me like I was a crazy man because we had the worst team in the NFL. But I never wavered in my attitude." Johnson, who has a degree in industrial psychology, was confident of a turnaround. His positive thinking paid off. In just four years, he transformed the league's twentieth-ranked defense into the No. 1 "D." In 1993 he also won the first of two consecutive Super Bowl championships. Yet less than a year later, on March 29, 1994, Jimmy Johnson quit the team. What went wrong?

In many ways pride killed this once hopeful-looking partnership. Unlike most NFL owners, Jerry Jones insisted on being actively involved in virtually every aspect of team management, except game planning. As the Cowboys owner, president, and general manager, he refused to give Johnson an unlimited budget or control of trading and drafting players. Always present on the sidelines, football's sanctum sanctorum, Jones unnerved the understandably territorial Johnson. By contractual arrangement, Jones and Johnson had to approve any team change the other wanted to make—but, as top dog, Jones always cast the decisive vote.

Everybody is prepared to enjoy a rich man's fall, and Jones set himself up by parading his $140-million toy around town. He grandstanded constantly. He had his own TV show, radio show, and newspaper column. From the club's tony headquarters in tony Valley Ranch, JJ (as Jones is known) seemed to enjoy thumbing his nose at the league, coaches, even fans.

For several years Jones had been trying to convince his fellow owners that each team should be allowed to keep its marketing and licensing fees, not share them equally among the other franchises. Finding little support for his ideas in the NFL, he inked a series of multimillion-dollar marketing deals with Pepsi, Nike, American Express, Dr Pepper, and AT&T to become Texas Stadium sponsors, contravening a league agreement. NFL Properties, the licensing and marketing arm of the league, sued Jones, the Cowboys, and Texas Stadium for $300 million in damages. Jones countersued in a federal court in New York, accusing the NFL of preventing the teams from conducting legitimate business and asking for $700 million in damages. In December 1996 the league, in an out-of-court settlement, gave Jones and his fellow owners the right to cut their own deals.

In Jones's view his star-studded football team is essentially a marketing tool. He has built one of the most profitable franchises in the league, and he intends to build an empire on it. Recognizing the primacy to get talent, Dallas operates on a star system: It pays to get the great ones and relies on them to win. Bolstered by his lucrative corporate sponsorships, Jones was able to sign flashy Deion Sanders in 1995 for $35 million over seven years. That included a huge $13 million signing bonus that circumvented the NFL salary cap. "The man's gone too far," grumbled San Francisco 49er's then president Carmen Policy. "He's gone out of control."

Jones is a classic example of the rogue leader, one whose ego keeps him from sharing power—or glory—with others. After the Cowboys' Super Bowl XXVII victory, the national spotlight was on both Jones and Johnson. But when asked to hold the Super Bowl trophy up together, Jones insisted that he alone perform the ceremony. Johnson's victory smile promptly withered to a surprised frown.

In another of many such instances, ESPN was covering the Cowboys' top brass during the 1992 NFL player draft. Although Dallas had already identified its picks, Jones told Johnson (the coach contends): "You know the [TV] camera is in the draft room today. So whenever we're about to make a pick, you look at me, like we're talking about it." Simply put, Jones wanted the world to know that he was the team's mover and shaker.

When asked, the peripatetic Jerry Jones says he doesn't recall such a conversation. But it is clear that Jones's need to be the team's Alpha male strained his relationship with Johnson, a proud man in his own right. If Jones was unwilling to share power down, Johnson was reluctant to share it up. "Johnson sometimes overheats at the thought of coaches he respects reading that he was assisted on a trade by Jones— by this rich guy who wants so badly to be cool and doesn't quite know how," wrote sportswriter Skip Bayless.

Johnson was also careless about showing respect to his boss in public. He openly called Jones "a frustrated football coach, everybody can see that." Johnson forgot that he served at Jones's discretion, even in matters of turf, and blew his cool, frequently threatening to quit every time Jones interfered.

Johnson is an avowed control freak with a rage to win. And Jones seemed to take a perverse delight in setting the volative Johnson off. Jones's tactic of purposely encouraging tension often left Coach Johnson confused about decisions ranging from player selection to coaching salaries. "Some people work better when they know what's going to happen, and some people work better when they don't know what's going to happen, and some don't work well unless they know exactly what's going to happen," Jones said. The whole point of such impenetrable statements seemed to be to remind Johnson that Jones was in charge, and Johnson was not.

Eventually Johnson had enough. "I've gone from angry and hostile to trying to be a good company man to trying to tell the truth to I really don't care. He owns the club," Johnson said. "What can I do?" Jones, also wearying of their constant sniping and sneering, leaked his intention to dump Johnson in favor of former Oklahoma University coach Barry Switzer. The former good buddies from Arkansas then took their frustrations out in the local press. On the front page of the *Fort Worth Star-Telegram,* one headline screamed: JERRY TO JIMMY: COMMIT OR QUIT. "I said to myself, I'm so tired of this," Johnson said. He told Jones, "It's time."

It was a good divorce, albeit a lousy marriage. In the end Johnson got what he wanted—escape from the man he had grown to dread, release from the last five years of his contract, and a $2 million golden parachute. And Jones got what he wanted—two Super Bowl championships and total control over the Cowboys franchise.

In truth, both men suffered from outsized egos and thin skins—a combination that makes co-leadership all but impossible. Psychologist James O'Connell of the outplacement firm of Drake Beam Morin says such people have an inflated sense of their own importance. They tend to downplay danger and let trouble build, until the enterprise crashes around them. Rather than bend, Jones and Johnson were willing to let their potentially lucrative partnership go down in flames.

Small-mindedness is often a factor in such failures. Jones admitted that he resented all the attention given Johnson. "I just couldn't put up with it," Jones told the *Financial Times*. "Every lack of recognition of how we got to where we were was like sticking pins in me. And I am sure that my lack of recognition of his contribution to how we got to where we were stuck pins into him."

After their parting, Dallas fans castigated Jones. Many predicted the end of America's Team. Skeptics scoffed when Jones brought in a new buddy, Barry Switzer. But in 1995 Dallas won its unprecedented third Super Bowl in four seasons and placed ten players in the Pro Bowl.

Johnson, for his part, relocated with his money to the Florida Keys, eventually hooking up with the Fox Network as a TV commentator. But his absence from coaching was short-lived. In January 1996 Johnson traded in the broadcast booth for owner H. Wayne Huizenga's offer of the keys to the Miami Dolphins empire. Like Jones, billionaire entrepreneur Huizenga had a whatever-it-takes commitment to winning a championship. He didn't hesitate to force out beloved coach Don Shula, a 26-year-veteran, and tap Johnson for the job.

In their initial meeting, Huizenga assuaged the worst of Johnson's fears. "I want a coach I can enjoy winning with," Huizenga told him. "I want to be your friend. There's no money in sports, so I have to have other reasons to be in it. I'm not Jerry [Jones]. I'm not a hands-on owner. I'm not going to bug you a lot—we might talk once or twice each week during the season—but I have to have a relationship with the man running my team, or it's not going to work."

"The owner," Peter King of *Sports Illustrated* reported, "wanted to be his friend, not his working peer and football adviser, as Jones had been—with disastrous consequences for Johnson—in Dallas." In addition Huizenga made Johnson the team's general manager in recognition of his uncanny ability to find diamonds in the rough and to turn borderline players into All-Pros. The Dolphins' new coach—a true co-leader at last—would make in excess of $3 million his first year.

As for Johnson's mood swings, Huizenga appeared unconcerned. Johnson's "charming, easy to be with," Huizenga said. "I felt I had to have him."

Johnson inherited a 9–7 team burdened with too many aging, high-priced underachievers. Under Shula the Dolphins failed to win a Super Bowl in the last 22 seasons of his tenure, 13 of which featured one of the game's greatest quarterbacks, Dan Marino. Despite two mediocre seasons (8–8 and 9–8), Miami fans hope that Johnson's reputation as a magnificent game-day coach and a magical trader can propel the team to a championship. The ever confident Johnson has only one goal in mind and that is winning another Super Bowl. "We should win one, two, three or four more games next season," he predicted of the 1998 season.

"We're looking for next year to be better and for the third year to be really competitive and maybe make it to the Super Bowl," owner Huizenga chimed in. Coach Johnson was certain his first two so-so seasons would eventually lead to a great success. "Pull out the clips," he said of his track record, "and see what happens."

The news clippings say that Johnson, over time, is indeed a winner. In his mid-50s, he understands fully that the hard-driving Huizenga, who founded Waste Management, Inc., Blockbuster Entertainment Corp., Republic Industries, and perhaps the biggest collection of sports properties anywhere (the Florida Panthers, Florida Marlins, and the Dolphins), will not tolerate failure. "As long as we win games, everything is fine," Johnson said, "As soon as we come up short, the honeymoon is over."

Meanwhile back in Dallas, America's Team stumbled through its first losing season since the Johnson era. The house that Jones and Johnson built was creaking, if not crumbling. As a result, Coach

Switzer was summarily dismissed, and Jones was tempted to become the team's sole leader once again—adding head coach to his titles of owner and general manager. "There is something in me that would like to coach," he said. "I don't back away from that at all. . . . I have to admit it would be extremely self-centered if I did coach the team. Still, the desire is sometimes there."

Wisely Jones resisted the urge. After an exhaustive search, he settled on his third rookie coach, Chan Gailey, the self-effacing offensive coordinator of the Pittsburgh Steelers. However, Jones insisted on retaining supreme authority over personnel matters. Gailey obviously has his work cut out for him.

Oil and Water in the Executive Suite

At 5:30 P.M. on January 17, 1996, Sumner Murray Redstone, the billionaire chairman of Viacom International Inc., ousted his No. 2, Frank J. Biondi, Jr. In a meeting of less than 20 minutes, Redstone told longtime deputy he was not providing the "nimble and aggressive" leadership the company needed. "When you have a CEO, unless you want to undermine him—and I never wanted to undermine Frank—you pretty much have to follow his course," Redstone told *Time* magazine. "I saw issues developing, and my sense was that they weren't being dealt with as aggressively as they should have been."

Industry observers reported that Redstone was especially disappointed with the performance of Paramount Pictures, the glitzy centerpiece of Viacom's $10 billion acquisition of Paramount Communications in 1994. The film studio released several flops in 1995 after an outstanding record the previous year led by the blockbuster *Forrest Gump.* According to the the *New York Times,* Redstone was irked that his No. 2 did not inject tighter operating control over the studio, despite several requests to do so. In addition Redstone was unhappy with the performance of Blockbuster Entertainment video and music stores, also acquired in 1994. The home-video distributor's earnings were faltering because of intense price competition in the domestic market.

Both Paramount and Blockbuster should have expanded more aggressively overseas, Redstone believed. Viacom, he felt, needed to function more like Australian media baron Rupert Murdock's News

Corporation, which was expanding its Fox network in Europe and had begun satellite distribution in Asia and Latin America. Exit Mr. Biondi.

"Frank's style was terrific for the old Viacom," Redstone said, "but we face enormous new challenges and opportunities." For scapegoat Biondi, the lesson was painfully clear: When you dance with a gorilla, the gorilla always leads.

Biondi joined a growing list of media chiefs dismissed by their companies. In the past few years, Viacom, Time Warner, Sony, and MCA have all forced out top-ranked executives. "This industry is more volatile and fastpaced than most," said Gerald R. Roche, chairman of Heidrick & Struggles, an executive recruiting firm. "That breeds restlessness on the part of boards and CEOs."

Nobody exhibits more restlessness than the hard-driving Sumner Redstone. The Boston billionaire overhauled a chain of drive-in movies into a $13 billion media conglomerate. Flinty and excitable, Redstone routinely scolded executives in public. The litigious lawyer launched a fierce takeover battle for Viacom. Shortly thereafter he hired Frank Biondi, the former head of Time Warner's Home Box Office unit.

From the start Wall Street loved the new team. With an Ivy League résumé (degrees from Princeton and Harvard Business School) and well grounded in the entertainment sector, nice-guy Biondi appeared to blend well with his new boss. The levelheaded manager's manager seemed the perfect complement for the volatile owner. So right was Biondi's addition to the partnership that, in the *New Yorker*, Ken Auletta referred to him as Redstone's "secret weapon."

The high-powered duo started off well. On the one hand, Redstone redoubled his considerable energies on the day-to-day affairs of his theater chain, National Amusements, Inc. Biondi, on the other hand, preferred a decentralist, arms-length approach to running Viacom, which then consisted of Simon & Schuster Publishing, the MTV and Nickelodeon networks, and Showtime cable network. In contrast to his hands-on boss, Biondi described himself as "much more of a delegator. [I] use good people and get out of their way."

The men demonstrated their very different strengths in various contractual negotiations. Biondi's even temper often led to prompt settlement of disputes, while the exacting, argumentative Redstone was able to launch full-scale frontal attacks on the likes of Time Warner and Tele-Communications Inc. But as acquisitions multiplied, Redstone seemed miffed that Biondi was receiving the lion's share of credit for various Viacom deals. "The publicity that anyone else got was of no concern to me," Redstone insisted later. "The fact is, the actual deals were made by me."

One thing was clear. As Redstone got more exposure to the media industry, he seemed to want more and more control. "When Sumner first bought Viacom, he asked few questions and left the running of the company to Frank and his people," said a former Viacom executive. "We were all waiting for the other shoe to drop—when Sumner was really going to take over the company."

In fact, as the largest shareholder of Viacom, Redstone had the proprietary right to run the business himself. "He owns the ball and bat," said Alan C. Greenberg, chairman of Bear, Stearns & Company, an adviser to Viacom in many of its commercial dealings. "His interests coincide with the interests of shareholders." But Redstone was also exhibiting the not uncommon owner-entrepreneur's reluctance to hand control over to a talented subordinate.

For the most part, Redstone cited differences in management style as the primary reason for Biondi's departure. "I would have preferred that Frank go out and fix it," Redstone said. "But he's not confrontational, not hands-on. . . . His [less aggressive] style was not working."

Redstone then elevated two young vice chairmen with limited backgrounds in the entertainment industry. However, most of the power remained with Redstone, who assumed the duties of chief executive. As to the charge that he would overcentralize Viacom management, the new CEO bristled: "I am not an autocrat, and I never have been." Nevertheless, he admitted to exercising "more oversight" in the future.

Meanwhile the investment community worried that Redstone, without a strong executive like Biondi to challenge his decisions, would have no checks on his considerable power as Viacom's controlling shareholder. Indeed many media analysts expressed shock over Biondi's ouster. "No one individual determines the future of a company," said John Tinker, who then covered the entertainment industry for the investment firm Furman Selz. "But running this company will be tricky for at least a while."

There were also questions about Redstone's age. When asked if his age would affect the firm's future, the then 72-year-old CEO responded: "If Bob Dole thinks he can run the country at age 72, then I can run Viacom." Colleagues didn't disagree. After all, the remarkably fit Redstone had a reputation for proving the critics wrong.

The good second even when ill-treated, Biondi did not share any hard feelings he might have had about his boss. "Sumner just decided he wanted to be totally involved," Biondi said. "He's having a lot of fun. He loves the publicity. He wants his day in the sun, and he's going to get it."

Only three months after his heave-ho from Viacom, the much respected Biondi got his own day in the sun. In April 1996 Seagram Co. CEO Edgar Bronfman, Jr., tapped Biondi to be chief of MCA Inc. (renamed Universal). Biondi's experience and easy authority were expected to improve the ho-hum performance of Universal's film, television, music, theme park, and publishing businesses. Billionaire Bronfman turned the tough operational issues over to the engagingly open Biondi. "Getting Frank was the culmination of building a new management," Bronfman explained. "[He] is great at setting business priorities."

Investors lauded Seagram's move. "Biondi brings a unique combination of talent," said analyst Jeffrey Logsdon of Seidler Co., an investment advisory firm. "There are not a lot of people [in entertainment] who know how to operate a company and also have good relationships with Wall Street."

Redstone also reacted positively to Biondi's new posting at Universal: "He will be a terrific addition to MCA and frankly be a lot of help to Edgar Bronfman." Yet even with Biondi's help, the Universal empire has been a disappointment. Although its music and theme park divisions performed well, the television and film units struggled. In late 1997 Bronfman sold most of the company's TV assets to entertainment mogul Barry Diller. The move was a blow to Biondi, who, though obviously chagrined, loyally described the spin-off as "a great deal." Still, many wondered whether the scion of the Bronfman family, who has often been characterized as a lightweight and a dilettante, was poised to part company with his second in command.

"Edgar may be polite, elegant and reluctant to throw elbows, but no one wants to win more than he does," said Biondi, who has the successful co-leader's gift for closely reading his boss. "One shouldn't underrate either his ability or conviction.

On November 16, 1968, Bronfman's resolve erupted when he fired Biondi. The move, in part, was prompted by the family's hefty $10.4 billion acquisition of PolyGram N.V., the world's largest music company. But in part, Bronfman's decision was Redstone-like, with the boss—once again—exercising his ownership prerogative and seizing tighter day-to-day control of the company. Showing no passion for power sharing, Bronfman declared, "There's really room for only one CEO and it's me."

Between Scylla and Charybdis

"All men are liable to error," philosopher John Locke once wrote. "And most are, in many points, by passion or interest, under temptation to it." It is shocking how often those in power are tempted to err by sharpening their knives against a potentially invaluable ally.

"Dress me slowly, I'm in a hurry!" Napoleon once remarked. That's the double bind of every ambitious co-leader: how to achieve some power and influence while maintaining loyalty to the leader. When titans clash, someone inevitably gets hurt, almost always the No. 2. Nonetheless, in the examples we've just seen, it may be the survivors such as Jerry Jones, Sumner Redstone, and Edgar Bronfman who begin to look like dinosaurs. The autocratic leader will have little or no place in the economy of the twenty-first century. It will be those leaders who can truly collaborate who will thrive.

14 | Recasting the Executive Suite

14 | Recasting the Executive Suite

Behind an able man there are always other able men.

—CHINESE PROVERB

As our earlier stories suggest, co-leadership is a two-way street. Every Bob Eaton must find his Bob Lutz, and vice versa. This is a painful truth for many hard-driving top executives to accept. But either because they lack the requisite skills or because the dream itself is so complex, many chieftains eventually realize that they can only achieve their vision collaboratively.

A half-century ago, General Leslie R. Groves could dream the Manhattan Project but, in truth, he couldn't do it unless he got J. Robert Oppenheimer to go along. The newly minted general desperately wanted the 38-year-old scientist because: "He's a genius . . . Oppenheimer knows about everything." While both men had considerable egos, Groves was able to craft co-leadership roles that allowed them to work independently and efficiently toward the same goal: the atomic bomb.

Today more and more successful enterprises have flexible power structures that have more to do with sharing responsibility than asserting control. Growing numbers of enlightened leaders realize that the talented, like cats, can't be herded—a fact General Groves reluctantly came to terms with in the New Mexico wilderness.

Not every top gun wants to share power, though. "I guess a significant number of CEOs don't want the No. 2 to be very close, because it's no fun being at the top if nobody's on the bottom," Warren Buffett, the legendary chairman of Berkshire Hathaway Inc., told *Fortune* in his refreshingly frank style. "Because the CEO dispenses all the favors, his biggest problem is to avoid being treated like God. Second is to avoid thinking he *is* God."

Early in Buffett's career, the so-called Oracle of Omaha demonstrated what he could do when it came to Wall Street. In the 1960s Buffett hooked up with a young attorney, Charles T. Munger. Over the years Munger has become known as the man behind Buffett's magic investing touch. The Los Angeles–based Munger converted Buffett from an old-fashioned Benjamin Graham value investor to the ultimate buy-and-hold value strategist. Berkshire Hathaway Vice Chairman Munger, now in his 70s, has been so effectively goading Buffett out of borderline investments that he now calls Munger "the abominable no man." "You have to calibrate with Charlie," the Oracle said in a *Fortune* interview, "because Charlie says everything I do is dumb. If he says it's really dumb, I know it is, but if he just says it's dumb, I take that as an affirmative vote." Two high-powered brains in almost uncanny sync, they have produced golden results for Berkshire investors.

Forging a co-leadership culture is largely a matter of attitude. While Napoleonic types fail miserably, Buffett and many other chiefs dampen their egos and create what management guru Charles Handy calls "membership communities." The newest member of the Berkshire community to share power is Louis Simpson, respected as a worthy backup to both Buffett and Munger. Buffett reveals just how true a co-leader Simpson is when he claimed that Simpson is "immediately available to handle [Berkshire's] investments if something were to happen to Charlie and me."

Redefining Responsibility

The resistance some top guns show to sharing power may reflect the traditional power split between CEO and COO. On paper the differences between them are very clear. The CEO is the absolute leader; the COO, the manager. The No. 1 is charged with doing the right thing, the No. 2 with doing things right. The leader is the grand strategist; the disciple, the master tactician. The CEO has the vision; the COO, hands-on control.

In many respects the chief operating officer's slot is the most forgotten job in American industry. And the executives in these slots have varying reasons for accepting the relative anonymity and other terms associated with being No. 2. For some COO status is the consolation prize in the race to the throne, as was originally the case with Bob Lutz at Chrysler. Other No. 2s disdain the glamour of the top job. They prefer the challenges of actually running various business units. Classic operating types, they typically despise certain elements of the CEO role: deal making, strategizing, and schmoozing with different interest groups. What motivates these COOs are the day-to-day dogfights of the marketplace.

For years cool-handed operators William Spencer and George Champion admirably served their respective masters, Walter Wriston of Citicorp and David Rockefeller of Chase Manhattan. For both co-leaders, star billing and the trappings of the executive suite were no great shakes. Today Larry D. Brady of the Chicago-based equipment maker FMC Corp., Textron's Lewis B. Campbell, Mobil's Eugene A. Renna, and Andrea Jung of Avon Products are presidents who perform admirably in the trenches and seem content, at least for now, to do so.

Still other deputies are enamored with the technical or functional challenges of a long-standing specialty. They may have come up the ranks from the cockpit, the oil fields, or the laboratories. These specialist COOs believe they can best contribute to the organization by fully exploiting their well-honed skills. For them technical job content is primary, generalist responsibilities secondary.

At Trans World Airlines, William F. Compton, a longtime pilot-cum-executive, fits that profile. The fiftyish president and COO has been instrumental in TWA's recent turnaround—no surprise given his background. Compton joined the airline in 1968 as a Boeing 707 pilot. He has flown everything from small twin-engined jets to jumbo jets and still manages to become airborne for a couple of days a month. From 1991 to 1995, he served as chairman of the Airline Pilots Association unit at TWA. As co-leader to CEO Gerald Gitner, Compton mines this rich background in overseeing TWA's flight operations, in-flight service, maintenance, and engineering.

A decade earlier another specialist COO, Thomas Paine, contributed greatly to Northrop Corp.'s technical prowess. After several years running the National Aeronautics and Space Administration, President Paine focused his considerable energies on developing high-performance aircraft.

Whatever their route to the executive suite, these invaluable men and women are committed team players. They tend to be enthusiastic, intelligent, and self-reliant in the pursuit of companywide objectives. However even in the best situations co-leaders face significant problems. No one makes it into the upper reaches of the corporate world without a healthy ego and strong opinions. Given that, even the most contented No. 2 may occasionally envy the No. 1 who collects all the accolades. "There is a certain pain to being a second banana, but you have to have an ability to sublimate your ego," conceded Peter Barton, former president and CEO of Liberty Media Corporation and righthand man to his mentor, Chairman John C. Malone. The discontented Barton, who left the company in 1997, used to keep a fake banana in his office as a joking reference to his No. 2 status.

Managing the boss can also be a delicate, if not treacherous, art. Anytime the co-leader opposes the chief, no matter how valid his or her position, the COO's job is at risk—not to speak of his or her prospects for succeeding to the top slot. This may intimidate or inhibit the No. 2, making him or her a less effective lieutenant and an even less likely CEO candidate.

Even the best executive can fall out of favor if he or she repeatedly crosses swords with the boss. Jacques Sardas, Goodyear Tire & Rubber's highly respected adjunct during the late 1980s, was fired because of his spats with then chairman and CEO Tom H. Barrett. "As number two, I had to sell my ideas a lot, and I had to be committed to the sacred cows of someone else," Sardas remembered. "I didn't want to be stuck in that position." He later moved on to run Sudbury, Inc., a Cleveland-area auto parts supplier.

While even the most principled dissent may put a career at risk, weak-kneed deputies do both themselves and their companies a disservice. The minute any co-leader begins to tailor his or her ideas to suit the boss, his or her sense of worth is diminished. And because no CEO is infallible, the company loses, too. Besides, whatever the cause, when the No. 2 begins withholding ideas or energy from the enterprise, it threatens his or her own chances for advancement.

As a result, the job of co-leader can become a management hot seat. COOs are constantly between a rock and a hard place: damned if they do and damned if they don't. Their first loyalty must always be to the company. It, after all, pays them their princely wages and reasonably expects them to give 100 percent to the job. But lieutenants who invest all their knowledge, talent, and expertise in a job may find themselves on the outs with a boss who, for good reason or none at all, feels threatened by the talented understudy. This *All About Eve* phenomenon is all too common.

Unquestionably co-leadership has its downside. "There isn't much good to say about being No. 2," said William Kagler, who in 1990, as president at Kroger Co., wanted a more specific timetable for his promotion to the top slot. As a result, he was axed. The truth is that even the savviest co-leader can make a fatal misstep at any time. Moreover, ambitious aides get antsy. A few years ago, Enron Corp. President Richard D. Kinder, long considered to be the likeliest successor to his good friend, Chairman Kenneth L. Lay, announced he was leaving the company after six years as second in command. Why? "I want to do more than be No. 2," he told the *Wall Street Journal*. No doubt a factor in Kinder's decision was a five-year extension of his boss's contract. (Today Kinder heads Kinder Morgan Energy Partners L.P.)

Fast-tracker Scott P. Marks, Jr., had a similar experience. As a well-respected vice chairman at First Chicago NBD, Marks helped shape the nation's fifth largest bankcard operation. But he resigned in November 1997, eager to head up a company. "My goal is to be a chief executive officer, or at a minimum in a position where I can aspire to CEO within a relatively short number of years," said the 51-year-old Marks. "It became clear that wasn't going to happen here."

Similarly G. Richard Thoman wanted to be No. 1 at a major corporation, and it wasn't in the cards at IBM. So when Xerox Corp. tapped him to become its president and COO—with the assurance that he would quickly ascend to the top slot, he left his comfortable berth at IBM. "I have to earn my way, but I came to Xerox to be chief executive," Thoman said later. "[Chairman Paul Allaire] and the Xerox board are positioning me for that." True to form, Thoman will replace Allaire as company CEO sometime during 1999. Allaire will remain as chairman, as is the custom at Xerox.

Nevertheless, the career shift wasn't easy for Thoman. It severed a long-standing relationship with Louis V. Gerstner, Jr., IBM's chairman and CEO. "He's been the biggest mentor in my professional career, no doubt about it," Thoman told the *Financial Times*. But Gerstner had made it clear that he wasn't going to leave the giant computer maker anytime soon. And at age 52, Thoman could no longer defer his lifelong dream of running his own show.

In 1997 feisty Eric Schmidt, in his early 40s, traded in a key executive position at Sun Microsystems Inc. to head troubled Novell Inc. A befuddled Sun CEO Scott G. McNealy remarked: "I never understood why he left the best job on the planet." Yet Schimdt, a world-class technovisionary, couldn't resist the greater challenge of turning around the world's fifth biggest software company.

Add to the list Bill Fields, heir apparent at behemoth Wal-Mart Stores, Inc., who jumped ship in 1996 to run the much smaller Blockbuster Entertainment Corp. The opportunity to jump-start Viacom's largest business promised self-renewal for Fields. According to *Fortune,* Fields was "bored, just plain bored with my work and everyday life" at Wal-Mart. (Later Fields traded Blockbuster in for Hudson's Bay Company, where he serves as president and CEO.)

Defections of top-notch co-leaders are inevitable. It's probably as hard to be co-leader to a proven, hard-driving No. 1 as it is to be top dog. If some fast-trackers don't want to wait forever, others tire of the heavy lifting. Hence, the average tenure of a chief operating officer is less than four years, according to executive recruiters Ward Howell International. Yet the road to the corner office almost always winds through a COO's office. Approximately 86 percent of U.S. CEOs served as COOs at some point in their careers. Like it or not, being a successful co-leader is a proven rite of passage.

Fortunately many No. 2s are completely comfortable being part of a vibrant management team, one that gives their businesses a powerful partnership. Besides Charlie Munger (Berkshire Hathaway), Craig Barrett (Intel), and Steve Ballmer (Microsoft), some of corporate America's most able alter egos include Rebecca Mark (Enron), Robert Bowman (ITT Corporation), Raymond J. Lane (Oracle Corp.), Ann Winblad (Hummer Winblad Venture Partners), Robert W. Pittman (America Online, Inc.), Stanley F. Druckenmiller (Quantum Fund), Herbert M. Allison, Jr. (Merrill Lynch & Co.), Marion

Sandler (Golden West Financial), Kenneth I. Chenault (American Express), and Sheli Rosenberg (Equity Group Investments, Inc.).

Talent in Tandem

The traditional two-tier CEO-COO structure, however venerable, is giving way to something more fluid. Although the division of power and responsibility is clear-cut on paper, in practice the roles are inextricably interwoven. Every leader has something of the manager, and every good manager has leadership qualities—or he or she would not have made it into the upper tier. Inevitably the CEO wears both leadership and managerial hats and, as a result, may occasionally tread on the COO's turf. At the same time, able No. 2s often can't resist flexing those leader's muscles and may assume some of the boss's prerogatives, with or without the boss's blessing.

Therefore, rather than clinging religiously to a division of tasks that is arbitrary at best, more and more firms are practicing dual- or co-leadership. They are encouraging overlapping strategic and operational responsibilities. At Chrysler, the two Bobs—Eaton and Lutz—confidently shared the mantle of leadership and management. But there are many other winning teams as well.

Henry Schacht and Richard McGinn have ably split command at Lucent Technologies, the $21 billion-a-year equipment maker that AT&T spun off in 1996. From the start Schacht, a former member of AT&T's board and the ex-chairman of the Cummins Engine Company, Inc., shared duties with McGinn, a former AT&T equipment executive. "Rich and I have been a partnership from the beginning, working toward a seamless succession," Schacht said. "That's a rare occurrence in the modern corporation."

Capitalizing on their different talents, Schacht worked Wall Street; McGinn, 12 years younger, coordinated operations and technology. However, their duties were often blurred. When one was tied up, the other filled in. In fact Chairman Schacht wouldn't talk strategy, do an interview, or pose for a photo session without his trusted president nearby.

"Power-sharing is, in fact, Mr. Schacht's forte," the *Wall Street Journal* wrote. "Over the first few months as Lucent CEO, [he] made it clear that his new 'partner' could one day succeed him. 'Henry has said to me that I'd see a big part of my job here as helping to make Rich the best CEO he can be someday,' " David Nadler of Delta Consulting Group, a Lucent adviser, remarked.

"He reached out his hand to me when we first met and said, 'I want to be your partner,' " McGinn reported of Schacht, "He's been a tremendous mentor and help to me." Under their combined direction, a stream of new products and patents flowed. "I feel we're more closely coupled to the people who run the company now," said Howard Katz, a scientist at Bell Labs. "I never had that sense with the old AT&T."

Thanks to their collective leadership, Lucent's stock soared after an initial public offering in early 1996 and a massive restructuring of the company's business. As Schacht intimated, he ceded his CEO post to the amiable but demanding McGinn in October 1997. The smooth succession was unusual in the technology sector, where companies such as Apple Computer have tended to play musical CEOs. Wall Street, for its part, applauded the flawless hand over. "Henry was brought in to show AT&T managers who had been there how to run a public company," said Gregory S. Geiling, an analyst with J. P. Morgan, told the *New York Times*. "You [had] the guy who's an absolute genius on the business side, and then you [had] Henry Schacht, who has tremendous amount of experience—No. 1, dealing with a public company and, No. 2, doing restructurings."

While Schacht remains the chairman (perhaps until his mandatory retirement in October 1999), he is enthusiastic about his co-leader's ascent. "I'm tremendously excited for Rich and for Lucent," Schacht said. "Rich and the board asked if I would stay with the board for this time, to play the part of being a helper, coach, listener, and supporter of Rich."

Helping, coaching, listening, and supporting are vital roles for leaders committed to co-leadership. In his new role, CEO McGinn has assumed more responsibility for strategy, with an emphasis on globalization and customer service. Yet McGinn continues to heed mentor Schacht. "We're learning how to become a really, really good company," McGinn said.

The Lucent changeover was a model of succession planning. The stock price skyrocketed as shareholders registered their approval. But succession continues to be a thorny issue at many organizations.

While succession planning is one of a board of directors' most important functions, many companies still get it wrong.

For every Lucent there is an AT&T (ironically Lucent's former parent). After numerous stops and starts, the telecommunications giant finally appointed a chairman and chief executive. In October 1997 C. Michael Armstrong, the former CEO of Hughes Electronics Corporation, became the first outsider CEO in the company's 120-year history. Taking a page out of Bob Eaton's primer on co-leadership, Armstrong immediately forged an alliance with longtime general counsel John D. Zeglis, who had pushed hard to succeed outgoing CEO Robert E. Allen. From the start the Harley-riding Armstrong made it very clear that he intended to share the running of AT&T with newly promoted President Zeglis. Repeatedly Armstrong stressed that the two planned "to operate as a team" in running the operations and most strategy and investment decisions. And, by all accounts, they continue to enjoy an excellent working relationship. "They're complementing each other well, and senior managers have found this encouraging," one company executive said. Last year the AT&T network expanded with its $37 billion merger of Tele-Communications Inc. So far the chemistry between Armstrong and TCI Chairman John Malone has been especially good.

In another exemplary case of co-leadership, wunderkind Michael Dell shares power with seasoned executive Mort Topfer. Dell pioneered the direct marketing of computers 15 years ago out of his University of Texas dorm room, to become the second biggest PC maker (behind Compaq). Topfer, in his 60s, joined Dell Computer Corp. as vice chairman in June 1994 after running Motorola's landmobile products division. From the start he brought a renewed sense of direction to the Austin, Texas, company.

"Topfer's managerial skills complement those of his boss," writes *Fortune*'s Rahul Jacob. "Dell has an instinctive feel for technology and marketing, while Topfer is an operations guy with a penchant for detail." Still in his early 30s, Dell has no trouble sharing strategic decision making with his older co-leader. For example, Topfer is charting the nearly $13 billion company's global push into Malaysia and other ripe foreign markets. According to Jacob, Dell "has delegated an enormous amount of responsibility to Topfer, whom he often describes as his 'co-CEO.' "

Michael Dell is now the richest man in Texas—richer than Ross Perot. His net worth at last report: roughly $13 billion. (He was actually richer at age 33 than Bill Gates was.) And yet Dell seems to take more satisfaction in building a cadre of deep leadership than in making money. When problems arise, he immediately seeks out the best people in the world to solve them. In December 1997 Dell added yet another co-leader, Vice Chairman Kevin B. Rollins, to his constellation of top executives. While Chairman Dell concentrates on overall strategy and technology and Topfer leads operations and the Europe and Asia-Pacific regions, Rollins, a former Bain & Co. consultant, heads Dell's Americas unit.

Until recently many organizations pooh-poohed the kind of serious succession planning described in these examples. All too often procrastination was the name of the game. However, the untimely deaths of Coca-Cola's Roberto Goizueta and Texas Instrument's CEO Jerry Junkins dramatized the importance of deep leadership and a clear backup plan. Maintaining an uninterrupted flow of co-leaders increasingly ranks as one of the most important tasks of any responsible chief executive and board of directors.

More and more, executive recruiters consider the promotion of co-leadership a must-have criterion for potential candidates for the corner office. "CEOs must be team leaders who inspire and develop other leaders throughout their organizations," said Thomas J. Neff, chairman of the search firm Spencer Stuart, U.S. Evidence of the surge in co-leadership comes from the Association of Executive Search Consultants, which reports that searches for co-leadership positions (that is, those slots just below CEO) rose by more than 50 percent in 1997. (At the same time, CEO and chairman searches dipped about 16 percent.) The dearth of senior executives can be traced to the reengineering and downsizing of the past decade.

In their efforts to recast the executive suite, enlightened chief executives are seeking co-leaders with shared values and similar vision. They seek what coauthors James C. Collins and Jerry I. Porras call, in their best-seller *Built to Last,* "alignment," an arrangement in which all the pieces of successful organizations work in concert. Visionary companies, the authors found, search for synergy and linkages. They put in place people who "reinforce each other to deliver a powerful combined punch."

Finding, then keeping, ambitious up-and-comers is never easy. Even thriving companies such as GE, Pepsico, and Disney have experienced major defections in recent years. A company such as IBM is especially vulnerable. As things stand today, the computer maker's bench strength is relatively weak. Many of its senior vice presidents are nearing retirement or are close in age to 55-year-old Chairman Gerstner, and junior executives are not being brought up quickly enough.

Two Heads are Better Than One—Sometimes

To build strength at the top, some firms are opting for a more radical (and possibly riskier) approach to co-leadership. They are formalizing their commitment to co-leadership by appointing co-equals to the corner office. Among those companies: Unilever, Warner Bros. Inc., J.C. Penney Company, Inc., Ralston Purina Co., and Bell Atlantic-GTE. However, the financial services sector is probably the most taken with the two-for-one trend.

At San Francisco–based Charles Schwab Corp., David S. Pottruck, its president and COO, shares the title of chief executive officer with company founder Charles Schwab. A former wrestler and football player at the University of Pennsylvania, Pottruck has long been acknowledged as one of corporate America's savviest operating executives. "It's time to recognize the role David's virtually been playing for the last 24 months," Schwab said at the time of Pottruck's elevation. "I need to have more attention, more help to lay out our strategic direction. David will be helping me more in that."

As co-CEO, Pottruck told the *Wall Street Journal* that Schwab would focus on the corporate vision, while he would concentrate more on strategy. Outsiders applauded this still unusual commitment to co-leadership. "It makes great sense," said Richard Strauss, an analyst at Goldman, Sachs & Co. "David is Chuck's right hand. He's a proven entity. The track record of Schwab in the time he has been there [14 years] speaks for itself."

Back East, Goldman, Sachs has had two pairs of co-CEOs. Morgan Stanley, Dean Witter & Discover Co. are run jointly by CEO Philip J. Purcell and President John J. Mack, although Purcell technically outranks Mack. Chase Manhattan also adopted a tandem approach to leadership. In December 1997 the nation's then largest bank surprised observers by committing 100 percent to co-leadership. Chase made Thomas C. Labrecque, its president and COO, a "totally co-equal partner" with its chairman and CEO, Walter V. Shipley. After the merger of Chase and Chemical Banking Corp. in 1996, most Chase executives (including Labrecque) had held secondary positions in the new structure. The creation of co-leaders confounded many industry watchers. "This is a total surprise to me," admitted Emanuel N. Mongenis, an executive recruiter at Heidrick & Struggles.

Many analysts read the coequal partnership as a signal that Labrecque is likely to succeed Shipley, who is slated to retire as chief executive in 2001. While Shipley did not confirm or deny that analysis, he seemed to be fully committed to sharing power with Labrecque. "We've developed a tremendous partnership," Shipley said. "We're very complementary to each other skill-wise."

As part of its top management makeover, Chase expanded its three-member office of the chairman (Shipley, Labrecque, and Vice Chairman William H. Harrison, Jr.) to a nine-member executive committee. By flattening the hierarchy, the bank claims that it is unleashing each of these co-leaders to maximize his or her contributions to the company. "These are all people we want to develop," Labrecque told the *Wall Street Journal*. In its succession planning, Labrecque said all candidates are being evaluated on their "team-building potential . . . how well they can lead, how well they manage their business, and how well they manage as a partnership."

Chase's cross-town rival, Citicorp, turned the most heads by teaming up with Travelers Group Inc. The recently christened Citigroup Inc. stands as the world's largest financial services company, with revenues of $72 billion. Sharing command of the financial powerhouse: co-CEOs John S. Reed from Citicorp and Travelers' Sanford I. Weill.

Meshing a commercial bank (Citicorp) with an investment bank and insurer (Travelers) cannot be easy. Sharing power in the executive suite may be even more challenging. Reed and Weill are used to running their own shows, and both have strikingly different personalities. Reed, who grew up in Argentina and Brazil (he is fluent in Spanish and Portuguese) has global and cerebral interests. An engineer by training and a classic buttoned-down banker, Reed is notoriously private, a person who is more interested in the big picture than nitty-gritty details. Brooklyn-born Weill is gregarious and outgoing—a people guy. Entrepreneurial and street smart, Weill tends to rely on intuition over analysis. The consummate hands-on manager, he tends to be less keen on strategizing than on getting things done.

Will this unusual partnership work? Can Reed and Weill sublimate their considerable egos and run Citigroup as coequals? "It totally depends on the chemistry and respect," said Jon Lukomnik, a senior pension fund executive. "It requires exceptional people. And Weill and Reed are exceptional people." Indeed both men seem committed to making the arrangement work. "I think we must work effectively together, and most importantly, be seen by our people to be working together," said John Reed. "It's like Mom and Dad in one house. If they differ on a single question, the kids know how to exploit it very well." Sandy Weill, for his part, said he knows how to work well with others. After all, he boasted, "I've been married to my wife for 43 years."

After the October 1998 ouster of James Dimon, Weill's protege and former co-CEO of Salomon Smith Barney, Citigroups investment bank, most experts remain skeptical that Weill and Reed can mesh comfortably in the executive suite. "It's inconceivable that these two could act in tandem for any length of time," warned Professor Samuel Hayes of the Harvard Business School. "They are both used to running their own shows." If the co-CEO structure is to work, both men will have to believe that they can make more of Citigroup together than they can separately.

The challenges of teaming strong personalities are considerable. Conflicts inevitably arise, and egos must always be added into the equation. As one cynic, Michael Feuer, founder and CEO of Office-Max, Inc., puts it: "If two chief executives think they can share power, they've been reading too much 'Goldilocks and The Three Bears.' "

The jury is still out on dual CEOs. But we do know that successful co-leadership cultures depend on mind-set and commitment. The true test of co-leadership is always the No. 1's willingness to share power with a potential ally. (A test of which we provided in the previous chapter.)

The accelerating trend toward megamergers, even global mergers, no doubt means there will be more co-CEOs in the future. How well, for instance, Bob Eaton and Jürgen Schrempp share power at DaimlerChrysler will be closely watched. The very existence of co-CEOs sends a powerful message that successful organizations are collections of talent, not solely reflections of the genius of one person, however gifted.

So far Eaton and Schrempp are saying, and doing, everything right. Both men claim they will continue to run their main business operations separately, with integration focusing on finance and purchasing. In addition, the reconfigured DailmerChrysler executive board has roughly equal numbers of Eaton people and Schrempp people—a good first step toward keeping power balanced in the corner suite. Moreover, both men speak respectfully of the teams of co-leaders the other had put together before the merger. That kind of mutual respect goes far to keep in check the organization's inevitable postmerger paranoia. Clearly having co-CEOs makes succession less problematical if one dies or is incapacitated. Although Eaton plans to retire in 2001, with the modesty that is one of the hallmarks of co-leadership, he concedes that "at any point I feel redundant, I will go."

15 Lessons for Co-Leaders

15

Lessons for Co-Leaders

From Gandhi to Mandela, from
the American patriots to the Polish
shipbuilders, the makers of revolutions
have not come from the top.
—GARY HAMEL, Co Author of
Competing for the Future

When everything's clicking, the relationship between a leader and co-leader is like a good marriage. There is the same affection, trust, and commitment to a common enterprise. Labor is divided easily, according to the gifts of both parties. Disagreements are resolved without acrimony and without loss of mutual respect.

Sometimes the only difference between a leader and a co-leader is the greater fame of the No. 1 and the size of his or her compensation package. Such alliances are true partnerships in which the pleasure of working together, and indeed the pleasure of being together, compensates the co-leader for living in the shadow of the more celebrated partner.

Disney CEO Michael Eisner had such a happy corporate marriage with co-leader Frank Wells before Wells's untimely death in a helicopter accident in 1994. Eisner would visit Wells's nearby office dozens of times a day, seeking his advice on virtually every decision. As Eisner told *Fortune* magazine in 1991, Wells loved to play "devil's advocate" and, by constantly challenging Eisner, helped him achieve their common goal in running Disney—making sure the best ideas won out. But what seems to have been the glue that made Eisner and

Wells such an extraordinary team was their easy camaraderie. As Wells explained, "For Michael, I make life easier. For me, he makes life more fun."

Many of our most successful enterprises are headed by happy couples—pairs in which the only obvious difference between the two is that the co-leader labors in relative obscurity. Such is the case with Steve Ballmer at software giant Microsoft. As Bill Gates told a reporter from *Forbes,* Ballmer is not only Gates's chief ally, "Steve is my best friend."

Checklist for Co-Leaders

What have we learned about being a great co-leader in looking at some of the best first lieutenants of all time, including such contemporary standouts as Microsoft's Steve Ballmer and Intel's Craig Barrett? If such distinguished co-leaders as Annie Sullivan, George Marshall, or the mythical Dr. Watson were here, these are the top 10 pieces of advice they might give us.

1. Know Thyself

Being No. 2 is just as hard as being No. 1, perhaps harder. The successful co-leader is one whose ego is strong enough to watch the kudos for his or her best work go to someone else. That isn't easy. If you can't reconcile yourself to relative anonymity, you shouldn't take the job. Co-leaders need flameproof egos. They need to be able to shrug off the indifference of others and ignore public slights (Chou En-lai was derided as Mao's "housekeeper." Bill Guthridge was sometimes described as Tonto to Dean Smith's Lone Ranger.) Which is not to say that successful co-leaders are all shrinking violets. At Coca-Cola, Donald Keough flourished as a charismatic, hands-on COO under baronial chairman and CEO Roberto Goizueta. Earlier when Coke chairman J. Paul Austin tapped Goizueta for the top job, he and Keough had agreed that the winner would hire the other. As soon as Goizueta was chosen, he assured Keough, "We're going to be partners." Keough told *Fortune* that he never regretted being No. 2, even in the face of offers for top slots elsewhere: "I've had all the psychic income I can handle in this job. . . . I knew this was my job, being president of Coca-Cola Co. If that isn't enough to satisfy your ego, you've got a problem."

If you don't have the right stuff to be a costar, however, best recognize that before you sign up. It's hard to feel too bad for someone who walked away from a job failure with a cash-and-stock package initially valued at $90 million, as Michael Ovitz did when he left Disney in 1996 after 14 months as president. But Ovitz's flop as a No. 2 took an enormous toll on his image—and thus his future marketability as well. Passed over for the top job at MCA, now Universal Studios, Ovitz looked long and hard for a firm niche in the entertainment industry, one that would restore some of the clout that once earned the former superagent the title "most powerful man in Hollywood." No sooner had he become No. 1 at Livent in 1998 than it filed for bankruptcy protection.

Prospective co-leaders who recognize that they can't work in someone else's shop do both the organization and themselves a favor. It's reasonable to assume that Ted Waitt, the maverick CEO of Gateway, would have been unhappy playing some secondary role at larger, more corporate Compaq Computer Corp., which negotiated with Waitt to buy Gateway in April 1997. An eccentric even by the standards of an eccentric industry, Waitt chose a Holstein cow as the original logo of the computer marketer he founded (a 1998 redesign retained only the cow's spots). Once described as a silicon cowboy, the 35-year-old billionaire's last-minute decision to pass on a $7 billion deal with Compaq reflects the kind of self-knowledge that keeps happy chiefs from turning into miserable deputies.

Not that a transition down the pyramid inevitably leads to misery. Who would have thought that CNN founder and legendary corporate egotist Ted Turner would have fit so smoothly into a supporting role at Time Warner? But time and experience can change a person's perspective, and the spotlight that seems irresistible at age 30 may look downright burdensome a few decades later.

2. Know Thy Leader

After searching your soul, you have decided you are ready to check your ego at the door and serve rather than star. But is your boss ready to let you? Top guns can subvert their lieutenants in dozens of ways. Some refuse to share intelligence, as both FDR and Lyndon Johnson did. Some refuse to share meaningful responsibility. Michael Eisner bonded with co-leader Frank Wells so completely that they collaborated in much of the decision making at Disney. Yet Eisner never gave

Michael Ovitz anything specific or significant to do during his brief tenure in Disney's No. 2 slot. Adding to Ovitz's woes, Eisner's other chief lieutenants apparently sabotaged the former superagent as well.

Some No. 1s are supportive for a time but grow increasingly uneasy as their chief lieutenants become more accomplished. Such bosses shoot down any subordinate who begins to shine too brightly. Compare how Lee Iacocca treated Bob Lutz at Chrysler, increasingly marginalizing the legendary auto designer, and how CEO Bob Eaton treated him at the same company. Unthreatened by the flamboyant Lutz, Eaton freed his No. 2 to perform brilliantly and basked in the reflected glory. No co-leader, however talented and hard working, can succeed without at least the tacit support of the person at the top.

In the best of all possible worlds, the CEO readies his or her deputy for succession and wholeheartedly supports his or her candidacy. But even when succession is not an issue, leaders and their co-leaders have a profoundly symbiotic relationship. As true partners, their fates are always correlated. As a result, you have to choose your prospective boss every bit as carefully as he or she chooses you.

3. Avoid Titanic Clashes

Every organization has a distinctive culture, a set of mutual assumptions that governs how it operates. A chief executive has the power to modify that culture by fiat, if he or she chooses. As a co-leader, you have no such power. Over time your influence may become such that you, too, can change the enterprise. But you must first master its culture. If you don't, you will be stymied at every turn. For example, an organization that goes by the book will not welcome your attempt to institute a creative new procedure, no matter how superior. The group will perceive it as an affront to tradition, a crime against institutional memory. You must first understand the entity you want to change. Failure to recognize the unwritten rules of the organization leads to frustration, bad decision making, and, all too often, the creation of dangerous and unnecessary opposition. Unfortunately Michael Ovitz learned these lessons the hard way.

4. Give Your Bosses What They Need, As Well As What They Want

For a co-leader no obligation is more important than speaking the truth to those in power. As chief insider, you have unique access to the person at the top, and you must tell him or her the truth as you see it, even when it hurts. To do so requires real courage, which may or may not be rewarded. General Pershing's receptivity to the truth was as much a factor in Marshall's success as his courage in speaking it. Such courage may give the fearless co-leader personal satisfaction, but remember, the person who points out the flaws in the boss's beloved new plan may do so at considerable peril.

Too many chieftains are like Sam Goldwyn, who insisted that his yes-men tell him the truth "even though it costs him his job." The result, of course, was that Goldwyn was usually spared the pain of hearing unpleasant truths, albeit at the cost of the honest feedback on which success depends. The wise leader welcomes the truth because he or she knows that first-rate information is essential to effective problem solving and good decision making. Wise leaders recognize that two heads really are better than one. But not all top dogs are wise. Executive suites are splattered, at least metaphorically, with the blood of too candid No. 2s or 3s. But tact is no crime either. The ability to make hard truths palatable is one that every long-lived co-leader has mastered.

5. Find Out What the Enterprise Needs Most and Deliver It Superbly

Some of the most distinguished co-leaders in the world are people who have transformed their organizations by making some crucial aspect of the operation their own. Intel's Craig Barrett is a prime example. As the chip maker's then head of manufacturing, Barrett caused productivity to soar and created a new industry standard. By assuming a critical area of responsibility and performing superbly, Barrett assured his succession to Andy Grove as Intel's CEO. (There is a risk that performing one aspect of the enterprise extraordinarily well will get you labeled an operations or marketing or finance type, but you can always prove you are a visionary once you get the top job.)

Organizations inevitably benefit from healthy competition among talented co-leaders hoping to impress their boards and bosses. That is never more true than when co-leaders know they are candidates for the top slot and that their performance is under especially intense scrutiny. At Avon Products, Inc., at least six executives were in 1997's in-house horse race to see who would succeed 64-year-old CEO Jim

Preston—three of them women. Executive Vice President Andrea
Jung had won kudos for giving the company what *Fortune* termed a
"marketing makeover," repositioning the venerable beauty business as
one "that takes women seriously." Edwina Woodbury, chief financial
and administrative officer, had won notice for the skill with which
she had streamlined the company and, in the process, found "ways to
free up cash for top-line growth." However, in December 1997 the
cosmetics maker tapped an outsider, Charles Perrin, former CEO of
battery maker Duracell International Inc. for the top spot. Nonetheless, Avon's female executives called it a fair fight, particularly Jung,
whose new job as president and COO not only made her one of the
first women COOs at a top U.S. company, but made her Perrin's
probable heir apparent. "I'm celebrating," said Jung of her promotion.

6. Don't Sell Your Soul (or Ruin Your Body)

One of the intrinsic problems of being an understudy is the pressure,
both internal and external, to become No. 1. Although the top gun
may suffer from fears of losing his or her primacy, he or she knows
what it is to star. The No. 1 role can seem irresistible to someone who
hasn't experienced both its pleasures and its shortcomings. Too often
ambitious adjuncts make a Faustian bargain. They give up everything
else in pursuit of top billing. They lose touch with their spouses. They
become strangers to their children. They turn their backs on work that
might bring them real satisfaction to engage in the kind of nonstop
court intrigue that still characterizes many corporations and other
organizations. Avocations are forgotten. Friends drop away. In extreme
cases parents are lost and barely mourned. While many apparently successful people are able to live this way for long periods of time, they
ultimately pay a terrible price. The community that supports and cares
for them begins to shrink. Worst of all, these frantic understudies are so
caught up in the organizational game that they fail to scrutinize their
own lives, to consider who they are and what they really need and to
make the changes that will prepare them for the next season of their
lives. However brilliant they may once have seemed, such people are
ultimately of limited value to the organization. At some point, their
obsessive ambition has cost them soul and substance.

As a condition to joining DreamWorks, Steven Spielberg insisted
that ample amounts of family time be built into his work routine.

Even as he was entering into an exciting new partnership with David Geffen and Jeffrey Katzenberg, a notorious workaholic, Spielberg was determined not to compromise his private life. Also aware of the importance of personal time, William Savoy, billionaire Paul G. Allen's thirty-something money manager, is an inveterate theater and concert goer. When Savoy is not tending the Microsoft cofounder's $22 billion fortune, he makes time for golf and other avocations, but he studiously avoids Seattle's frenzied, big-money charity scene. "My work persona is built around one person," Savoy told the *Wall Street Journal*. "I don't want my social life to be that too."

Similarly Intel CEO Craig Barrett not only does a superior job, he is obviously a complex, well-rounded human being. He has a life outside the chip maker—an extraordinarily active one that includes strenuous hiking and cycling, often with his wife, Barbara. Instead of haunting Intel's offices in Santa Clara, California, he chooses to commute once a week from his home in Phoenix. He retreats monthly to the ranch he and his wife own in western Montana. When Barrett assumed the top job at Intel, he brought to the position not just his demonstrated talent and experience, but a panoply of less obvious assets, such as self-awareness and personal equilibrium that serve both him and the company. The late Frank Wells loved Disney, but he had a private life as well, which included scaling some of the world's highest peaks. Barrett, too, sets goals and challenges for himself apart from those set by his superiors. That kind of self-possession and independence has leadership written all over it, whatever title the individual may have.

7. Lead As Well As Follow

In relating to the leader, a great co-leader routinely shows the good follower's virtues of loyalty, courage, and trustworthiness. But he or she must have all the skills and attributes of a leader as well. As first lieutenant, the co-leader is a model for the others in the organization. He or she knows how to serve the boss's needs without fawning. If the organization takes a wrong or immoral turn, a first-rate deputy does whatever is necessary to try to set it right. If that effort fails, the great co-leader maintains his or her personal integrity even at the cost of a job.

In addition to acting as checks on executive hubris, savvy cohorts function as talent spotters, always on the lookout, as George Marshall and Win Smith were, for able individuals who can be helped to become outstanding members of the team. Great first mates know how to find the right niche for others in the group. Great co-leaders are good mentors, and they also know how to translate for both the boss and the other members of the organization—they are good communicators.

Great co-leaders also understand the frustrations of the work-place. They make sure good work is recognized. They find ways to remove the impediments to good work, including onerous red tape and corrosive organizational values that encourage people who should be collaborators to undermine one another. In short they stem the tide of Dilbert postings in the workplace. Exceptional costars both revel in the details of the enterprise and understand the big pic-ture. They constantly find new ways to implement the organization's vision by better deploying its assets, most importantly, its people. One result is that great co-leaders enhance the very status of followership, which is no less important to the group than leadership.

8. Know When to Stay Put

Not everyone was meant to be No. 1. The temptation to star is so ingrained in our culture that many people feel compelled to take top positions for which they are poorly suited. Sometimes an extraordi-narily gifted person lacks the charisma for the top slot, the executive patina or the communications skills (the ability to sell the organiza-tion to the public, for instance) that being No. 1 usually requires. (Interestingly a number of contemporary CEO/entrepreneurs are compensating for their lack of personal charisma by hiring costars with flash and fire, as low-profile founder Stephen Kahng did at Power Computing Corp. when he tapped the flamboyant Joel Kocher.) Sometimes an individual has all the necessary attributes for the cor-ner office except the stomach for the job. Leading a company in a time of accelerating change, under unprecedented scrutiny from boards and shareholders, is not a job everyone wants. Contemporary CEOs live with the knowledge that they may be heroes one minute and zeros the next. All the glory may be theirs, but so is all the blame.

Look at the extraordinary beating AT&T chairman Robert E. Allen took in the press in 1996 and 1997. John R. Walter, who briefly succeeded Allen, was also pilloried. Among the blows Walter had to endure: reading in the national press a board member's judgment that he lacked "the intellectual leadership" for the job. There are outstanding men and women who would rather not risk being that large a target. There are top-notch individuals who want to build something great without taking ultimate responsibility and without being under constant public scrutiny. If they are smart, as Amy Tucker and Steve Ballmer are, such people continue in the role of costar.

9. Know When to Walk Away

Like leaders, co-leaders must learn when to say no. The second in command who discovers that his or her leader is involved in illegal or immoral behavior must counsel the chief and, if that fails, walk away. There are No. 1s who become unworthy of a decent person's loyalty. George Stephanopoulos toiled day and night to get Bill Clinton elected in 1992 and worked hard on the 1996 campaign as well. But the young adviser clearly felt Clinton had moved too far to the right in order to win reelection, and so he moved on to become a TV commentator.

Some bosses simply require too much of their aides. Such harried and harassed deputies often act much like abused children, redoubling their efforts to please their abuser. Charles Huang's 1995 film, *Swimming with Sharks,* is a fascinating black comedy about just such an unhealthy relationship between a monstrous Hollywood studio executive and his ambitious assistant. Certain causes are worthy of extraordinary sacrifices. J. Robert Oppenheimer worked so hard he damaged his already precarious health in the course of leading the Manhattan Project. But when a chief executive becomes so demanding that he or she threatens the health and sanity of his or her subordinates, the healthy co-leader says, "No more."

There are other reasons for leaving a supporting spot as well. At some point, most deputies decide they are ready to be No. 1, either at another existing organization or as the head of an enterprise they create for themselves. Sometimes that decision is hastened by the discovery that the co-leader is no longer the heir apparent that he or she was thought to be. In a relationship as interdependent as that between No. 1 and 2, chemistry is all. Relationships change, and the wise co-leader knows when the magic that once galvanized a great partnership has fizzled. Alex Mandl shocked Wall Street in 1996 when he suddenly resigned as No. 2 at AT&T to become CEO of a small, untested communications firm now called Teligent. Not long after Robert Allen named ill-fated outsider John Walter as AT&T president and Allen's likely successor, another up-and-comer at the telecommunications giant, Joseph P. Nacchio, quit as president of its residential long-distance division to become CEO of one of the hottest upstarts in telecommunications, Qwest Communications International.

Another common reason for moving on is a co-leader's desire to start the next stage of his or her life, instead of waiting for an entrenched No. 1's retirement. Some top dogs become so addicted to power that they can't step down (Armand Hammer at Occidental Petroleum comes immediately to mind). Almost half of all CEOs remain on the job for 10 or more years. For a deputy feeling his or her nascent power, a decade may seem like a lifetime.

10. Define Success on Your Terms

Success is one of the most seductive lures imaginable in a culture as preoccupied with winning and celebrity as ours. And yet much of the time most of us allow the terms of success to be determined by others. How many people of questionable talent continue to flock to Hollywood or Nashville in hopes of becoming a star? Albert Einstein had priceless counsel on this matter. "Try not to become a success," he said, "but rather try to become a man of value."

To accept a conventional definition of success is to lose what control any of us has over his or her destiny. Success in the sense of becoming a star is so dependent on luck as to be the equivalent of winning the lottery. The wise person defines success not in terms of being famous or anything else that we can only get from others, but in terms he or she can influence. You can't make yourself into the next Tom Cruise. But you can nurture a talent for acting into a craft that can be practiced in hundreds of satisfying ways, from teaching to doing regional theater.

Wise people find work that they love and do it well. They find people and causes they can believe in and serve them with all their heart and mind. They give their love and their energy to enterprises that improve people's lives, not diminish them. They find ways to savor all of life, not just the rewards of work. They realize that having fun is one of the litmus tests of a worthwhile enterprise. If, in the course of that, they become as rich and famous as Bill Gates or Michael Eisner, so be it. But even if they earn only modest rewards by conventional standards, they have found a way to live well.

Creating a Co-Leadership Culture

The once-popular image of the CEO was that of an all-powerful titan surrounded by a pack of pygmies—in the early days, who knew the name of anyone at the Ford Motor Co. but Henry Ford? Now as then, we need strong leaders who boldly pilot their organizations through increasingly choppy waters. But what more and more organizations are discovering is that they *don't* need pretentious bigwigs who behave like sultans and silence potentially invaluable co-leaders who dare to dissent, have better ideas than theirs, or compete with them for the spotlight.

"We can do as partners what we cannot do as singles," Daniel Webster once said. Enlightened employers are breeding grounds for, in behavioral scientist Peter M. Senge's words, "thinking partners," people who work for positive change at every level of the enterprise. These organizations consistently demonstrate the ability to forge a co-leadership culture. There's nothing magic about their approach. But here are 10 common strategies that encourage power sharing and co-leadership.

1. Celebrate the Enterprise, Not Celebrity

The planting of the American flag on Iwo Jima is probably the most famous image of World War II. It also captures the essence of the Marine Corps' special esprit in a single frame—a faceless team of men struggling to achieve a larger goal. Indeed two of the men have their backs turned to the camera, two are seen only from the side, and the fifth is hidden except for his arms and hands, which support the flag. There are no famous generals here, just five anonymous riflemen making a turning point in modern history.

Like the Marines, some of the country's best-run businesses (General Motors, McDonald's, Westinghouse, and Xerox, to name a few) are directed by all but invisible leaders and co-leaders. The people who run these enterprises rarely show up in *People* magazine. "There are no superstars at Wal-Mart," says low-key CEO David

Glass, a 23-year company veteran. "It's our people who make the difference *collectively*."

2. Foster Togetherness

Successful organizations avoid people who suck all the energy out of the enterprise without giving anything back. They discourage capricious self-interest. Bound by a common vision, these dynamic communities practice inclusion with a vengeance. At General Electric, CEO Jack Welch insists on a "boundaryless" organization in which information can come from anywhere, not just from the top.

Until recently teamwork had never been associated with the star culture at Fidelity Investment, best known for famed stock picker Peter Lynch. But eventually runaway egos and runaway growth at the Boston-based mutual fund giant began to hurt the firm's performance. "When you grow . . . quickly you can let the collegiality and the esprit get away from you," Robert C. Pozen, head of Fidelity's fund management group, told the *Financial Times*. To recapture the collegial spirit, the company has instituted free lunches several times a week for all employees. The theory is that these will encourage candid, broad-based talk about where the firm is and where it should be going. At the same time, teams of analysts have quietly replaced the big-name stock pickers of the past.

"Prima donnas need not apply," U.S. Robotics chairman Casey Cowell advises every prospective hire. Cowell says it is a commitment to teamwork that has allowed the $2 billion modem maker's remarkable growth. An expert at leveraging the talents of his co-leaders, Cowell concentrates on long-term planning and shares power with a team of key executives led by COO John McCartney. "In a sense, I do almost nothing—nothing directly," Cowell said in a *Business Week* interview.

3. Cultivate Egalitarianism

In strong co-leadership cultures, caste distinctions are kept to a minimum. CEOs and other top executives do not share in the divine right of kings. "Elitism is an expensive salve that doesn't work," warns Dow Chemical chairman Frank Popoff. "You thrive by having smart, dedicated people. Don't ever think you can divide the company into haves and have-nots, thinkers and doers." Debbi Fields of cookie fame agrees: "There is a lesson that lies in the foundation of my business—there is no such thing as an insignificant human being. To treat people that way is a kind of sin, and there's no reason for it, none."

Predictably the executive offices are modest at Dow Chemical, Mrs. Fields Inc., and many other companies with co-leadership cultures. Absent, too, are cushy executive dining rooms. Such firms understand that they will benefit if senior managers mingle daily with lower-echelon workers in the company cafeteria or beside the lunchwagon.

Ken Iverson, CEO of Nucor Corp., says the steelmaker has grown to $3.6 billion in annual sales as a result of "70 percent culture and 30 percent technology." Middle managers are few at Nucor, and everyone gains, or loses, with the company. In 1982, for instance, the company experienced a rare subpar year, and Iverson slashed his own expected salary of $450,000 by more than three-fourths.

4. Strengthen Self

Healthy co-leaders are supremely self-confident people who are prepared to sacrifice for something or someone bigger than themselves. They view themselves as every bit as talented as their more highly acclaimed superiors—and they often are. It is their superior self-esteem that enables them to succeed. Insecure people do not make good co-leaders.

While self-esteem may be inherited, like height or eye color, proponents of co-leadership believe it can also be nurtured. According to a recent annual report, GE systematically cultivates self-confident men and women "by turning them loose, giving them independence and resources, and encouraging them to take big swings." The payoff? "Self-confident people are open to good ideas regardless of their source and are willing to share them," CEO Jack Welch contends. "Their egos don't require that they originate every idea they use, or get credit for every idea they originate."

5. Nurture Trust

Trust is the coin of the realm in any partnership. It is as important as vision and common sense. Of course, chemistry also counts. The Dean Smith–Bill Guthridge partnership at North Carolina survived three decades because of their similar backgrounds, beliefs, and values. But without trust, Guthridge says, "I would have left a long time ago."

Building credibility is a two-way street. When looking for a chief operating officer, credentials are not as important as trust, Charles Wang, cofounder and CEO of $3.9 billion Computer Associates, told *Forbes*. The blunt, aggressive Chinese refugee described co-leader and COO Sanjay Kumar as "someone I absolutely trust."

Trust tends to flourish in organizations that stay focused on the tasks at hand. When everybody's busy advancing the goals of the organization, there's little time for the constant intrigue that breeds mistrust and undermines collaboration in many enterprises.

6. Purvey Hope

"A leader must be a dealer in hope," Confucius once said. CEOs committed to co-leadership are experts at restoring people's faith in the future, especially the faith of talented people who have been undervalued or mistreated by the organization.

Transition is an ideal time to infuse new hope. Upon joining Merck & Co. in 1996, Chairman Raymond V. Gilmartin gathered his top senior managers together and asked them: "What do you think are the major issues to resolve? If you had my job, what would you focus your time on?" As an outsider, the amiable newcomer sought to inject hope of genuine power sharing into a notoriously turf-conscious culture. Within three months, Gilmartin chose 12 people for his co-leadership team. "The way . . . I operate is to be receptive to other people's ideas and to basically respect what they do," Gilmartin told *Business Week,* adding, "I get a lot in return." And so do the stockholders. Since his arrival, the value of the pharmaceutical giant's shares have skyrocketed.

In assessing Gilmartin's consensus-building style, Merck director William G. Bowen said: "He went in with the idea this was going to be a partnership. He was eager to release the talent that was there." By creating a wave of optimism, the new chairman quickly transformed his organization.

7. Institutionalize Dissent

Abraham Lincoln's success as president was due to a number of remarkable traits, not the least of which was his rare ability to listen carefully to his constituents. Almost every day he threw open the doors of the White House for his "public opinion baths." Dozens of people dropped in to voice their concerns. In addition he solicited hundreds of letters, most of which he responded to himself in long-hand. These exchanges gave Lincoln uncanny insight into the public mind and enabled him to react to it in an informed way.

Perhaps the single most important characteristic of any co-leadership culture is a similar willingness to solicit the truth. Organizations that appreciate the power of disharmony and the importance of speaking out have an enormous edge over those that prefer the comfort of unanimity. Smart organizations recognize the cost of insights unshared and constructive criticism unspoken. Wise organizations don't wimp out. They welcome honest dissent within the ranks. Of course, all sides can't prevail in a debate, but all opinions can contribute to shaping the right answer. The co-leader who is willing to speak up shows precisely the kind of initiative that real leadership is made of.

8. Redefine Loyalty

Every leader requires allegiance. In a recent survey, a large group of CEOs said loyalty was what they most wanted in those who reported to them. In today's unsettled, boss-a-year environment, leaders place an understandable premium on fidelity. But at what cost?

Blind devotion often backfires. Befriending the wrong boss can be hazardous to one's career. Many co-leaders have been done in by their overly close association with a flawed chief. John Zeglis's strong ties to Robert Allen may have cost him the top job at AT&T, while Al Gore could lose his bid for the presidency because he has been a flawed leader's loyal lieutenant.

Genuine co-leadership abhors toadyism. But loyalty can mean walking a tightrope of personal and institutional interests and obligations. Strong boards sometimes help by giving co-leaders an alternative entity to be loyal to, but, ultimately, questions of loyalty must usually be resolved the old-fashioned way: by measuring what is asked of you against your most basic values.

9. Balance Power

As Sophocles wrote, Power shows the man. The thoughtful and imaginative use of power is a hallmark of great leaders. "Strange as it sounds, great leaders gain authority by giving it away," Vice Admiral James B. Stockdale of the Hoover Institute has said. There's real clout in generosity: We get power by deeding it to others.

First-rate chiefs recognize that leadership is not a zero-sum game. Yet striking the proper power balance is not easy. Sharing authority requires a sure touch. As Bill Walsh, the highly successful ex-coach of the San Francisco 49ers, once observed: "Too little and you become a figurehead, too much and you squelch creativity." In World War II both Roosevelt and Churchill rarely countermanded their generals, while Hitler constantly second-guessed the German military.

10. Build Team Goals

"We are all in this alone," comic Lily Tomlin once quipped. Co-leaders beg to disagree. They understand that fostering esprit requires people to think beyond themselves. Colleagues are not competitors.

"There's more to life than competing," said Olympic champion Jackie Joyner-Kersee. "If I can cheer someone on, I'm willing to do that." By establishing team goals and encouraging people to work collaboratively, co-leaders dampen potentially debilitating intramural competition. "Where you want the contest, is not among people, but among *ideas,*" U.S. Robotics' Casey Cowell has said.

Looking Ahead

As we enter the new millennium, leadership is undergoing a dramatic transformation. Aware that we have long lived in what Robert H. Frank and Philip J. Cook aptly termed *The Winner-Take-All Society* (the title of their best-selling book), we are finally beginning to question the time-honored assumption that any great institution is the work of one person, however great.

Another, perhaps more accurate prism through which the new organizational reality may be viewed transcends No. 1s and No. 2s. It considers relationships at all levels of the organization. The New Economy is characterized by camaraderie grounded in shared accomplishment. It is powered by teams of people working toward a common goal, doing exciting work, and doing it collaboratively. In this brave new world, one of leadership's most important challenges is to understand and manage these multiple relationships as true partnerships. Leaders who fail to do so risk losing any organization's most important resource—its talent.

That CEOs and other top dogs have lost some of their luster is evidenced in many ways. The No. 1 job in most organizations is no longer a sinecure. CEOs are being replaced more quickly and more often than ever before. They are also increasingly having to make concessions, including promising to step down by a certain date, in order to find first-rate successors.

As top executives have lost the aura of infallibility, co-leaders have gained in reputation. We all know how much is accomplished by the men and women behind the throne. Also helping democratize our ideas of leadership is the proliferation of the Silicon Valley model for success. Whatever their titles, people stay in the best high-tech companies because the work is exciting and because they choose to. In these profoundly nonhierarchical organizations, people are too engaged in the creative work at hand to think of themselves as either a No. 1 or No. 2 or No. 3. In these companies roles and titles tend not to be fixed. Instead all the cards are in the air, and one good idea is all it takes to turn today's co-leader into the CEO of tomorrow's hottest startup.

The value of co-leadership also becomes increasingly clear as we shift our emphasis from rewarding good work to doing good work. Co-leaders aren't masochists. They don't choose to work for and with others because it hurts. They do it because they understand that nothing is more joyful than doing something important with others whom you respect. George Marshall once said that there was no limit to the amount of good people could accomplish as long as they didn't care who received the credit. If you are concerned about the credit, you are paying too much attention to something other than the task.

Writer Roger Rosenblatt captured the spirit of the great co-leader in a wonderful tribute to the late George Burns. The cigar-smoking comic made a career of working in the shadow of his marvelously ditzy wife, Gracie Allen. Like other great costars, Burns understood the personal and professional rewards that come only as a result of collaboration.

As Rosenblatt writes, "The essence of the straight man is that he gives. He gives the best lines, the stage, the spotlight. By giving, he creates the show—the entire show, including all the performances.

. . . And he gets by giving. It takes a certain kind of person to do that—one who is willing to diminish his part for the good of the whole."

The generosity of the great co-leader is grounded in a profound understanding that we are all in this together. We need community as surely as we need water, food, or air. It is only in fruitful alliances with others that we can do great things and put down, if only for a time, the burden of self.

No wonder satisfied co-leaders don't care about the credit. They are having too much fun creating the show. In a great partnership, everybody wins.

Acknowledgments

First, a word about the development of this book. Our friend and colleague Patricia Ward Biederman labored with us from the start of this project in 1994. Despite the pressures and success of her own writing projects, Pat gave our ideas flight and elegance. She not only read and critiqued our source materials but also helped fashion the overall presentation of this book. Her passion for co-leadership accompanied us every step along the way. To say that she was a true collaborator would not be an exaggeration.

■

Many other people also helped make this book possible. A very special thanks goes to Kristin Hohenadel. Her painstaking research clarified earlier versions of this manuscript. Marie MacCord also assisted on selected research assignments.

In the academic community, we are especially indebted to Spencer Johnson, Ed Perkins, Jerry Porras, and Bill Hamilton, who reviewed various segments of our work. Other scholars who offered invaluable insights were Kirby Warren, Ed Schein, Stan Davis, George Parker, Robert Kelley, and Dan Boylan. George Kanahele deserves particular credit for his critique of the Bernice Pauahi Bishop material. Gussie Bento and Michael Chun of the Kamehameha Schools were also extremely helpful as were their counterparts at the Bishop Museum. Besides Ed Perkins's classic *Wall Street to Main Street*, Win Smith, Jr., Selina Morris, Ron Young, and Lee Roselle of Merrill

Lynch made the co-leadership tandem of Charlie Merrill and Win Smith come alive.

A microscopic version of our thinking first appeared in *Across The Board*. Our thanks go to Al Vogl for permitting us to incorporate this earlier piece. Our efforts were also influenced by a number of excellent writers who are duly cited in the Notes. They include: Bob Lutz, Micheline Maynard, Paul Eisenstein, Daniel McGinn, Jeffrey Young, Richard Nixon, John McCook Roots, Kai-yu Hsu, Dick Wilson, Han Suyin, Forrest Pogue, Doris Kearns Goodwin, Howard Gardner, Ed Cray, Larry Bland, Leonard Mosley, Helen Elmira Waite, Richard Harrity, Ralph Martin, Nella Braddy, Joseph Lash, Steve Tally, Richard Berke, Lee Pace, Bill Cole, Ron Green, Jr., Dwight Chapin, Dick Rockne, Candace Putnam, Michael Pointer, Skip Bayless, Mark Landler, and Geraldine Fabrikant. Our heartfelt thanks go to this special group of people.

For similar reasons, we are enormously grateful to many co-leaders, but especially Al Gore, Bob Lutz, Bill Guthridge, Amy Tucker, Dick Tomey, and Homer Smith, who gave us a better understanding of the power of great partnerships.

For their gifted editorial assistance and devotion to this project, we are indebted to Henning Gutmann and Renana Meyers of John Wiley & Sons. Their keen interest in this subject boosted our enthusiasm. Others rendering special assistance include Marie Christian, Jenny Okano, Debbie Miyagi, Suzanne Yamada, Claire Huismann, and Kathleen Deselle. Our longtime friend and agent Bill Leigh clarified our earlier ideas and handled all negotiations. Barbara Monteiro helped bring the book to market. Martha Miller's competence, diligence, and unfailing good cheer through successive versions of the manuscript contributed greatly to its completion.

Last but not least, our wives, Nery and Grace, have been at our side throughout this project. *Co-Leaders* would not be what it is without them. They each read and commented on the entire manuscript and helped reshape its principal arguments. To these most loving and constructive critics goes a very special *Mahalo*.

Notes

Unless indicated in the notes below, quotations were from interviews with the authors or their associates.

Preface
viii   Daniel Webster at the signing of the Declaration of Independence, Philadelphia, July 4, 1776.

Chapter 1: The Case for Co-Leaders

3   Jeffrey Young, "The George S. Patton of Software," *Forbes,* 27 January 1997, 88.

4   For more on the importance of organizational collaboration, see Warren Bennis and Patricia Ward Biederman, *Organizing Genius: The Secret of Creative Collaboration* (Reading, Mass.: Addison-Wesley, 1997), and David A. Heenan, "Second Bananas," *Across the Board* (February 1996): 26–28.

7   Andy Grove, "Taking on Prostate Cancer," *Fortune,* 13 May 1996, 72.

8   "Transitions," *Chief Executive* (November 1997): 79. See, too, Nikhil Deogun, "Coke's Deep Management Bench Assures Market While Its Chief Is Hospitalized," *Wall Street Journal,* 10 September 1997, B2, and David Greising, *I'd Like the World to Buy a Coke: The Life and Leadership of Roberto Goizueta* (New York: John Wiley & Sons, 1998).

8   Nikhil Deogun, "Advice to Coke People from Their New Boss: Don't Get Too Cocky," *Wall Street Journal,* 9 March 1998, A1, A11.

8   Betsy Morris, "Doug is It," *Fortune,* 25 May 1998, 74.

8   On Ivester's reluctance to appoint an heir apparent, see Morris, "Doug is It," 84.

9   The upward mobility of No.2s is presented by Ward Howell International in Christine Foster, "Couples," *Forbes,* 2 December 1996, 18–20.

10   Neal Templin, "Passed Over for the No. 1 Job at Chrysler, He Parked His Pride and Thrives as No. 2," *Wall Street Journal,* 3 April 1995, B1.

10   See Robert E. Kelley, "In Praise of Followers," *Harvard Business Review* (November–December 1988): 142–148, and *The Power of Followership: How to Create Leaders People Want to Follow and Followers Who Lead Themselves* (New York: Currency/Doubleday, 1992).

11   Micheline Maynard, "Lutz's Career on Final Lap," *USA Today,* 26 May 1998, 5B.

12   The description of Stephen Kahng and Joel Kocher at Power Computing and the related quotes are from Peter Burrows, "Power Duo," *Business Week,* 21 April 1997, 127.

12   Erma Bombeck's remarks are from Erma Bombeck, "Erma Bombeck Quotes," in http://www.cp-tel.net/miller/Bill Lee/quotes/Bombeck.html.

13   Tim Weiner, "For 'the Ultimate Staff Guy,' a Time to Reap the Rewards of Being Loyal," *New York Times,* 20 March 1997, B13.

14   Harvey Araton, "A Loyal Aide Takes Pride in the Feat," *New York Times,* 16 March 1997, 31.

14   Keith Bradsher, "A Different Sort of Scion," *New York Times,* 20 September 1998, BU6.

17   Mary H. Krout, *The Memories of the Honorable Bernice Pauahi Bishop* (New York: The Knickerbocker Press, 1908), 228–229.

17   Robert Lenzner and Stephen S. Johnson, "Seeing Things as They Really Are," *Forbes,* 10 March 1997, 122.

18   The information on U.S. CEO compensation is from Bethany McLean, "Where's the Loot Coming From?," *Fortune,* 7 September 1998, 129.

18   For more on the salary differential between Chrysler and Daimler executives, see Thane
        Peterson, "A Giant Leap for the New Europe," *Business Week,* 18 May 1998, 42, and Greg
        Steinmetz and Gregory L. White, "Chrysler Pay Draws Fire Overseas," *Wall Street Journal,* 26
        May 1998, B1.

18   "Call It Executive Overcompensation," *Business Week,* 21 April 1997, 162.

Chapter 2: The Two Bobs: Sharing the Driver's Seat

24   See Edward A. Robinson, "America's Most Admired Companies," *Fortune,* 3 March 1997,
        F-2. Also Jerry Flint, "Company of the Year: Chrysler," *Forbes,* 13 January 1997, 83, and "The
        Top Managers of 1996," *Business Week,* 13 January 1997, 60. Also see "Industry Rankings of
        the S&P 500," *Business Week,* 24 March 1997, 120–121. In addition, *Fortune's* fifteenth
        Annual Corporate Reputations Survey listed Chrysler as the "most admired" firm in the
        motor vehicle and parts industry.

24   Paul A. Eisenstein, "Lutz Helped Revive Chrysler's Fortunes," *Washington Times,* 19 March
        1993, G1. See, too, his "Straight Shooting," *Cigar Aficionado* (Summer 1996): 185, and "At
        Chrysler, It's Time to Bulk Up," *Investor's Business Daily,* 22 October 1996, A4.

24   Neal Templin, "Passed Over for the No. 1 Job at Chrysler, He Parked His Pride and Thrives
        as No. 2," *Wall Street Journal,* 3 April 1995, B1.

24   For more on Bob Lutz's career, see Robert A. Lutz, *GUTS* (New York: John Wiley & Sons,
        1998); "CEO Award Winners—Automobile Industry," *Wall Street Transcript,* 19 July 1993; Alex
        Taylor III, "Will Success Spoil Chrysler?," *Fortune,* 10 January 1994; Bill Vlasic and David
        Woodruff, "Chrysler's Most Valuable Player?" *Business Week,* 22 January 1996; Micheline May-
        nard, "Lutz: Taking Life by Barnstorm," *USA Today,* 17 May 1996, B1; and John Lynker, "Lutz's
        Training, Experience Make Top-Drawer Executive," *Washington Times,* 29 March 1996.

25   Eisenstein, "Lutz Helped Revive Chrysler's Fortunes," G1.

25   Jay Akasie, "To Go or Not to Go . . .," *Forbes,* 8 September 1997, 20.

26   Lutz, *GUTS,* 5.

26   Paul Eisenstein, "Book Offers Another View of the 'Iacocca Legacy,' " *Christian Science Mon-
        itor,* 3 August 1995, 9. See, too, Doron Levin, *Behind the Wheel At Chrysler: The Iacocca Legacy*
        (New York: Harcourt Brace, 1995).

26   Vlasic and Woodruff, "Chrysler's Most Valuable Player?"

26   Maynard, "Lutz," 2B. Eisenstein, "Lutz Helped Revive Chrysler's Fortune," G1.

27   Tom Denomme, "Fighting Bob," *Business Week,* 16 October 1995, 95. Bob Eaton's arrival at
        Chrysler is described in J. P. Donlon, "Eaton Hits a Few Speed Bumps," *Chief Executive*
        (November 1997): 26–33.

27   The comments about the Chrysler difference and the Port Huron experience are from "Can
        Chrysler Keep It Up?," *Business Week,* 25 November 1996, 108–120; Donlon, "Eaton Hits a
        Few Speed Bumps," 30.

27   Lutz, *GUTS,* 40; Denomme, "Fighting Bob"; Ibid., 90; See, too, Donlon, "Eaton Hits a Few
        Speed Bumps," 30.

28   Lutz, *GUTS,* 39.

29   Daniel McGinn, "Just Fine, Thanks," *Newsweek,* 22 June 1998, 56.

29   Lutz, *GUTS,* xii.

29   Maynard, "Lutz," 2B.

30   Eisenstein, "Lutz Helped Revive Chrysler's Fortunes."

30   The platform teams approach is variously described. See, for example, Vlasic and Woodruff,
        "Chrysler's Most Valuable Player?"; Denomme, "Fighting Bob"; and "Can Chrysler Keep It
        Up?," 112–116.
        Chrysler's impressive production timetable is reported in Micheline Maynard and James R.
        Healey, "Detroit's Dazzling Performance," *USA Today,* 18–20 April 1997, B2.

31   Vlasic and Woodruff, "Chrysler's Most Valuable Player?," 64; Templin, "Passed Over," B1;
        Lutz, *GUTS,* 32; The $1,000–$1,500 cost advantage was offered by Lutz in Flint, "Com-
        pany of the Year," 85.

31   Taylor, "Will Success Spoil Chrysler?"; Micheline Maynard, "At Chrysler: The Bobs' Man-
        agement Style Spells Success," *USA Today,* 13 January 1997, 4B.

31   Haig Simonian, "The Man Who Saved Chrysler's Skin," *Financial Times,* 14–15 February
        1998, IX.

31   See Lutz's remarks on "the ritualistic B.S." in Taylor, "Will Success Spoil Chrysler?," 88;
        "Can Chrysler Keep It Up?," 109.

32   Taylor, "Will Success Spoil Chrysler?," 88. See, too, Denomme, "Fighting Bob," 89.
32   Eisenstein, "Lutz Helped Revive Chrysler's Fortunes."
32   Micheline Maynard, "Chrysler Shuffles Lineup of Executive," *USA Today*, 6 December 1996, 1B; Eisenstein, "Straight Shooting," 189; Micheline Maynard, "Eaton Pulls Through With Poise, Skill," *USA Today*, 19 May 1995, 2B.
33   Denomme, "Fighting Bob," 95.
33   Gabriella Stern, "Chrysler's President Rejects Kerkorian's Reaching Out, Says He Isn't Interested," *Wall Street Journal*, 10 September 1995, A4; "The Gloves are Coming Off at Chrysler," *Business Week*, 2 October 1995, 62. See also Denomme, "Fighting Bob," 95.
34   Denomme, "Fighting Bob," 95; Maynard, "Eaton Pulls Through," 2B.
34   Eaton's career is outlined in Denomme, "Fighting Bob," 90.
34   For more on the CEO poll, see Josh McHugh, "Find a Better Way," *Forbes*, 13 January 1997, 90–91.
35   Maynard, "At Chrysler."
35   Taylor, "Will Success Spoil Chrysler?," 88; Lutz, *GUTS*, 155; "Can Chrysler Keep It Up?," 112.
35   Jerry Flint, "The Car Chrysler Didn't Build," *Forbes*, 12 August 1966, 89–91.
36   Flint, "The Car Chrysler Didn't Build"; Lutz, *GUTS*, 212. See, too, pages 195, 200–201.
36   Vlasic and Woodruff, "Chrysler's Most Valuable Player," 65.
36   Robert Lutz, speech to the American International Club of Geneva, Switzerland, 3 March 1997; Marjorie Sorge, "Time to Listen to the 'Kinky' Guys," *Automotive Industries*, 1 September 1996, 5.
36   Flint, "Company of the Year," 84.
36   Lutz, speech to the American International Club of Geneva.
37   Lutz, *GUTS*, 36, 238–239.
37   Rachel Konrad, "Exec Says this is Last Year with Automaker," *Detroit Free Press*, 6 January 1998, 3.
37   Lutz's description of himself as "Chief Coaching Officer" is from his speech to the American International Club of Geneva; Angelo B. Henderson, "Chrysler Moves Lutz, With No Hints on New No. 2," *Wall Street Journal*, 6 December 1966, A4.
38   Bill Vlasic, "An Efficiency Nut at the Wheel," *Business Week*, 9 February 1998, 78; Robyn Meredith, "An Obsessive Cost-Cutter Takes Charge at Chrysler," *International Herald Tribune*, 3–4 January 1998, 9.
38   Meredith, "An Obsessive Cost-Cutter."
38   Ibid.; "Chrysler: Priority Shifts to Quality," *USA Today*, 20 January 1998, 3B, and Vlasic, "An Efficiency Nut," 76.
39   Daniel Howes, "New Chrysler Chief to Attack Problems," *Detroit News*, 16 December 1997.
39   Lutz, *GUTS*, 112; McGinn, "Just Fine," 56; Micheline Maynard, "Lutz's Career on Final Lap," *USA Today*, 26 May 1998, 5B; Eisenstein, "Lutz Helped Revive Chrysler's Fortunes."
39   Lutz, *GUTS*, 180.
40   Donlon, "Eaton Hits a Few Speed Bumps," 32.
40   For more on the Chrysler-Daimler merger, see Douglas Lavin, " 'Daimler' is Roadworthy," *Wall Street Journal*, 8 May 1998, A14; Bruce Horowitz, "Merge Obstacle Course Puts Eaton to the Driving Test," *USA Today*, 7 May 1998, 3B; and Micheline Maynard, "Each Firm Would Benefit from Other's Strengths," *USA Today*, 7 May 1998, 1A.

Chapter 3: Cyberstars: Ballmer Is to Gates What Barrett Is to Grove
43   Norman Pearlstine, "The Man and the Magic," *Time*, 29 December 1997, 8.
43   The estimate on PC household use is from J. P. Donlon, "The Fourth Comes Forth, *Chief Executive*," October 1988, 31.
45   For a discussion of America's most "valuable" company, see Allan Sloan, "Bragging Rights," *Newsweek*, 27 July 1998, 35.
45   For more on the origins of Microsoft, see Bill Gates with Nathan Myhrvold and Peter Rinearson, *The Road Ahead* (New York: Viking, 1995).
45   For an excellent discussion of Steve Ballmer's contributions, see Jeffrey Young, "The George S. Patton of Software," *Forbes*, 27 January 1997; James Wallace and Jim Erickson, *Hard Drive: Bill Gates and the Making of the Microsoft Empire* (New York: John Wiley & Sons, 1992), 163–164.
45   Gates, *Road Ahead*, 43.
46   Steve Ballmer, the recruiter, is examined in "Wired for Hiring: Microsoft's Slick Recruiting Machine," *Fortune*, 5 February 1996, 124; His recruiting philosophy and *InfoWorld* interview are reported by Wallace and Erickson, *Hard Drive*, 260.

46   Bill Gates, video interview, National Museum of American History, Smithsonian Institution, 1997; Young, "George S. Patton," 88.

46   For more on Microsoft lingo, see Ken Barnes and Associates, "Microspeak LEXICON," jeeem@rocketmail.com, 1995–1998.

46   "The Embalmer" moniker is discussed in "Technology's Very Richest," *Forbes ASAP*, 6 October 1997, 60.

47   The Microsoft executive's description of Ballmer at Harvard is from Wallace and Erickson, *Hard Drive*, 164. Ballmer's role in the partnership is discussed in "Bill's Co-Pilot," *Business Week*, 14 September 1998, 77.

47   Young, "George S. Patton," 90.

48   For more on "Bashing Big Blue" and the Windows launch, see Gates, *Road Ahead*, 47–63.

48   Young, "George S. Patton," 88. See also Brent Schlender, "What Bill Gates Really Wants," *Fortune*, 16 January 1995, 34.

49   The reports on various Windows sales are from Ballmer's Keynote Address to the 1997 PC Expo, 17 December 1997, reprinted by the Microsoft Home Network.

49   An assessment of the Netscape/Java alliance is found in "Microsoft vs. Netscape: Round One," *Fortune*, 8 July 1996, 70.

49   Brent Schlender, "Javaman: The Adventures of Scott McNealy," *Fortune*, 13 October 1997, 2. See, too, "Sun and Microsoft: A Simmering Dispute," *The Economist*, 21 February 1998, 67.

49   Young, "George S. Patton," 86, 90.

50   Steve Hamm, with Amy Cortese and Susan B. Garland, "In Search of the Real Bill Gates," *Time*, 13 January 1997, 6.

50   Schlender, "What Bill Gates Really Wants," 13.

50   Hamm, "In Search of the Real Bill Gates," 9, and 6, respectively.

51   Young, "George S. Patton," 92.

51   Ibid., 18. See, too, "In Search of the Real Bill Gates," 15.

51   Gates, *Road Ahead*, 43. For more on the Microsoft culture, see James K. Glassman, "Gates Leads Economy," *Honolulu Advertiser*, 8 October 1997, A12.

52   "In Search of the Real Bill Gates," 17; Gates, *Road Ahead*, 35.

52   James Surowiecki, "In Praise of an Organization Man," *Wall Street Journal*, 30 March 1998, A18.

52   Kevin Maney, "Grove Sets New Course with Intel," *USA Today*, 27 March 1998, 1B. For more on Intel and the Grove philosophy, see Andrew S. Grove, *Only the Paranoid Survive: How to Exploit the Crisis Points* (New York: Currency/Doubleday, 1996). See, too, David Kirkpatrick, "Intel's Amazing Profit Machine," *Fortune*, 17 February 1997. For a less than kind picture of the company, see Tim Jackson, *Inside Intel* (New York: Dutton, 1998).

52   Louise Kehoe, "Grove Hands Over Control of Intel After 11 Years at the Top," *Financial Times*, 27 March 1998, 15.

53   Louise Kehoe, "Not a Grove in the Valley," *Financial Times*, 28/29 March 1997, 7.

53   Steve Lohr, "Intel's Chief Steps Down After 11 Years," *New York Times*, 27 March 1998, C1. See, too, Brent Schlender, "The Incredible, Profitable Career of Andy Grove," *Fortune*, 27 April 1998, 34.

54   "Intel Begins Transition as Grove Quits as CEO," *International Herald Tribune*, 27 March 1998, 13; " 'Man of the Year' Gets Out While the Getting is Good," *Barron's*, 30 March 1998, 12; Lohr, "Intel's Chief Steps Down," C4. For a contrary opinion, see Andy Reinhardt, "Who Says Intel's Chips Are Down?," *Business Week*, 7 December 1998, 103.

54   Julie Schmit, "Intel's Next CEO 'Ready to Flex His Muscle,' " *USA Today*, 27 March 1998, 5B; Schlender, "The Incredible, Profitable Career of Andy Grove," 35.

54   Professor Nix's recollection of Barrett is found in Margaret D. Williams, "Intel's Barrett Thrives in Andy Grove's Shadow," *Computer News Daily*, 13 May 1997.

54   See, for example, David Einstein, "Intel's Craig Barrett Adds Title of President," *San Francisco Chronicle*, 21 May 1997. See, too, Barrett's interview with Sam Whitmore, "Barrett Makes Plans for Intel," *The Site*, Ziff-Davis TV Inc., 1997; Williams "Intel's Barrett Thrives."

55   For an excellent description of a typical Barrett plant visit, see Dean Takahashi, "A Demanding Boss Goes on Tour," *Upside, Today!* 1 October 1997; Andy Reinhardt, "Intel's Detail Man Craig Barrett," *Dataquest*, 30 June 1997.

55   "Intel," *Business Week*, 22 December 1997, 73; Kirkpatrick, "Intel's Amazing Profit Machine," 63.

56   Don Clark, "A Big Bet Made Intel What It is Today: Now It Wagers Again," *Wall Street Journal*, 7 June 1995, A1.

56   Schmit, "Intel's Next CEO," 5B; Clark, "A Big Bet," A4.

56   "Q&A with Intel's Craig Barrett—Part II," *Electronic Buyers' News,* 1997. See, too, Brent Schlender, "The New Man Inside Intel," *Fortune,* 11 May 1998, 161; Tom Quinlan, "Intel's Chief: New Chip at One Helm, But Off the Old Block," *Seattle Times,* 24 May 1997; Clark, "A Big Bet," A4.

56   For more on Intel's hard line and the AMD and DEC run-ins, see Jackson, *Inside Intel;* Clark, "A Big Bet"; and Josh McHugh, "Don't Mess With Me," *Forbes,* 23 March 1998, 42.

57   Andy Reinhardt, "Intel's Detail Man Craig"; Dean Takahashi, "Barrett Inside," *Upside* (November 1997): 158–168.

57   Grove's description of Washingtonians may be found in Takahashi, "Barrett Inside."

57   Andy Grove, "My Turn: Breaking the Chains of Command," *Newsweek,* 3 October 1983, 23.

58   Grove, *Only the Paranoid Survive,* 162, and 115, respectively.

58   Takahashi, "Barrett Inside," 158–168.

58   Takahashi, "Barrett Inside"; Dean Takahashi, "Intel's Barrett Moves Nearer to the Top Job," *Wall Street Journal,* 14 January 1997, B1.

58   "Key to Success: People, People, People," *Fortune,* 27 October 1997, 232; Kara Swisher, "Oh, What a Tangled Web Silicon Valley Moguls Weave," *Wall Street Journal,* 5 March 1998, B6; Schlender, "The New Man Inside Intel," 163.

59   The Intel succession scenario is outlined in Dean Takahashi, "Grove is Yielding Top Spot at Intel at a Pivotal Point," *Wall Street Journal,* 27 March 1998, B1; "Intel Names Fourth President, Possible Grove Heir," *USA Today,* 2 September 1997, B1.

59   Joshua Cooper Ramo, "A Survivor's Tale," *Time,* 29 December 1997, 72.

Chapter 4: Winthrop H. Smith: A Breed Apart

63   For an excellent description of turn of the century capitalism, see Jonathan R. Laing, "Thank you, Clarence," *Barron's 75th,* 20 May 1996, A7; Maggie Mahar, " 'You Must Buy Stocks,' " Ibid., A12; Bridget O'Brian, "Easy But Sleazy," *Wall Street Journal,* 26 May 1996, R12; and Dave Kansas, "Taking Stock," Ibid., R1.

64   For more on Charles Edward Merrill, see esp. Edwin J. Perkins, *Wall Street to Main Street: Charles Merrill and the Quest for Middle Class Investors* (London: Cambridge University Press, forthcoming). See, too, Daniel Gross, *Forbes' Great Business Stories of All Time* (New York: John Wiley & Sons, Inc., 1996), esp. 91–105. Other sources are supplied mainly by Merrill Lynch, namely: Henry Hecht, ed., *A Legacy of Leadership: Merrill Lynch, 1884–1985* (New York: Merrill Lynch, 1985); "The World of Merrill Lynch," a Merrill Lynch brochure, 1994; Joseph Nocera, *A Piece of the Action: How the Middle Class Joined the Money Class* (New York: Simon and Schuster, 1994); "Merrill Lynch & Co., Inc.," *International Directory of Company Histories, Vol. II* (Chicago: St. James Press, 1990); "Charles Edward Merrill," *Forbes,* 1 November 1947; "Brokerage Supermarket," *Business Week,* 8 November 1947; "Merrill Lynch Adds an 'Inc.' to Its Name," *Business Week,* 13 December 1958; "Charlie Merrill Always Called Them Right," *Fortune,* May 1972; Robert Sobel, "The People's Choice," *Barron's,* 19 February 1997, 23; and a series of articles in the *Commercial & Financial Chronicle.*

64   Gross, "Forbes' Great Business Stories," 95. See, too, Hecht, *Legacy of Leadership,* 21–22.

64   Interview with Winthrop H. Smith, 16 November 1956, ML Files.

65   Hecht, *Legacy of Leadership,* 41. See, too, Gross, 96; Hecht, *Legacy of Leadership,* 42.

66   Hecht, *Legacy of Leadership,* 30.

66   Hecht, *Legacy of Leadership,* 56. See, too, Smith's interviews, 16 November 1956, ML Files, and his "Reminiscences of Charles E. Merrill," ML Files.

67   Hecht, *Legacy of Leadership,* 60. See, too, Smith, "Reminiscences."

67   Hecht, *Legacy of Leadership,* 61; The "department store of finance" charge is variously reported. See "Merrill Lynch & Co., Inc.," 424. The firm's "We the People" campaign and its trailblazing marketing efforts are examined in "Brokerage Supermarket." See, too, "Merrill Lynch Adds an 'Inc.' to Its Name."

67   For more on the firm's Ten Commandments, see "The World of Merrill Lynch."

68   Smith, "Reminiscences." For more on Merrill's health problems, see Perkins, *Wall Street to Main Street,* chap. 11.

70   Merrill Lynch's system of remote-control management is discussed in Perkins, *Wall Street to Main Street,* chap. 11. See, too, "Brokerage Supermarket." The "What Everybody Ought To Know" campaign is described in Gross, *Forbes' Great Business Stories,* 101. The firm's "Own Your Share of America" program is discussed in Kansas, "Taking Stock," R6.

70 J. P. Donlon, "Merrill Cinch," *Chief Executive* (March 1998): 31. See also, Martin Schifrin, "Merrillizing the World," *Forbes,* 10 February 1997, 147–151.

71 The estimate of current U.S. stock ownership was reported by David Hale of Zurich Kemper Investments in James L. Tyson, "America's Consuming Love Affair with Stocks," *Christian Science Monitor,* 17 October 1997, 11.

71 For more on the 1956 Ford Motor stock offering, see Kansas, "Taking Stock," R6; Hecht, *Legacy of Leadership,* 85.

71 See "Merrill Lynch Adds an 'Inc.' to Its Name," 134.

72 Merrill to Smith, 18 February 1946, ML Files.

72 Perkins, *Wall Street to Main Street,* chap. 11, 4.

72 Merrill to Smith, 5 February 1947, ML Files.

73 Merrill, handwritten notes, ML Files; Merrill to Smith, 15 December 1951, ML Files.

73 Merrill to Smith, 20 September 1943, ML Files. See, too, Merrill to Smith, 9 May 1953, ML files.

73 Smith, "Reminiscences."

73 Merrill to Smith, 9 May 1953, ML Files.

73 Merrill to Smith, 23 December 1954, ML Files; Merrill to Smith, 9 December 1954, ML Files.

74 Merrill to Smith, 30 December 1954, ML Files.

74 Hecht, *Legacy of Leadership,* 19. See, too, Merrill's "Closing Remarks" at the ML Managers Conference, October 19–20, 1953.

74 Smith, "Reminiscences"; Merrill to Smith, 23 November 1955, ML Files.

75 Hecht, *Legacy of Leadership,* 19. See, also, Smith, "Reminiscences."

75 Hecht, *Legacy of Leadership,* 19.

75 Sobel, "The People's Choice," 23.75

000 See Edmund Lynch, Jr., interview, undated, ML Files; See Robert Rooke interview, 27 November 1956, ML Files.

76 Herbert Melcher interview, 29 November 1956, ML Files.

76 Hecht, *Legacy of Leadership,* 89.

76 See Perkins, *Wall Street to Main Street,* 6; Smith, "Reminiscences."

77 Charlie Merrill's dubbing partnerships "antiques" is variously reported. See, for example, Gross, *Forbes' Great Business Stories,* 103. See, too, "Merrill Lynch Adds an 'Inc.' to Its Name," 130; Ibid.

77 Ibid., 126.

78 "Brokerage Supermarket"; Smith, speech at the University Club, New York, 20 March 1946, 10.

78 Winthrop Smith, Jr.'s remarks are from a 1998 interview with the authors. See, too, his 1982 interview, 11, 39, and 41, ML Files.

79 Smith's award was presented in *Forbes,* 15 November 1957.

79 Merrill Lynch Annual Report, 1957, 3.

79 Winthrop Smith, Jr., interview with authors. See, too, his 1982 interview, 3, ML Files.

80 Ed Lynch, Jr., undated interview, ML Files; Hecht, *Legacy of Leadership,* 89.

Chapter 5: Chou En-lai: The Elastic Bolshevik

83 For an excellent description of the October 1st ceremonies, see John McCook Roots, *Chou: An Informal Biography of China's Legendary Chou En-Lai* (New York: Doubleday & Company, Inc., 1978), 101, and Kai-yu Hsu, *Chou En-lai: China's Gray Eminence* (New York: Doubleday & Co., 1968), 190–191.

84 For a physical comparison of Mao and Chou, see Hsu, *Chou En-lai,* 238.

84 Two well-documented biographies of Mao Tse-tung are Stuart R. Schram, *Mao Tse-Tung,* rev. ed. (New York: Simon and Schuster, 1966), and Jerome Ch'en, *Mao and the Chinese Revolution* (London: Oxford University Press, 1965). See, too, *Encyclopedia Britannica,* Vol. 4, 465–469 (Chicago: Encyclopedia Britannica, Inc., 1979). For more of Chou's development, see Chae-Jin Lee, *Zhou Enlai: The Early Years* (Stanford, Calif.: Stanford University Press, 1994), Li Tien-Min, *Chou En-lai* (Taipei: Institute of International Relations, 1970), Hsu, *Chou En-Lai,* chap. 1–4, and *Encyclopedia Britannica,* Vol. 12, 456–458.

84 Mao's famous "political power" quote is variously cited. See *Encyclopedia Britannica,* Vol. 12, 465.

86 Mao's complaint of limited input in the CCP is treated in Richard Nixon, *Leaders* (New York: Warner Books, Inc., 1982), 236–237.

86   *Encyclopedia Britannica,* Vol. 12, 457.

87   For Mao's rejection of Marxist-Leninist dogma, see Roots, *Chou,* 58; the scorched land strategy is discussed in Hsu, *Chou En-lai,* 109.

87   Chou's early criticism of Mao is discussed in Hsu, *Chou En-lai,* 84–85, 109–110.

87   Chou's subsequent appreciation of Mao's military tactics are examined in Roots, *Chou,* 58–65, and Hsu, *Chou En-lai,* 111.

88   Chou's sense of Mao's people skills is examined in Roots, *Chou,* 156; Ibid., 66.

89   Chou's support of Mao is from Dick Wilson, *Zhou Enlai, A Biography* (New York: Viking Penguin Inc., 1985), 122. Also see Hsu, *Chou En-lai,* 111. Chou's appreciation of Mao's strategic insight is discussed in Roots, *Chou,* 156.

89   Chou's comments to Henry Kissinger may be found in Nixon, *Leaders,* 233. His views on adversity are from Richard Nixon, *In the Arena: A Memoir of Victory, Defeat, and Renewal* (New York: Simon and Schuster, 1990), 103–104. Chou's conversion to Mao is outlined in Roots, *Chou,* 65–66, 162–163; Ibid., 157.

89   Wilson, *Zhou Enlai,* 162; Nixon, *Leaders,* 228.

89   Nixon, *In the Arena,* 14.

89   Han Suyin, *Eldest Son* (New York: Hill and Wang, 1994), 125.

90   Hsu, *Chou En-lai,* 130.

90   The convergence of the Chou-Mao strategy may be found in various sources. See, for example, Suyin, *Eldest Son,* 197 and Hsu, *Chou En-lai,* 92–93, 207, and 224; Mao's "hundred flowers" remarks may be found in *Encyclopedia Britannica,* Vol. 12, 468; Sun Yat-sen's "heap of sand" commentary is reported in Nixon, *Leaders,* 244.

91   For an excellent discussion of General Marshall's China exploits, see Suyin, *Eldest Son,* 192–194. See, too, Sterling Seagrave, *The Soong Dynasty* (New York: Harper & Row, 1985), 396–403; Chiang Kai Shek's comments are from Wilson, *Zhou Enlai,* 157. Also see Seagrave, *Soong Dynasty,* 356, and Roots, *Chou,* 85.

91   Wilson, *Zhou Enlai,* 156.

91   Suyin, *Eldest Son,* 390.

92   Henry Kissinger's glowing accolades are from *Time,* 19 January 1976, as reported in Roots, *Chou,* 154. Chou's negotiating principles are discussed in Hsu, *Chou En-lai,* 205.

92   Suyin, *Eldest Son,* 194.

93   Richard Nixon, *The Memoirs of Richard Nixon* (New York: Grosset & Dunlap, 1978), 577. See, too, Nixon, *In the Arena,* 359; Kissinger, *Time,* 554.

93   Nixon, *Leaders,* 223.

93   Ibid., 231.

93   Nixon, *Memoirs,* 558.

93   Nixon, *Leaders,* 238.

94   On the personality differences between Chou and Mao, see Nixon, *Leaders,* 237; Ibid., 226–227.

94   Chou's classical upbringing is discussed in Nixon, *Leaders,* 227; Hsu, *Chou En-lai,* 204.

94   For a discussion of Chou's incredible vitality, see Suyin, *Eldest Son,* 408.

94   Chou's tough negotiating style is discussed in Hsu, *Chou En-lai,* 163; Nixon, *Leaders,* 226, and 221, respectively.

94   Roots, *Chou,* 156.

95   Chou's indispensability to Mao is presented in Roots, *Chou,* 157.

95   Wilson, *Zhou Enlai,* 298–299.

95   Roots, *Chou,* 102; Suyin, *Eldest Son,* 197.

95   Wilson, *Zhou Enlai,* 299.

96   Ibid., 123; Hsu, *Chou En-lai,* 244; Ibid., 178.

96   The relationship between the two men is examined in Wilson, *Zhou Enlai,* 164–165, 218.

96   Suyin, *Eldest Son,* 391; Wilson, *Zhou Enlai,* 123; Nixon, *Leaders,* 237.

97   Nixon, *Leaders.* See, too, Wilson, *Zhou Enlai,* 290.
      The discussion of Chou's funeral arrangements and the subsequent anniversary celebration are from Wilson, *Zhou Enlai,* 290.
      The reports of Chou's final days are from Nixon, *Leaders,* 247, and Wilson, *Zhou Enlai,* 290, 299; Suyin, *Eldest Son,* 396.

97   Wilson, *Zhou Enlai,* 299.

98   Nixon, *Leaders,* 248.

Chapter 6: George C. Marshall: Selfless Leadership
See especially the monumental four-volume biography of General Marshall by the late Forrest C. Pogue. Completed in 1987 after 30 years of labor and the review of 3.5 million pages of research material, The Viking Press publications include: *George C. Marshall, Volume I: Education of a General, 1880–1939* in 1963, followed by *Volume II: Ordeal and Hope, 1939–1942* in 1965; *Volume III: Organizer of Victory, 1942–1945* in 1973; and finally, *Volume IV: Statesman, 1945–1959*. Additional source material may be obtained from the George C. Marshall Research Foundation in Lexington, Virginia. See, too, *Encyclopedia Britannica*, Vol. 11, (Chicago: Encyclopedia Britannica Inc., 1979), 534–535.

101   For more on the China assignment, see Katherine Tupper Marshall, *Together: Annals of an Army Wife* (New York: Tupper & Love, 1946); John McCook Roots, *Chou: An Informal Biography of China's Legendary Chou En-lai* (New York: Doubleday & Co., 1978), 94; and Sterling Seagrave, *The Soong Dynasty* (New York: Harper & Row, 1985), 396–431.

101   For more on Marshall's post–World War II exploits, see James Patterson, *Grand Expectations: The United States, 1945–1974* (London: Oxford University Press, 1996). See, too, Albert R. Hunt, "The Greatest Man Churchill and Truman Ever Met," *Wall Street Journal*, 1 September 1994, A13.

102   America's wartime resurgence is described in Doris Kearns Goodwin, *No Ordinary Time* (New York: Touchstone, 1995), 608. See, too, Hunt, "The Greatest Man."

102   Pogue, *Organizer of Victory*, xi; the *Time* magazine excerpt may be found in Leonard M. Mosley, *Marshall: Hero for Our Times* (New York: Hearst Books, 1982), 356–357.

103   Marshall's success in managing such difficult personalities is reported in Mosley, *Marshall*, 356.

103   Marshall's interruption from retirement is from Roots, *Chou*, 94.

103   For more on Marshall's preparation for China, see Larry I. Bland, ed., *The Papers of George Catlett Marshall: Volume I* (Baltimore: Johns Hopkins University Press, 1981), 299; Pogue, *Statesman*, x–xi.

104   Ibid., x–xi; For more on the similarities between Marshall and the Duke of Wellington, see Ibid., x.

104   For more on the China assignment, see Roots, *Chou*, 94, and Seagrave, *Soong Dynasty*, 431.

105   For more on Marshall's insistence that his junior officers dissent, see Pogue, *Ordeal and Hope*, ix.

106   Marshall's early years are described in Ed Cray, *General of the Army: George C. Marshall, Soldier and Statesman* (New York: Norton, 1990); Pogue, *Education of a General*, xv, and *Encyclopedia Britannica*, Vol. 11.

106   Howard Gardner, *Leading Minds* (New York: Basic Books, 1995), 151.

106   Marshall's appraisal is from a 31 December 1964 document found in Bland, *Papers of George Catlett Marshall*, 92–93.

107   Gardner, *Leading Minds*, 152.

107   Ibid.

107   Marshall's "special fitness" is from Cray, *General of the Army*, 64, and Pogue, *Education of a General*, 164; M. A. Stoler, *George C. Marshall: Soldier—Statesman of the American Century* (Boston: Twayne, 1989), 40. See too, Gardner, *Leading Minds*, 153.

108   Marshall's admonitions to Pershing are from Gardner, *Leading Minds*, 148. His admission of "a great mistake" is from Bland, *Vol. I*, 129.

108   For more of the similarities between Marshall and Pershing, see Mosley, *Marshall*, 84, and Gardner, *Leading Minds*, 153.

108   Bland, *Vol. I*, 298–299.

109   Gardner, *Leading Minds*, 153; Lance Morrow, "George C. Marshall: The Last Great American?" Smithsonian, August 1997, 115.

109   Marshall's second marriage is discussed in *Encyclopedia Britannica*, 53, and Marshall, *Together*. For an excellent discussion of the general, see Cray, *General of the Army*, and Morrow, "George C. Marshall," 105–121. See also *George C. Marshall: Interviews and Reminiscences for Forrest Pogue*, ed. by Larry I. Bland, George C. Marshall Research Foundation (Lexington, Virginia: 1991).

109   *Encyclopedia Britannica*, 535.

110   Mosley, *Marshall*, 121–122. See, too, Goodwin, *No Ordinary Time*, 22.

110   Gardner, *Leading Minds,* 148.
110   Mosley, *Marshall,* 127. See, too, Bland, *Vol. I,* 641–642.
111   For more on Marshall's appointment, see Goodwin, *No Ordinary Time,* 23, and Mosley, *Marshall,* 128; Ibid.
111   Bland, *Vol. I.,* 714.
111   The sorry state of the U.S. military is described in Goodwin, *No Ordinary Time,* 23, and *Encyclopedia Britannica,* Vol. 11.
112   The military budget debate is from Goodwin, *No Ordinary Time,* 23–24.
112   Morgenthau's remarks are from Cray, *General of the Army,* 155, and Pogue, *Ordeal and Hope,* 30–31.
112   Mosley, *Marshall,* 139.
112   The smoothing of feelings between Marshall and Roosevelt is from Goodwin, *No Ordinary Time,* 24.
113   Ibid., 24.
113   Ibid., 23–24.
113   Ibid., 607.
113   Mosley, *Marshall,* 269.
113   Goodwin, *No Ordinary Time,* 608.
114   Gardner, *Leading Minds,* 157.
114   Bland, *Vol. II,* 530–531.
114   General Omar N. Bradley reveals Marshall's rejection of book offers in Pogue, *Ordeal and Hope,* xi, Pogue, *Education of a General,* x–xiii, and Morrow, "George C. Marshall," 106.
115   Pogue, *Organizer of Victory,* xi.
115   Roots, *Chou,* 94.
115   Bland, *Vol. II,* 3.
115   Goodwin, *No Ordinary Time,* 565.
115   For more on the president's role as a talent scout, see Goodwin, *No Ordinary Time,* 609, and Pogue, *Organizer of Victory,* xii–xiii.
116   Marshall's ability to select outstanding commanders is discussed in Goodwin, *No Ordinary Time,* 22, Pogue, *Ordeal and Hope,* 269, and by General Omar Bradley in Pogue, *Organizer of Victory,* xi–xii.
116   Pogue, *Organizer of Victory,* xii.
116   Eric Larrabee, *Commander in Chief: Franklin Delano Roosevelt, His Lieutenants and Their War* (New York: Harper & Row, 1987), 11.
116   Goodwin, *No Ordinary Time,* 240.
117   Ibid., 349.
117   Bland, *Vol. I,* 202; Bland, *Vol. II,* 621.
117   Mosley, *Marshall,* jacket flap.
117   Bland, *Vol. II,* 31.
118   John Gardner, *On Leadership* (New York: Free Press, 1990), 52.
118   Operation Overlord is examined in Goodwin, *No Ordinary Time,* 478.
118   Ibid.; Mosley, *Marshall,* 255.
118   Pogue, *Organizer of Victory,* 269–270.
119   *Marshall,* 265–266.
119   Morrow, "George C. Marshall," 106. See, too, Gardner, 159.
119   Pogue, *Organizer of Victory,* 348–349.
119   Mosley, *Marshall,* 341.
120   Ibid., 401.
120   "George Marshall: Straight Shooter," *U.S. News & World Report,* 16 March 1998, 64–67; Winston Churchill's description of the Marshall Plan may be found in Evan Thomas, "The Plan and the Man," *Newsweek,* 2 June 1997, 36.
121   For more on Senator McCarthy's smear tactics, see Cray, *General of the Army,* 723. Eisenhower's anemic defense of Marshall is discussed in David Hallberstam, *The Fifties* (New York: Villard, 1993), 1250–1251.
121   Stoler, *George C. Marshall,* 130.
121   Mosley, *Marshall,* 521–523.
121   Ibid.

Chapter 7: Bernice Pauahi Bishop: A Legacy Second to None
Authors' note on Hawaiian spelling: Although in this chapter we chose to use traditional English, modern linguists have distinguished more vowel sounds in spoken Hawaiian than did the missionaries who first produced the language in printed form. For example, several diacritical marks have been developed to show some of the more subtle distinctions of sound. For example, a hamza between vowels indicates a glottal stop. A macron over a vowel indicates a long vowel sound.

125 *The 1993 Annual Report,* Kamehameha Schools/Bernice Pauahi Bishop Estate, Honolulu, 12.

125 Ibid.

126 The princess's directive is cited in George H. S. Kanahele, *Pauahi:The Kamehameha Legacy* (Honolulu: Kamehameha Schools Press, 1986), 173. See, too, Mary H. Krout, *The Memories of Hon. Bernice Pauahi Bishop* (New York:The Knickerbocker Press, 1908. Reprinted by Kamehameha Schools Press, Honolulu, 1958), 226; and Cobey Black and Kathleen D. Mellen, *Princess Bernice Pauahi Bishop and Her Legacy* (Honolulu: Kamehameha Schools Press, 1965), 100.
For more on Bishop Estate, see Alix M. Freedman and Laurie P. Cohen, "Hawaiians Who Own Goldman Sachs Stake Play Clever Tax Game," *Wall Street Journal,* 25 April 1995,A1. In recent months, considerable controversy has surrounded the estate, particularly over the alleged shenanigans of the current trustees. See, for example,Todd S. Purdum, "Hawaiians Angrily Turn on a Fabled Empire," *New York Times,* 14 October 1997,A1; Paul M. Barrett, "Tempest Erupts Over Secretive Hawaiian Trust," *Wall Street Journal,* 10 October 1997, B1; and Susan Essoyan,"Shaken Trust," *Los Angeles Times,* 17 October 1997, D1.

128 Excellent histories of the Hawaiian Islands may be found in many places. See esp. Rita Ariyoshi, "Hawaii: Our Island Home," in *The Best of Aloha* (Honolulu: Island Heritage Publishing, 1990), chap. 1. See, too, Alan Gavan Daws, *Shoal of Time: A History of the Hawaiian Islands,* (Honolulu: University of Hawaii Press, 1974); Helen Bauer, *Hawaii, The Aloha State* (Honolulu: The Bess Press, 1982); A. Grove Day, *Kamehameha, First King of Hawaii* (Honolulu: Hogarth Press Hawaii, 1974); E. S. Craighill Handy et al., *Ancient Hawaiian Civilization* (Tokyo: Charles E. Tuttle Co., 1973); Ralph S. Kuykendall, *The Hawaiian Kingdom, Vol. I* (Honolulu: University of Hawaii Press, 1938); Ralph S. Kuykendall and A. Grove Day, *Hawaii: A History* (Englewood Cliffs, N.J.: Prentice-Hall, Inc., 1976); Joseph G. Mullins, *Hawaiian Journey* (Honolulu: Mutual Publishing Co., 1978); Robert B. Goodman, Gavan Daws, and Ed Sheehan, *The Hawaiians* (Norfolk Island, Australia: Island Heritage Limited, 1970); David W. Forbes, *Encounters with Paradise: Views of Hawaii and Its People, 1778–1941* (Honolulu: Honolulu Academy of Arts, 1992); and *Encyclopedia Britannica,* Vol. 8 (Chicago: Encyclopedia Britannica, Inc, 1979), 673–676.

129 Kuykendall, *Hawaiian Kingdom, Vol. I,* 195.
Bernice Pauahi Bishop's early years are recounted in Julie Stewart Williams, *Princess Bernice Pauahi Bishop* (Honolulu: Kamehameha Schools/Bernice Pauahi Bishop Estate, 1992). See, too, Bernice Pauahi Bishop's *Child Diary I, January 11, 1843 to May 14, 1844,* Bernice Pauahi Bishop Museum Library, Honolulu; Bernice Pauahi Bishop, *Child Diary II, June 3, 1844, to October 6, 1846,* Bernice Pauahi Bishop Library, Honolulu; Black and Mellen, *Her Legacy,* and Harold Winfield Kent, *An Album of Likenesses* (Honolulu, Bernice Pauahi Bishop Museum, 1972).

129 Williams, *Princess Bernice,* 18. For more on Mr. and Mrs. Amos Starr Cooke, see Mary Atherton Richards, *Amos Starr Cooke and Juliette Montague Cooke* (Honolulu: The Daughters of Hawaii, 1941).

130 The Cookes' influence on the curricula is from Black and Mellen, *Her Legacy,* 26–27.

130 Ibid., 28, 31.

130 Ibid., 29.

130 Williams, *Princess Bernice,* 44, and Black and Mellen, *Her Legacy,* 32; Krout, *Memories,* 47.

131 For more on Charles Reed Bishop, see Harold W. Kent, *Charles Reed Bishop, Man of Hawaii* (Palo Alto, Calif.: Pacific Books, 1965); Kent, ed., *Charles Reed Bishop: Letter File* (Honolulu: 1972); and Caroline Curtis, *Builders of Hawaii* (Honolulu: Kamehameha Schools Press, 1986).

131 "Hawaii," *Encyclopedia Britannica,* Vol. 8 (Chicago: Encyclopedia Britannica, Inc., 1979), 673.

131 Williams, *Princess Bernice,* 49, and Krout, *Memories,* 42.

131 Kanehele, *Pauahi,* 72.

132 Mullins, *Hawaiian Journey,* 58. The impact of sugar on the Hawaiian economy is discussed in Lawrence H. Fuchs, *Hawaii Pono: A Social History* (New York: Harcourt, Brace & World, Inc.), esp. chap. 2. See, too, Edwin P. Hoyt, *Davies: The Inside Story of a British-American Family in the Pacific and Its Business Enterprises* (Honolulu:Topgallant Publishing Co., 1983), chap. 12.

132 Kent, *Man of Hawaii*, 329. See, too, Black and Mellen, *Her Legacy*, 127. For a less flattering opinion of Bishop, see Bob Dye, "Charles Reed Bishop: The Man Pauahi Trusted," *Honolulu*, January 1998, 28–68.
132 Kanahele, *Pauahi*, 101.
133 Ibid., 120.
133 Kent, *Man of Hawaii*, 63. See, too, Kanahele, *Pauahi*, 121–122; Kent, *Man of Hawaii*, 64, and Kanahele, *Pauahi*, 122.
133 Bernice Pauahi's early marital duties are discussed in Williams, *Princess Bernice*, 57–62.
133 Black and Mellen, *Her Legacy*, 68.
134 Mrs. Bishop's accumulation of land is treated in "The Land of Kamehameha Schools/Bernice Pauahi Bishop Estate," special publication of the Kamehameha Schools/Bernice Pauahi Bishop Estate, Honolulu, Hawaii, revised June 1989. See, too, Kanahele, *Pauahi*, 164–166.
134 Kamehameha V's appeals and Princess Pauahi's responses are from Williams, *Princess Bernice*, 64. See, too, Black and Mellen, *Her Legacy*, 73–74.
135 The likelihood of Princess Pauahi's ascension is examined closely in Kanahele, *Pauahi*, esp. chap. 5.
135 Krout, *Memories*, 204.
135 Bishop's managerial qualifications are discussed in Kanahele, *Pauahi*, 89–92; Ibid., 84.
135 Ibid., 45, 114, 170–171.
136 Kent, *Letter File*, 56, 70–72.
136 Kanahele, *Pauahi*, 117–118, 176.
136 For more on the creation of other Hawaiian trusts, see Linda Ching, *'Ano Lani* (Honolulu: Hawaiian Goddesses Publishing Co., 1993), 140. See, too, Robert Midkiff, "Hawaiian Sovereignty: A Brief Overview," address to the Social Science Association, 6 December 1993, and Bob Krauss, *McInery* (Honolulu: The McInerny Foundations, 1981), 85–87. Also, refer to Kanahele, *Pauahi*, 176.
137 Kanahele, *Pauahi*, 172.
137 Ibid., 187.
137 The princess's funeral services are reported in Williams, *Princess Bernice*, 76–77, Krout, *Memories*, 221–227 and Kanahele, *Pauahi*, 89–91, 189–193.
138 Kanahele, *Pauahi*, 191.
138 "The Last of Her Race: In Memoriam of Bernice Pauahi Bishop," 30 October 1884.
138 Charles Reed Bishop's enduring contributions to Hawaii are presented in Kent, *Man of Hawaii*, 31, 165–171, and also *Letter File*, vii. See, too, Krout, *Memories*, 165–171.
139 Krauss, *McInerny*, 86.
139 Kent, *Man of Hawaii*, 157; Ibid., 159; Ibid., 165.
139 Kent, *Letter File*, 35, and *Man of Hawaii*, 150–151; Kent, *Letter File*, 22, and *Man of Hawaii*, 165.
139 Kent, *Man of Hawaii*, 162, 161.
139 Kent, *Letter File*, 20.
140 Kent, *Man of Hawaii*, 329.
140 Black and Mellen, *Her Legacy*, 129.
140 *1994: The Year in Review, Kamehameha Schools/Bernice Pauahi Bishop Estate*, Honolulu, 1994, 3.
140 Williams, *Princess Bernice*, 78, and Krout, *Memories*, 228–229.

Chapter 8: Anne Sullivan Macy: The Miracle Worker
143 For an interesting discussion of Kim Powers's remarkable career, see Susan Jaques, "Breaking the Sight and Sound Barrier," *Good Housekeeping*, March 1996, 24.
144 Walt Belcher, "TV Tuesday Extra!" *Tampa Tribune*, 10 October 1995; Jaques, "Breaking the Sight and Sound Barrier," 24.
145 For more on Helen Keller and Anne Sullivan Macy, see Robert M. Bartlett, *They Dared to Live* (New York: Association Press, 1943); Helen Elmira Waite, *Valiant Companions: Helen Keller and Anne Sullivan Macy* (Philadelphia: Macrae Smith Co., 1959); Van Wyck Brooks, *Helen Keller: Sketch for a Portrait* (New York: E. P. Dutton & Co., 1956); Richard Harrity and Ralph G. Martin, *The Three Lives of Helen Keller* (Garden City, N.Y.: Doubleday & Company, 1962); *Notable American Women 1607–1950: A Biographical Dictionary, Vol. II* (London: Oxford University Press, 1971, 481–483; and Dorothy Herrmann, *Helen Keller: A Life* (New York: Alfred A. Knopf, 1998).
145 Anne Sullivan Macy's early years are discussed in Bartlett, *They Dared to Live*, chap. 2. See, too, "Anne Sullivan Macy" in Elizabeth F. Hoxie, *Encyclopedia Britannica, Vol. 17* (Chicago:

Encyclopedia Britannica Inc., 1979), 481–483; Nella Braddy, *Anne Sullivan Macy: The Story Behind Helen Keller* (New York: Doubleday, Doran E. Company, 1940); Mary Jo Salter, "The Achiever," *New York Times Magazine,* 24 November 1996, 61; Deborah G. Felder, *The Hundred Most Influential Women of All Time* (New York: Citadel Press, 1995), 65–68; Helen Keller, *The Story of My Life* (New York: Doubleday, 1954); Keller, *Midstream: My Later Life* (Westport, Conn.: Greenwood Press, 1929); Keller, *Teacher: Anne Sullivan Macy. A Tribute to the Foster Child of Her Mind* (New York: Doubleday, 1995); and Joseph P. Lash, *Helen and Teacher: The Story of Helen Keller and Anne Sullivan Macy* (New York: Delacorte Press, 1980).

See, too, Alexander Woollcott's classic essay, "In Memoriam: Annie Sullivan," *Atlantic Monthly,* March 1939, 305–308. For a comparable essay, see Roger Rosenblatt, "New Hopes, New Dreams," *Time,* 26 August 1996.

145   Bartlett, *They Dared to Live,* 77. See, too, Senator Margaret Chase Smith and H. Paul Jeffers, *Gallant Women* (New York: McGraw-Hill Book Co., 1968), 78.

146   Waite, *Valiant Companions,* 17.

146   Houston Peterson, ed., *Great Teachers: Portrayed by Those Who Studied Under Them* (New Brunswick, N.J.: Rutgers University Press, 1946), 3–4.

146   Smith and Jeffers, *Gallant Women,* 79.

147   Keller, *Story of My Life,* 242.

147   Harrity and Martin, *Three Lives,* 30.

148   Peterson, *Great Teachers,* 4; Woollcott, "In Memoriam," 306.

148   For more on the doll incident, see Waite, *Valiant Companions,* 35.

148   Harrity and Martin, *Three Lives,* 8; Smith and Jeffers, *Gallant Women,* 80.

148   Brooks, *Sketch,* 18.

149   Philip S. Foner, ed., *Helen Keller: Her Socialist Years* (New York: International Publishers, 1967), 8.

149   Harrity and Martin, *Three Lives,* 9. See, too, Smith and Jeffers, *Gallant Women,* 80.

149   The water incident is widely discussed. See, for example, Waite, *Valiant Companions,* 61–62.

149   Peterson, *Great Teacher,* 7.

149   The T-e-a-c-h-e-r incident is recounted in many places. See, for example, Smith and Jeffers, *Gallant Women,* 82.

150   Waite, *Valiant Companions,* 63; Harrity and Martin, *Three Lives,* 32.

150   See Waite, *Valiant Companions,* 71.

150   Keller, *Teacher,* 67.

150   Peterson, *Great Teachers,* 8.

151   Lash, *Helen and Teacher,* 82–83.

151   Waite, *Valiant Companions,* 88–89.

151   Harrity and Martin, *Three Lives,* 34.

151   Ibid., 33.

152   Lash, *Helen and Teacher,* 80.

152   Waite, *Valiant Companions,* 94.

152   *Notable American Women 1607–1950: A Biographical Dictionary, Vol. II* (London: Oxford University Press, 1971), 481; Keller, *Midstream,* 108. See also, Brooks, *Sketch,* 74.

153   Helen Keller's many benefactors are identified in Waite, *Valiant Companions,* 118.

153   Ibid., 119–120.

153   Harrity and Martin, *Three Lives,* 10. See also Waite, *Valiant Companions,* 122.

154   Keller, *Story of My Life,* 61.

154   Bartlett, *They Dared to Live,* 79.

154   Waite, *Valiant Companions,* 182.

155   A description of Keller's graduation ceremonies is from Smith and Jeffers, *Gallant Women,* 76.

155   Keller, *Midstream,* 25.

155   Ibid., 33.

156   Waite, *Valiant Companions,* 198.

157   Helen Keller's devotion to the blind is examined in Waite, *Valiant Companions,* 208–209. Her quote is from *Teacher,* 247.

157   Harrity and Martin, *Three Lives,* 109.

158   The exchange between Helen Keller and Polly Thompson is from Woollcott, "In Memoriam," 308.

158   Keller, *Teacher,* 227–228.

158   Bartlett, *They Dared to Live,* 79–80.

158   Braddy, *Anne Sullivan Macy,* 350.

159 Sullivan's accomplishments are summarized in *Newsweek,* 31 October 1936.

159 Lash, *Helen and Teacher,* 105–106, 236–237.

160 Harrity and Martin, *Three Lives,* 109. See, too, Keller, *Teacher,* 88–89; Keller, *Teacher,* 119. An excellent discussion of Sullivan's personality is also found in Brooks, 50–51.

160 Lash, *Helen and Teacher,* 116.

160 Joseph Lash contrasts Sullivan and Keller in *Helen and Teacher,* 106.

160 For more on "optimism," see Helen Keller, *Optimism: An Essay* (New York: T.Y. Crowell and Co., 1903); Keller's comments on pessimism are from Brooks, *Sketch,* 56.

161 Keller, *Teacher,* 140.

161 Lash, *Helen and Teacher,* 1; Ibid., 71.

161 Ibid., 329; Ibid., 311.

161 Keller, *Teacher,* 82–83.

162 Ibid., 86, 152.

162 Harrity and Martin, *Three Lives,* 10. See, too, Brooks, *Sketch,* 57–58; Ibid., 10.

162 Keller, *Midstream,* 108. Also see, Brooks, *Sketch,* 74.

162 Keller, *Midstream,* 50.

162 Maria Montessori's "creator of the soul" quote is from Felder, *Hundred Most Influencial Women,* 66. The subsequent exchange is from Brooks, *Sketch,* 19, and Lash, *Helen and Teacher,* 418.

162 Harrity and Martin, *Three Lives,* 109. See, too, Brooks, *Sketch,* 85.

163 *Newsweek,* 31 October 1936. Also see Keller, *Midstream,* 346; Keller, *Teacher,* 82.

163 Harrity and Martin, *Three Lives,* 109.

163 Felder, *Hundred Most Influential Women,* 68. See, too, Smith and Jeffers, *Gallant Women,* 82, and Keller, *Teacher,* 23.

Chapter 9: Al Gore: Hail to the Co-Chief

167 Steve Tally, *Bland Ambition* (New York: Harcourt Brace Jovanovich, 1992), 220.

167 See Brian Sibley, *C. S. Lewis Through the Shadowlands: The Story of His Life with Joy Davidman* (Grand Rapids, Mich.: Fleming H. Revell, 1994).

167 John Adams "insignificant" quote is from Edgar Wiggins Waugh, *Second Consul* (Indianapolis: Bobbs-Merrill Co., 1956), 38. His criticism of George Washington is from Tally, *Bland Ambition,* 5.

168 Michael V. DiSalle and Lawrence G. Blochman, *Second Choice* (New York: Hawthorn Books, 1966), 14.
For other useful insights to the American vice presidency, see David Halberstam, *The Best and the Brightest* (New York: Random House, 1972); Joel K. Goldstein, *The Modern American Vice Presidency: The Transformation of a Political Institution* (New Jersey: Princeton University Press, 1982); and Francis X. Clines, "Hail to the Veep, Head and Shoulders Above the Chest," *New York Times,* 28 May 1995, sec. 4, 1.

168 *Of Thee I Sing* is discussed in DiSalle and Blochman, *Second Choice,* 15, and Tally, *Bland Ambition,* 255.

168 Goldstein, *Modern American Vice Presidency,* 10; Ibid., 146.

168 Tally, *Bland Ambition,* xii–xiii.

169 Tally's insightful description of veeps is from *Bland Ambition,* xiii. See, too, Goldstein, *Modern American Vice Presidency,* 135–139, and DiSalle and Blochman, *Second Choice,* 13–15.

169 Ibid., 312.

169 John Nance Garner's vivid description is from DiSalle and Blochman, *Second Choice,* 14. See, too, Clines, "Hail to the Veep," sec. 4, 1. Alan Simpson is quoted in Claudia Dreifus, "Exit Reasonable Right," *New York Times Magazine,* 2 June 1996, 27.

170 The vice presidential perks are recounted by Tally, *Bland Ambition,* 179–185.

170 Tally, *Bland Ambition,* 183.

170 Ibid., 319; Ibid., 319–320.

170 Waugh, *Second Consul,* 166.

171 Alan Brinkley, "The Perpetual Man of the Hour," *New York Times,* 3 September 1995, sec. 2, 28. See, too, David G. McCullough, *Truman* (New York: Simon & Schuster, 1992).

171 Waugh, *Second Consul,* 166.

171 Tally, *Bland Ambition,* 294. See, too, Goldstein, *Modern American Vice Presidency,* 136–137; Clines, "Hail to the Veep," sec. 4, 1.

171 Tally, *Bland Ambition,* 323. See, also, DiSalle and Blochman, *Second Choice,* 16; Ibid., 329.

172 Halberstam, *Best and the Brightest,* 533.

172   Goldstein, *Modern American Vice Presidency,* 146.

172   Halberstam, *Best and the Brightest,* 533.

172   LBJ's shabby treatment of Hubert Humphrey is discussed in Halberstam, *Best and the Brightest,* 533–535, 660–661. See, too, Goldstein, *Modern American Vice Presidency,* 148–149, and Tally, *Bland Ambition,* 332.

172   DiSalle and Blochman, *Second Choice,* 16; Hubert Humphrey's frustrations are discussed in Tally, *Bland Ambition,* 334. See also Goldstein, *Modern American Vice Presidency,* 148–149.

173   For more on Gore, see Betty Burford, *Al Gore: United States Vice President* (Hillside, N.J.: Enslow Publishers, Inc., 1994), and Hank Hillen, *Al Gore, Jr.: His Life and Career* (New York: Birch Lane Press, 1992).

173   For a pronouncement of Clinton's vice presidential criteria, see Gov. Bill Clinton and Sen. Al Gore, *Putting People First* (New York: Times Books, 1992), 199. For more on the Clinton-Gore partnership, see Warren Bennis and Patricia Ward Biederman, *Organizing Genius: The Secret of Creative Collaboration* (Reading, Mass.: Addison-Wesley, 1997), esp. 104–107, 114–116.

173   Susan Page, "Loyal Gore Steadfast in His Support," *USA Today,* 26 January 1998, A1; Richard L. Berke, "The Gore Guide to the Future," *New York Times Magazine,* 22 February 1998, sec. 6, 35.

174   David Wessel and Rick Wartzman, "Clinton Decision to Offer Balanced-Budget Plan was Strongly Opposed by Top Democrats, Aides," *Wall Street Journal,* 16 June 1995, A12. See, too, Albert R. Hunt, "Albert Gore Warms up for 2000," *Wall Street Journal,* 12 September 1996, A17; Page, "Loyal Gore," A2.

174   Richard L. Berke, "The Good Son," *New York Times Magazine,* 20 February 1994, 33.

174   Goldstein, *Modern American Vice Presidency,* 147.

174   Berke, "The Good Son," 44. See also Joe Klein, "Second Bananahood," *Newsweek,* 21 October 1996, 42, and Eleanor Clift, "Gore: Playing Second Fiddle," *Newsweek,* 25 January 1993, 35; Richard L. Berke, "Clinton Can Now Sing, 'Me and My Shadow President,' " *New York Times,* 14 December 1997, sec. 4, 1. See, too, J. F. O. McAlliston, "A Veep who Leaves Prints," *Time,* 2 September 1996, 37–38.

175   Todd S. Purdum, "What Kind of Democrat?" *New York Times Magazine,* 19 May 1996, 36.

175   Ibid.; Ibid., 36.

176   For more on Gore's involvement in high-tech issues, see Gene Koprowski, "The ASAP Interview: Vice-President Al Gore," *Forbes ASAP,* 4 December 1995, 134–137. See also John Simons, "How a Vice President Fills a Cyber-Cabinet: With Gore—Techs," *Wall Street Journal,* 13 March 1998, A1.

176   See Senator Al Gore, *Earth in the Balance: Ecology and the Human Spirit* (Boston: Houghton Mifflin Company, 1992).

176   Richard L. Berke, "Murmur of Gore's Ambition Becomes Louder," *New York Times,* 22 April 1996, C10; Gore's discussion of Newt Gingrich is from Ian Fisher, "Not Taking New York for Granted, Gore Campaigns in Brooklyn," *New York Times,* 5 June 1996, A13.

177   For more on Gore's influence on White House appointments, see Burford, *Al Gore,* 114, Peter J. Boyer, "Gore's Dilemma," *The New Yorker,* 28 November 1994, 105, and Berke, "Murmur," C10.

177   Burford, *Al Gore,* 114; "Al Gore," *Time,* 17 June 1996, 68.

177   Berke, "The Good Son," 30; Bill Nichols, "The Heir Apparent Has Solid Record and Stolid Image," *USA Today,* 29 August 1996, 6A; Berke, "The Good Son," 30. See, too, Christina Nifong, "Gore is Right-Hand Man—and then Some," *Christian Science Monitor,* 8 October 1996, 10, and David S. Broder, "Gore Sets a New Standard for the Vice Presidency," *International Herald Tribune,* 27 August 1996, 1.

177   John F. Kennedy's advice to VPs is found in Michael Medved, *The Shadow Presidents* (New York: Times Books, 1979), 273. See Bruce Clark, "Gore Maintains a Low Profile," *Financial Times,* 26 January 1998, 4. Halberstam, *Best and the Brightest,* 663.

178   Dan Quayle, "Make Family Time," *USA Weekend,* 12–14 April 1996, 14. See, too, Richard Benedetto, "A Wiser Quayle Offers His Advice," *USA Today,* 12 August 1996, 10A, and Maureen Dowd, "The Education of Dan Quayle," *New York Times Magazine,* 14 April 1996, 142–143.

178   Mindy Fetterman, "Nation's Chief Gets Mostly Good Marks," *USA Today,* 28 April 1991, B1.

178   Tally, *Bland Ambition,* 399. For more on the Quayle paradox, see Richard Morin, "The No. 2 Man is seen as a Poor Second," *Washington Post National Weekly Edition,* 13–19 May 1991, 37.

179   Berke, "The Good Son," 30. See, too, David Shribman, "What Gore Needs to Win in 2000,"
       Fortune, 23 December 1996, 48; Peter J. Boyer, "Gore's Dilemma," *The New Yorker,* 28
       November 1994, 100–110.
179   Page, "Loyal Gore," A2.
179   *Time's* citation is in the 17 June 1996 issue, 68. David Broder, "Gore's 'Dilemma' as No. 2,"
       Honolulu Advertiser, 2 April 1997, A12. See, too, "The President *Loves* the Guy," *Fortune,* 17
       October 1997, 62, and Berke, "Clinton Can Now Sing," WE1.
180   Bob Woodward, " 'Solicitor in Chief' Gore Raked in Big Money for the Democrats," cited
       in *International Herald Tribune,* 3 March 1997, 1. Gores's self-defense may be found in Bill
       Nichols, "Fund-Raising Opens Gore to a Barrage of Questions," *USA Today,* 4 March 1997,
       7A. See also Jack Germond and Jules Witcover, "Gore Could Be Hurt by Campaign Abuses,"
       Honolulu Star-Bulletin, 29 February 1997, A16, and Alison Mitchell, "Gore's Fund-Raising
       Casts a Political Shadow," *New York Times,* 3 March 1997, 1.
181   Tally, *Bland Ambition,* 304; Berke, "The Good Son," 44.
181   Albert Gore III's accident is described in Clinton and Gore, *Putting People First,* 214–215.
       Also see Burford, *Al Gore,* 87–89; Gore, *Earth in the Balance,* 14.
181   The quotes or impressions of Presidents Harding, Jefferson, Adams, and Pierce are from A. E.
       Hotchner, "Grouse Under Pressure: The White House was No Picnic," *New York Times,* 8
       October 1995, 7.
181   See John Milton Cooper, Jr.'s excellent essay, "The Presidency: Out of the Shadowlands,"
       Wall Street Journal, 22 May 1995, A12.

Chapter 10: Bill Guthridge: Invisible but Invaluable
185   For an excellent assessment of the assistant coach's role, see Frank Blackman, "Coaches'
       Right-Hand Men," *San Francisco Examiner,* 29 December 1991, C1.
186   For more on Bill Guthridge's early career, see esp. Kevin Quirk, "Silent Partner," *Charlotte
       Observer,* 11 March 1982, 1C. See, too, Sam Register, "Bill Guthridge: He Doesn't View
       Assistant's Job as a Stepping Stone to Head Coach," *Carolina Blue,* 24 January 1981, 2; Larry
       Keech, "Carolina's Quiet Man," *Greensboro News & Record,* 16 March 1977; A. J. Carr,
       "Olympic Dream Fulfilled," *Raleigh News & Observer,* 6 July 1976; A. J. Carr, "Invisible but
       Invaluable," *Raleigh News Observer,* 23 June 1981; Frank Dascenzo, "Guthridge's Decisions,"
       Durham Sun, 22 April 1976; Mark Whicker, "Bill Guthridge: Everyone's Heir Apparent
       Content to be No. 2," *Chapel Hill Newspaper,* 19 December 1973; Bill Cole, "Forgotten
       Man," *Winston-Salem Journal,* 20 March 1997, C1; and Lee Pace, "The Man behind the
       Man," *Carolina Court* (Chapel Hill: Tar Heel Sports Marketing, 1995).
186   Caulton Tudor, "Staying Power," *Raleigh News & Observer,* 20 December 1990.
186   Pace, "Man behind the Man," 76. See, too, Tudor, "Staying Power"; Sam Donnellon, " 'Second-
       to-One' Guthridge," *Norfolk Virginian Pilot,* 24 January 1988, D1; "Guthridge Stays with
       Heels," *Durham Herald,* 14 March 1978, Adam Davis, "Bill Guthridge Has No Regrets
       About Turning Down Head Coaching Jobs," *Carolina Blue,* 16 March 1996; Harvey Araton,
       "A Loyal Aide Takes Pride in the Feat," *New York Times,* 16 March 1997; and Quirk, "Silent
       Partner," 1C.
187   Register, "Bill Guthridge," 2. See also Pace, "Man behind the Man," 71.
187   Ibid.
188   David Perlmutt, "The No. 1 No. 2," *Charlotte Observer,* 10 February 1996, 12A.
188   Davis, "Bill Guthridge Has No Regrets."
190   For more on Guthridge's role, see Bill Cole, "Guthridge is Silent Partner," *Winston-Salem
       Journal,* 13 February 1983, D2, and Quirk, "Silent Partner," 1C.
190   Guthridge's "I'm the only one" interview is amplified in Brock Page, "Working for Dean
       Smith and Selling Carolina, Bill Guthridge 'Has Best Job in the Country,' " *Carolina Blue,* 4
       February 1995, 19.
190   Bob Gretz, "Guthridge Remains Beacon of Stability," *Chapel Hill Newspaper,* 24 February
       1988.
190   *Carolina Blue,* 22 March 1997, 2. See, too, Cole, "Forgotten Man," C4.
191   For more on Guthridge's daily regimen and his attention to detail, see Pace, "Man behind
       the Man," 71–76.
191   Pace, "Man behind the Man," 73.
192   The Grgurich affair was reported in Tom Friend, "Tarkanian Era Hovers in the Rafters,"
       New York Times, 28 October 1994, B13. See, too, Mike Fitzgerald, "Tim Grgurich: A Tribute
       to All Key Assistants," *Honolulu Star-Bulletin,* 7 June 1995, C1.

193   For more on the Lotz situation, see Pace, "Man behind the Man," 66.

193   Perlmutt, "No. 1 No. 2," 12A.

194   Dean Smith's coaching innovations are discussed in "1995 Carolina Men's Basketball," 22–26.

194   "1995 Carolina Men's Basketball," 25–26; Timothy W. Smith, "Thomas is Kentucky, Except on the Court," *New York Times,* 29 March 1997, 26; "1995 Carolina Men's Basketball," 22.

194   Pace, "Man behind the Man," 74.

194   Ibid., 76.

194   Tudor, "Staying Power," 2C; For more on the philosophical similarities between Guthridge and Smith, see Ibid., 2C.

195   "1995–1996 Carolina Men's Basketball," 30.

195   Interview with Bill Cole; Pace, "Man behind the Man," 71.

195   Pace, "Man behind the Man," 65.

196   Donnellon, "Second-to-One," D5.

196   Page, "Working for Dean Smith," 19.

196   Donnellon, "Second-to-One."

197   For more on the pluses and minuses of coaching see, too, Register, "Bill Guthridge," 2.

197   Richard Moll, *The Public Ivys: A Guide to America's Best Public Undergraduate Colleges and Universities* (New York: Penguin Books, 1985, revised 1996).

197   Donnellon, "Second-to-One."

198   Dick Patrick, "Smith: Ignores Pleas, Tearfully Steps Down," *USA Today,* 10 October 1997, 2.

198   Patrick, "Smith," C1.

198   Barry Jacobs, "Bill Guthridge: Second Banana Never Expected Top Billing," *New York Times,* 10 October 1997; Patrick, "Smith," C2.

198   Jacobs, "Bill Guthridge," and Alexander Wolff, "No Question," *Sports Illustrated,* 16 February 1998, 71.

198   David Droschak, "At Age 60, Guthridge Gets Challenge," *Associated Press,* 10 October 1997.

199   "Guthridge Coaching Style Will Be Similar to Smith's," *Carolina Blue,* 18 October 1997, 18.

199   Rudy Martzke, "Guthridge Holding UNC Fort for Ford," *USA Today,* 10 October 1997, C2. See, too, Mike Lopresti, "Lasting Loyalty No. 1 Victory." *USA Today,* 10 October 1997, C3, and James Surowiecki, "In Praise of an Organization Man," *Wall Street Journal,* 30 March 1998, A18; Droschak, "At Age 60," 2.

199   Wolff, "No Question," 71.

200   John Kilgo, "The Head Coach Runs the Ship," *Carolina Blue,* 21 February 1998, 2; Wolff, "No Question," 72.

Chapter 11: Amy Tucker: Hoop Dreams

204   Richard Zoglin, "The Girls of Summer," *Time,* 12 August 1996, 50; Peter Boylan, "Better than Men," *Honolulu,* August 1996, 122.

204   Candace Putnam, "Stanford Women Wrote Book about Great Expectations," *San Jose Mercury News,* 21 March 1996, 5D.

205   "Women's Coach Tara VanDerveer," ed. by NBA Publishing Ventures, in *USA Today,* 3 July 1996, 9E.

205   "1995–1996 Stanford University Basketball," 10. See esp. Steve Raczynski, "A Season of Change," 5–6.

206   Dwight Chapin, "Low-Key Tucker Buoys Stanford," *San Francisco Examiner,* 29 March 1996, B1.

207   Dick Rockne, "An Experiment in Chemistry," *Seattle Times,* 21 March 1996, C1.

207   Dick Patrick, "Stanley's Temp Job Could Reopen Doors," *USA Today,* 11 March 1996, 9F. See, too, Candace Putnam, "Stanley is Remaining Focused on the Job at Hand," *San Jose Mercury News,* 15 March 1996, Special Section: NCAA Basketball: Your Guide to the College Tournament, 2CC, and Dwight Chapin, "Glad to be Back on the Bench," *San Francisco Examiner,* 6 February 1998, A13.

207   Rockne, "Experiment in Chemistry," C5.

208   "1995–1996 Stanford University Basketball," 11.

208   Rockne, "Experiment in Chemistry," C5.

208   Chapin, "Low-Key Tucker," and Ron Green, Jr., "VanDerveer Now Stanford's 'Distant Assistant,' " *Charlotte Observer,* 28 March 1996, 6B.

208   Rockne, "Experiment in Chemistry," C5. See, too, Chapin, "Low-Key Tucker," and Green, "VanDerveer Now Stanford's 'Distant Assistant.' "

208 Rockne, "Experiment in Chemistry."
209 Green, "VanDerveer Now Stanford's 'Distant Assistant,' " 6B.
209 Ibid.
209 Rockne, "Experiment in Chemistry," C1; Miki Turner, "Going for Gold," *Coaching Women's Basketball* (July/August 1996): 19.
209 Green, "VanDerveer Now Stanford's 'Distant Assistant,' " 6B.
209 Ibid.
210 Chapin, "Low-Key Tucker."
210 For more on the University of California's hiring of Stanley, see Gwen Knapp, "Bears Make the Gutsy Hire," *San Francisco Examiner,* 11 April 1996, and Dwight Chapin, "Glad to be Back," A13. For more on her first year at Cal, see Michelle Smith, "Rebuilding," *Coaching Women's Basketball* (May/June 1997): 20–23.
211 Steve Wieberg, "Perfect Ending for USA: 111–87 Win," *USA Today,* 5 August 1996, 10C. See also "1995–1996 Stanford University Basketball," 9; Turner, "Going for Gold," Zoglin, *Time,* and Alexander Wolff, "Road Show," *Sports Illustrated,* 22 July 1996, 94–97.
211 "Women's Coach Tara VanDerveer," 9E.
211 Wieberg, "Perfect Ending."
211 Chapin, "Glad to be Back." See, too, Green, "VanDerveer Now Stanford's 'Distant Assistant,' " 1B.
212 Jody Meacham, "A World Beyond Stanford," *San Jose Mercury News,* 30 April 1996, 2D. See, too, Steve Wieberg, "Suddenly, the Future is Now," *USA Today,* 6 August 1996, 3C.
212 Dwight Chapin, "Olympic Coach Discovers Life Away from Stanford," *San Francisco Examiner,* 7 July 1996, D1.
212 Green, "VanDerveer Now Stanford's 'Distant Assistant,' " 6B; Ann Killion, "As Stanford Soars, so Does Tucker's Stock," *San Jose Mercury News,* 27 February 1996, 1D. See, too, Turner, "Going for Gold."
212 Wieberg, "Suddenly the Future is Now," 3C.
213 Chapin, "Olympic Coach," D1. For a first-hand account of her Olympic year, see Tara VanDerveer with Joan Ryan, *Shooting from the Outside: How a Coach and Her Olympic Team Transformed Women's Basketball* (New York: Avon, 1997). See, too, Sara Corbett, *Venus to the Hoop: A Gold-Medal Year in Women's Basketball* (New York: Doubleday, 1997).
213 Putnam, "Stanford Women."
213 Rockne, "Experiment in Chemistry," C5. See, too, Chapin, "Olympic Coach."
213 Rockne, "Experiment in Chemistry," C5.
213 Candace Putnam, "Tucker Signs 3-Year Deal as Stanford Assistant," *San Jose Mercury News,* 27 April 1996, 1C. See, too, Killion, "As Stanford Soars"; Putnam, "Tucker Signs," 9C. See, too, Killion, "As Stanford Soars."
213 Coach VanDerveer's fondness for Stanford is cited in Holly Woodard, "Stanford Signs VanDerveer to Five-Year Coaching Deal," *USA Today,* 29 March 1997, 7C.

Chapter 12: Dr. Watson and Sherlock Holmes: Fiction's Most Famous Pair
219 Among the many useful Holmesian references, see T. S. Blakeney, *Sherlock Holmes, Fact or Fiction* (London: John Murray, 1932); M. Brilliant and M. Brilliant, *The Man Who Was Sherlock Holmes* (London: John Murray, 1924); Allen Eyles, *Sherlock Holmes: A Centenary Celebration* (New York: Harper & Row Publishers, 1986); Trevor H. Hall, *Sherlock Holmes and His Creator* (New York: St. Martin's Press, 1977); Lesley Henderson, ed., *Twentieth-Century Crime and Mystery Writers,* 3rd ed. (Chicago: St. James Press, 1991); Ian McQueen, *Sherlock Holmes Detected* (New York: Drake Publishers, 1974); Michael Pointer, *The Public Life of Sherlock Holmes* (New York: Drake Publishers, 1975), 95; Donald A. Redmond, *Sherlock Holmes, A Study in Sources* (Montreal: McGill-Queen's University Press, 1982); Colin Bruce, *The Strange Case of Mrs. Hudson's Cat and Other Science Mysteries Solved by Sherlock Holmes* (Reading, Mass.: Addison-Wesley, 1997).
220 Michael Pointer, *The Sherlock Holmes File,* (New York: Drake Publishers, 1975), 98–99. Important biographies of Dr. Watson include S. C. Roberts, *Doctor Watson* (London: Faber & Faber, 1931), and Michael Hardwick, *The Private Life of Dr. Watson* (New York: E. P. Dutton, Inc., 1983). See too, Marcia Muller and Bill Pronzini, ed., *Detective Duos* (London: Oxford University Press, 1997).
220 There are more than 30 book-length studies of Doyle and his work. Among the best are John Dickson Carr, *The Life of Sir Arthur Conan Doyle* (New York: Harper & Row, 1949);

Don Richard Cox, *Arthur Conan Doyle* (New York: Frederick Ungar Publishing Co., 1985); Charles Higham, *The Adventures of Conan Doyle* (New York: W. W. Norton & Co., 1976); Jacqueline A. Jaffe, *Arthur Conan Doyle* (Boston: Twayne Publishers, 1987); Pierre Nordon, *Conan Doyle: A Biography* (New York: Holt, Rinehart and Winston, 1967); and Hesketh Pearson, *Conan Doyle: His Life and Art* (New York: Taplinger Publishing Co., 1977). Also see Arthur Conan Doyle, *Sir Arthur Conan Doyle, Memories and Adventures* (Boston: Little, Brown, and Co., 1924); Jean Conan Doyle, *Epilogue;* Adrian Conan Doyle, *The Life of Sir Arthur Conan Doyle* (London: John Murray, 1949); and Ira B. Nadel and William W. Fredeman, ed., *Victorian Novelists after 1885* (Detroit: Gale Research Co., 1983). See, too, Tom Huntington, "The Man Who Believed in Fairies," *Smithsonian,* September 1997, 107–114.

220 Jaffe, *Arthur Conan Doyle,* 15.

221 Hall, *Sherlock Holmes and His Creator,* 79.

221 Ely Liebow, *Dr. Joe Bell: Model for Sherlock Holmes* (Bowling Green, Ohio: Bowling Green University Popular Press, 1982), *preface.*

221 Liebow, *Dr. Joe Bell: Model for Sherlock Holmes,* 3–4.

222 Doyle, *Memories and Adventures,* 69, and 5, respectively.

222 For more on the Doyle method, see Henderson, *Twentieth-Century Crime,* 332, and Frank N. Magill, ed., *Critical Survey of Mystery and Detective Fiction* (Pasadena, Calif.: Salem Press, 1988), 535.

222 Jaffe, *Arthur Conan Doyle,* 49.

222 Professor Moriarty's description is reported in Eyles, *Sherlock Holmes,* 30.

223 Pointer, *The Public Life,* 14; Eyles, *Sherlock Holmes,* 31.

223 For more on the growing popularity of crime novels, see Michele Ross, "Mystery Book Trends," *Christian Science Monitor,* 30 September 1996, 10–11. See, too, Cox, *Arthur Conan Doyle,* 178–179, and Nadel and Fredeman, *Victorian Novelist,* 93.

223 Cox, *Arthur Conan Doyle,* 178. See, too, Eyles, *Sherlock Holmes,* 6; Henderson, *Twentieth-Century Crime,* 332. See, too, Cox, *Arthur Conan Doyle,* 180.

224 For an excellent overview of Doyle's characters, see Redmond, *Sherlock Holmes, A Study in Sources.*

224 Henderson, *Twentieth-Century Crime,* 332.

224 "Sherlock Holmes on the Screen," *Arthur Conan Doyle on Sherlock Holmes: Speeches at the Stoll Convention Dinner, an Exchange of Rhymed Letters,* with an introduction by Roger Lancelyn Green (London: Favil Press, 1981), 5–7.

225 George Grella and Philip B. Dematteis, "Sir Arthur Conan Doyle," in *Victorian Novelists after 1885,* Nadel and Fredeman, ed., 93.

225 McQueen, *Sherlock Holmes Detected,* 16. For an interesting comparison of the writer and Holmes and Watson, see Cox, *Arther Conan Doyle,* 182–183. See, too, Pointer, *Sherlock Holmes File,* 95; Nordon, *Conan Doyle,* 279–285; Hall, *Sherlock Holmes and His Creator,* 88–90; and Nadel and Fredeman, *Victorian Novelists,* 92–93.

225 Adrian Conan Doyle, *Life of Sir Arthur Conan Doyle,* 15–16, and Higham, *Adventures of Conan Doyle;* 10. Lady Conan Doyle, "Conan Doyle was Sherlock Holmes," *Pearson's Magazine,* vol. 78 (December 1934): 574–577.

225 Cox, *Arthur Conan Doyle,* 182–183.

226 Pointer, *Sherlock Holmes File,* 95.

226 The importance of Watson's role is also well discussed in Eyles, *Sherlock Holmes,* 7.

226 Eyles, *Sherlock Holmes,* 7; Pointer, *Sherlock Holmes File,* 7; Pearson, *Conan Doyle,* 91.

226 Nordon, *Conan Doyle,* 268; Jaffe, *Arthur Conan Doyle,* 38.

227 Eyles, *Sherlock Holmes,* 7; Nordon, *Conan Doyle,* 270.

227 Pointer, *Sherlock Holmes File,* 103; *Hound of the Baskervilles,* vol. I, 243; Blakeney, *Sherlock Holmes, Fact or Fiction,* 1.

227 See Pointer, *Public Life,* 14, and Pearson, *Conan Doyle,* 22.

227 Ross, "Mystery Book Trends," 11.

228 See "His Last Bow," vol. II, 1086.

Chapter 13: Clash of the Titans

232 Deanna Kizis, "Welcome to Hollyfeud!," *BUZZ: The Talk of Los Angeles* (December/January 1997): 82. Also see James Sterngold, "When the Executives Not the Stars, Get the Hollywood Spotlight," *New York Times,* 16 December 1996, C11.

232 Bruce Orwall, "Disney Says Michael Ovitz is Resigning as President," *Wall Street Journal,* 13 December 1996, A6.

233 Ovitz's severance package is estimated by Bruce Orwall in "He's Ba-ack! Ovitz's Thumb is in Malls, Stadium," *Wall Street Journal,* 27 March 1998, B1; Ibid., A3. See, too, Eben Shapiro and Bruce Orwall, "Entertainment Chiefs Lack Understudies," *Wall Street Journal,* 6 January 1997, B1.

233 Richard Nixon, *In The Arena: A Memoir of Victory, Defeat, and Renewal* (New York: Simon and Schuster, 1990), 14.

235 For an excellent summary of the relationship between Jerry Jones and Jimmy Johnson, see Skip Bayless, *The Boys* (New York: Simon & Schuster, 1993), and his "Such Good Friends," *Sports Illustrated,* 12 July 1993. For more on Jerry Jones, see Jim Dent, *King of the Cowboys* (Holbrook, Mass.: Adams Publishing, 1995).

235 Bayless, "Such Good Friends," 69.

235 Patricia Sellers, "So You Failed Now Bounce Back!," *Fortune,* 1 May 1995, 55.

236 Richard Hoffer, "Cowboys for Sale," *Sports Illustrated,* 18 September 1995, 62.

237 Peter King, "Bad Blood," *Sports Illustrated,* 11 April 1994, 36. See, too, Bayless, "Such Good Friends," 68.

237 Bayless, "Such Good Friends," 74.

237 Ibid.

237 Ibid., 73–74.

237 Ibid., 76; King, "Bad Blood," 41.

238 Sellers, "So You Failed," 62.

238 Todd Shapera, "The Creaking House that Jerry Built," *Financial Times,* 15–16 November 1997, XI.

239 Peter King, "From the Heart," *Sports Illustrated,* 22 January 1996, 40.

239 Ibid.

239 Ibid., 41.

239 For more on Coach Johnson's joining the Miami Dolphins, see Thomas George, "Arrogant, Cocky and Good," *New York Times,* 15 September 1996, 25; Charlie Nobles, "An Energetic Johnson Motivates the Dolphins," *New York Times,* 13 August 1996, B2; Paul M. Johnson, "Starting Over," *Petersen's Pro Football, Annual 1996 Issue,* 36; and Meg Grant, "Shark Among Dolphins," *People,* 19 September 1996, 215; Coach Johnson's prediction of more wins is found in *Honolulu Advertiser,* 20 December 1996, C5.

239 Tom Pedulla, "Dolphins Focus on the Future," *USA Today,* 11 December 1996, 4C.

239 "Miami Dolphins," *Sports Illustrated Pro Football '96,* 137.

240 Mike Freeman, "Jerry Jones Considering Another Hat: The Coach's," *New York Times,* 21 September 1997, sec. 1, 27.

240 For more on the Redstone-Biondi affair, see Mark Landler, "Viacom Chief Ousted; Paramount's Performance a Factor," *New York Times,* 18 January 1996, C1; Landler with Geraldine Fabrikant, "Sumner and His Discontents," *New York Times,* 19 January 1996, C1; Laura Landro and Mark Robichaux, "Redstone Fires Biondi as CEO of Viacom," *Wall Street Journal,* 19 January 1996, A3; Landro and Robichaux, "Redstone's One-Man Show Opens at Viacom," *Wall Street Journal,* 19 January 1996, B1; Claudia Eller and James Bates, "Relaxed Fix," *Los Angeles Times,* 25 June 1996, D2; Richard Zoglin, "A Firing at Fort Sumner," *Time,* 29 January 1996, 56; Thomas R. King, "Biondi's Task: Making Peace with Redstone," *Wall Street Journal,* 24 April 1996, B1. Redstone's quotes are from Zoglin, "A Firing," 56.

241 Landler, "Viacom Chief Ousted," C1.

241 Mark Landler with Geraldine Fabrikant, "Consolidation in the Media Turns Chiefs into Casualties," *New York Times,* 5 February 1996, C1.

241 For more on Redstone's early success, see Landro and Robichaux, "Redstone's One-Man Show."

241 Zoglin, "A Firing," 57.

241 Eller and Bates, "Relaxed Fix," 06. For more on the personality differences between the two men, see Landro and Robichaux, "Redstone's One-Man Show."

242 Landler with Fabrikant, "Consolidation in the Media," C3.

242 Landler with Fabrikant, "Sumner and His Discontents," C4.

242 Ibid., C1. See, too, John Gapper, "Star of His Own Show," *Financial Times,* 22 June 1998, 8.

242 Landro and Robichaux, "Redstone's One Man Show," B1.

242 Landler with Fabrikant, "Sumner and His Discontents," C4.

242 Landler, "Viacom Chief Ousted," C17.

243 Landler with Fabrikant, "Sumner and His Discontents," C1, and Zoglin, "A Firing," 57. For an update on the Biondi-less Viacom, see Elizabeth Lesly, with Gail DeGorge and Ronald

Grover, "Sumner's Last Stand," *Business Week,* 3 March 1997, 66. For more on the recent reversal of Redstone's fortunes, see Robert Lenzner and Peter Newcomb, "The Vindication of Sumner Redstone," *Forbes,* 15 June 1998, 49–56.

243   Zoglin, "A Firing," 57.

243   Eller and Bates, "Relaxed Fix," D6. See, too, King, "Biondi's Task," B10.

243   David Lieberman, "Former Viacom Chief Biondi to Head MCA," *USA Today,* 24 April 1996, 2B.

243   King, "Biondi's Task," B10; David Lieberman and Chris Woodyard, "Universal's Boss Talks Back to Critics," *USA Today,* 20 April 1998, B1.

244   Jonathan R. Laing, "Lights! Camera!," *Barron's,* 27 April 1998, 36.

244   Bernard Weinraub, "Shifting Priorities Lead to Biondi's Dismissal," *New York Times,* 17 November 1998, G1.

244   For more on the difficulties of blending powerful personalities, see "Sharing the Limelight," *The Economist,* 18 April 1998, 59.

Chapter 14: Recasting the Executive Suite

247   Warren Bennis and Patricia Ward Biederman, *Organizing Genius: The Secret of Creative Collaboration* (Reading, Mass.: Addison-Wesley, 1997), 174.

248   John Huey, "Secrets of Great Second Bananas," *Fortune,* 6 May 1991, 64.

248   Ann Davis, "Meet Mr. Munger: Shrewd Investor with Odd Investment," *Wall Street Journal,* 19 November 1997, B1. See, too, Robert Lenzner and David S. Fondiller, "The Not-So-Silent Partner," *Forbes,* 22 January 1996, 78; Brent Schlender, "The Bill & Warren Show," *Fortune,* 20 July 1998, 61.

248   Thomas A. Stewart, "Brain Power," *Fortune,* 17 March 1997, 107; "This Sage Isn't from Omaha," *Business Week,* 1 April 1996, 40.

248   For more on the traditional CEO-COO division of responsibilities and the related weaknessess, see Warren Bennis, *The Unconscious Conspiracy: Why Leaders Can't Lead* (San Francisco, Jossey-Bass Publishers, 1989).

249   Besides the forgotten job notion, Columbia's Robert Lear calls the COO position "the most insecure job in the company." See his similarly titled article in *Chief Executive* (January/February 1990): 14.

250   Geraldine Fabrikant, "A Supporting Actor Takes Center Stage," *New York Times,* 15 May 1996, C1. See, too, Mark Robichaux, "Peter Barton, 'Second Banana,' at TCI, Quits," *Wall Street Journal,* 2 April 1997, B1.

250   Bernard Condon, " 'Jack Likes the Test,' " *Forbes,* 21 October 1996, 206.

251   Alecia Swasy, "Failing to Win Chief Executive's Throne Can Leave Heirs at a Loss," *Wall Street Journal,* 10 July 1990, B1; Peter Fritsch, "Enron's President, Kinder, Will Leave at End of the Year," *Wall Street Journal,* 27 November 1996, B5.

251   Matt Murray, "Marks, First Chicago Bank-Card Whiz, Resigns to Seek Top Post Elsewhere," *Wall Street Journal,* 17 November 1997, B12.

251   Kenneth N. Gilpin, "Xerox Hires I.B.M. Officer as President," *New York Times,* 13 June 1997, C1. See, too, Bart Ziegler, "Success at IBM Gives Thoman Edge at Xerox," *Wall Street Journal,* 13 June 1997, B1.

252   Richard Waters, "Xerox's Heir Apparent," *Financial Times,* 7 June 1997, 6.

252   "There's No Looking Back for Eric Schmidt," *Business Week,* 1 September 1997, 87.

252   Patricia Sellers, "Wal-Mart's Big Man Puts Blockbuster on Fast Forward," *Fortune,* 25 November 1996, 112.

252   The Ward Howell International research on COO turnover and advancement is cited in Christine Foster, "Couples," *Forbes,* 2 December 1996, 18–20.

253   John J. Keller, "Lucent Technologies Choose McGinn to Succeed Schacht as Chief Executive," *Wall Street Journal,* 7 October 1997, B17. McGinn aired his esteem for Schacht on "The Nightly Business Report," 29 January 1998.

254   See John J. Keller, "An AT&T Outsider and a Veteran Join to Run New Spinoff," *Wall Street Journal,* 14 October 1996, A2. For more on the Lucent partnership, see "For Lucent, A Shining Moment," *Business Week,* 21 April 1997, and Seth Schiesel, "Lucent: A Sassy Spinoff Enjoys a Lot of Luck," *New York Times,* 13 April 1997, F1.

254   Steve Rosenbush, "Lucent Technologies CEO passes Torch," *USA Today,* 7 October 1997, 52; Andrew Kupfer, "Is Lucent Really as Good as It Seems?," *Fortune,* 26 May 1997, 110.

254   Seth Schiesel, "Lucent's Chief Executive Post Awarded to Expected Heir," *New York Times,* 7 October 1997, C2. See, too, Schiesel, "Lucent: A Sassy Spinoff," sec. 3, 1.

254   Ibid.
254   Ibid.
255   "New Boss New Plan," *Business Week,* 2 February 1998, 132; John J. Keller, "AT&T Armstrong Has a Long Agenda," *Wall Street Journal,* 3 December 1997, A3.
255   Rahul Jacob, "The Resurrection of Michael Dell," *Fortune,* 18 September 1995, 124. Also see "Whirlwind on the Web," *Business Week,* 7 April 1997, 132; Ibid. See, too, Andy Serwer, "Michael Dell Rocks," *Fortune,* 11 May 1998, 59–70.
256   "Casting for a Different Set of Characters," *Business Week,* 8 December 1997, 39. See, too, Tom Neff's "Leadership Now: What's Constant? What's Changing?" Spencer Stuart's *Perspectives on Leading Business Issues* (Spring 1997): 9; The findings of the Association of Executive Search Consultants are discussed in Ibid., 38.
256   James C. Collins and Jerry I. Porras, *Built to Last* (New York: HarperBusiness, 1994), 202, 214.
257   Patrick McGeehan, "Charles Schwab's Pottruck Will Share Title of CEO with Company Founder," *Wall Street Journal,* 2 December 1997, B5.
257   Ibid.
258   Stephen E. Frank, "Chase Shakes Up Its Top Management," *Wall Street Journal,* 17 December 1997, A3. See, too, Timothy L. O'Brien, "Chase Revises Management Structure," *New York Times,* 17 December 1997, C1; and Matt Murray, "Tom Labrecque, Left for Dead in a Merger, Found Alive and Well," *Wall Street Journal,* 25 November 1998, A1.
258   McGeehan, "Charles Schwab's Pottruck."
258   Frank, "Chase Shakes Up."
259   David Lieberman, "Experts Doubt Co-CEOs Can Share Power," *USA Today,* 7 April 1998, B1; Saul Hansell and Leslie Wayne, "The Contrasting Styles of Citigroup's Co-Chiefs," *International Herald Tribune,* 8 April 1998, 11; Leslie Scism, Anita Raghavan, and Stephan Frank, "Weill and Reed Merge Their Firms; Can They Also Merge Their Egos," *Wall Street Journal,* 7 April 1998, A1.
259   "Big Merger Pushes Dow Past 9000," *Honolulu Advertiser,* 7 April 1998, A1.
259   Luisa Kroll, "You Have Been Merged," *Forbes,* 6 October 1997, 18.
259   For more on the difficulties of the dual-CEO arrangement, see Claudia H. Deutsch, "When Two Take the Top Seat," *New York Times,* 18 March 1990, sec. 3, pt. 2, 25; Matt Marshall, "Two Chiefs Blur Thyssen/Krupp Hoesch Merger," *Wall Street Journal,* 23 January 1998, B11A; Tracy Corrigan and John Authers, "Sharing Power at the Top May Prove the Biggest Threat," *Financial Times,* 8 April 1998, 17; Tony Jackson, "Double Means Trouble," *Financial Times,* 9 June 1998; Adam Bryant, "Co-Chief Executives: Can Two be a Crowd?," *New York Times,* 2 August 1998, sec. 3, 4; and Paula Dwyer, "Someone Has To Be the Boss," *Business Week,* 16 November 1998, 184.
260   Karen Lowry and JoAnn Muller, "The Auto Baron," *Business Week,* 16 November 1998, 84.

Chapter 15: Lessons for Co-Leaders
264   John Huey, "Secrets of Great Second Bananas," *Fortune,* 6 May 1991, 64.
264   Jeffrey Young, "The George S. Patton of Software," *Forbes,* 17 January 1997, 86.
264   Huey, "Secrets of Great Second Bananas," 70.
265   Steve Lohr, "Still Running with the Cows," *New York Times,* 22 September 1997, C6.
267   Warren Bennis, "Followers Make Good Leaders Good," *New York Times,* 31 December 1989, C1.
268   "Why Avon Called a 'Nonwoman,' " *Business Week,* 16 March 1998, 51. See, too, Leslie Wayne and Kenneth N. Gilpin, "Avon Calls on a Man to Lead It," *New York Times,* 12 December 1997, C1; "No Avon Lady—Yet," *Fortune,* 12 January 1998, 36.
269   Kara Swisher, "An Unusual Gatekeeper Gravels Paul Allen's Fortune," *Wall Street Journal,* 9 April 1998, B1.
269   Craig Barrett's athletic pursuits are discussed in Marilyn Chase, "Some Fitness Plans Designed by People Who Actually Do Them," *Wall Street Journal,* 5 January 1998, B1.
270   Stephen Kahng's management style was reported in Peter Burrows, "Power Duo," *Business Week,* 21 April 1997, 127. See, too, Julie Schmit, "Power Computing to enter PC market," *USA Today,* 3 September 1997, 2B. For additional information on CEO tenure in office, see Tom Neff and Dayton Ogden, "Third Annual Route to the Top: Pinball Wizards," *Chief Executive* (January/February 1998), esp. 34. Also, "Wanted: A Few Good CEOs," *Business Week,* 11 August 1997, 64–70. See, too, Dun Gifford, Jr., "CEO Turnover," in "Briefings from the Editors," *Harvard Business Review* (January–February 1997): 9–10.

271   The criticism of John Walter was variously reported. See, for example, "Career Track," *Chief Executive* (January/February 1998): 38.

273   For more on "thinking partners," see Peter M. Senge, "Communities of Leaders and Learners," *Harvard Business Review* (September–October 1997): 32.

273   For more on the Marine Corps approach, see Thomas E. Ricks, *Making the Corps* (New York: Scribner, 1997), and David H. Freedman, "Corps Values," *Inc.,* April 1998, 54–64.

274   John Huey, "Wal-Mart: Will It Take Over the World?" *Fortune,* 30 January 1989, 56.

274   General Electric's *1995 Annual Report,* 3.

274   Jane Martinson and John Authers, "Teams Shine as the Star Culture Fades," *Financial Times,* 24 April 1998, 21.

274   Casey Cowell, "Casey Cowell's Modern Operandi," *Business Week,* 11 November 1996, 107; Ibid., 104.

275   David A. Heenan, *The New Corporate Frontier* (New York: McGraw Hill, 1991), 157; James C. Collins and Jerry I. Porras, "Making Impossible Dreams Come True," *Stanford Business School Magazine,* July 1989, 17.

275   Daniel Gross, "Doing Business by the Book, *Hemispheres,* November 1997, 49. See, too, Ken Iverson with Tom Varian, *Plain Talk: Lessons from a Business Maverick* (New York: John Wiley & Sons, 1997).

275   General Electric's *1995 Annual Report,* 2.

276   Christine Foster, "Couples," *Forbes,* 2 December 1996, 20.

276   Gilmartin's approach is examined in "Mr. Nice Guy with a Mission," *Business Week,* 25 November 1996, 132–142; Ibid., 132. See, too, John Helyar and Joann S. Lublin, "Do You Need an Expert on Widgets to Head a Widget Company?," *Wall Street Journal,* 1 January 1998, A10.

276   Helyar and Lublin, "Do You Need an Expert?" A10.

277   For more on Abraham Lincoln's listening skills, see David Herbert Donald, *Lincoln* (New York: Simon & Schuster, 1995).

277   The importance of loyalty is discussed in a survey by Goodrich & Sherwood Associates, New York–based consultants, in "Blind Devotion Wanted?" *Wall Street Journal,* 22 July 1997, A1.

277   For more on Admiral James Stockdale's view on power, see his *A Vietnam Experience: Ten Years of Reflection* (Stanford, Calif.: Hoover Institution, Stanford University, 1984).

278   Bill Walsh, "Holy Macro," *Forbes ASAP,* 26 August 1996, 30.

278   Lily Tomlin's remarks are from "Lily Tomlin Quotes," http://members.aol.com/NLB409/quote.html.

278   Jackie Joyner-Kersee's views on competing are from Lynne Joy McFarland, *21st Century Leadership: Dialogues With 100 Top Leaders* (Long Beach, Calif: The Leadership Press, 1997), 77; Cowell, "Modern Operandi," 107.

278   See Robert H. Frank and Philip J. Cook, *The Winner-Take-All Society* (New York: Free Press, 1995).

280   Roger Rosenblatt, "The Straight Man," *Modern Maturity,* July–August 1996, 20.

Index

Heenan, David A.   HD57.7
Co-leaders: the power of   H458c
great partnerships